TRANSCENDING
Boundaries

TRANSCENDING
Boundaries

Multi-Disciplinary Approaches to the Study of Gender

•

Edited by **Pamela R. Frese**
and **John M. Coggeshall**

Bergin & Garvey
New York • Westport, Connecticut • London

Copyright Acknowledgments

The authors would like to thank the Royal Anthropological Institute of Great Britain and Ireland for permission to reprint an expanded version of " 'Ladies' behind bars: a liminal gender as cultural mirror" that originally appeared in 1988 in *Anthropology Today* 4(4): 6–8. We would also like to thank the Metropolitan Museum of Art for permission to use a photograph of "St. Emerentia with Virgin and Child and St. Anne" (Gift of J. Pierpont Morgan, 1916; [16.32.208]).

Library of Congress Cataloging-in-Publication Data

Transcending boundaries : multi-disciplinary approaches to the study
  of gender / edited by Pamela R. Frese and John M. Coggeshall.
      p.   cm.
  Includes bibliographical references and index.
  ISBN 0-89789-230-5—ISBN 0-89789-231-3 (pbk.: alk. paper)
  1. Sex role. 2. Sex differences (Psychology) I. Frese, Pamela
R. II. Coggeshall, John M.
  HQ1075.T75   1991
  305.3—dc20   90-39154

British Library Cataloguing in Publication Data is available.

Library of Congress Catalog Card Number: 90-39154
ISBN: 0-89789-230-5
    0-89789-231-3 (pbk.)

First published in 1991

Bergin & Garvey, One Madison Avenue, New York, NY 10010
An imprint of Greenwood Publishing Group, Inc.

Printed in the United States of America

The paper used in this book complies with the
Permanent Paper Standard issued by the National
Information Standards Organization (Z39.48-1984).

10 9 8 7 6 5 4 3 2 1

Contents

Illustrations

Acknowledgments

This book represents for both of us the outcome of a long intellectual and personal exploration of the concept of gender and the social consequences of that conceptualization. Several special people have greatly aided us during the course of our careers to explore beyond disciplinary boundaries to consider ideological and social constructs in a new light.

Pam is especially indebted to Roy Wagner and Vic and Edie Turner for opening intellectual frontiers to exploration and leading the way on forays into other ways of thinking about the world and the discipline of anthropology.

Mike would like to thank Charlotte Frisbie, who first introduced a narrow-minded undergraduate to the significant but overlooked ethnographic world of women's voices. More importantly, through her professionalism, Charlotte has served as an ideal academic mentor and role model. Her guidance and support through the years have been greatly appreciated.

Finally, both Pam and Mike would like to thank their respective spouses, Simon Gray and Cathy Robison, whose patience and understanding through this project truly made it possible.

To all these special people we dedicate this book.

The preparation of this manuscript benefited from the financial assistance provided by the College of Wooster in a summer aid-in-research grant. We would also like to thank Carolyn Rahnema for her patience and skills on the word processor.

Introduction

God created man in his image. In the image of God he created him. Male
and female he created them.

Genesis 1:27

Since these words were written, indeed even before, humans have defined through
culture the biological differences between the sexes. As the images from the
Judeo-Christian world view indicate, the way cultures perceive genders and
gender relationships ultimately impacts deeply on every aspect of culture.

This volume explores the ways in which the boundaries of gender constructs
shape and influence cultural ideology and social interaction. The integrating
perspective is the general assumption of anthropology that human society and
cultural beliefs must be studied as a system of complex, interrelated parts.
Feminist scholars from a variety of disciplines share an assumption that gender
must be viewed as a social and cultural construct and that sexual asymmetry,
as a cultural construction, can be altered. All the contributors to this volume,
from a variety of disciplines, are united in their concern with the process of
sexual differentiation; that is, how "feminine" and "masculine" are defined
and how these definitions contribute to perceptions of social reality.

The early focus in gender studies in anthropology was in part an assumption
that women participate in a hidden culture in the private domain, a voiceless
segment of most societies and one traditionally overlooked in ethnographies.
Edwin Ardener expressed this concern in his seminal consideration of the exclusion of women from social models used by both male and female anthro-

pological researchers. Ardener argues that "the models of a society made by most ethnographers tend to be models derived from the male portion of that society" (1972:138) and that these bounded models that are provided by men do not necessarily reflect the beliefs of the unheard segment of the population, the women. Implicit in his argument is that ethnographers, both male and female, were operating under models reflecting male concerns:

Our women ethnographers may then be expressing the "maleness" of their subject when they approach the women of other societies. It may well be, too, that their positive reluctance to deal with the problem of women is the greater because they sense that its consideration would split apart the very framework in which they conduct their studies. (1972:155)

The first generation of scholars to consider these issues primarily focused on the investigation of the definition and social role of "female." In one of the first contributions to cross-cultural studies of "female," Michelle Z. Rosaldo and Louis Lamphere introduce a fundamental point now taken for granted by most feminist scholars:

today, it seems reasonable to argue that the social world is the creation of both male and female actors, and that any full understanding of human society and any viable program for social change will have to incorporate the goals, thoughts, and activities of the "second sex." (1974:2)

Henrietta A. Moore traces the transformation of anthropological studies on women to the current feminist perspective. She argues that:

Feminist anthropology is more than the study of women. It is the study of gender, of the interrelations between women and men, and of the role of gender in structuring human societies, their histories, ideologies, economic systems and political structures. Gender can no more be marginalized in the study of human societies than can the concept of "human action," or the concept of "society." It would not be possible to pursue any sort of social science without a concept of gender. (1988:6)

More recent developments in interdisciplinary feminist criticism (Spector 1986; Showalter 1989) reflect this need to understand both male and female from the feminist perspective. That is, "gender studies" has replaced "women's studies" in a maturing of the discussion, for scholars recognize that both genders need to be included for a more holistic understanding of gender categories and their social ramifications.

This newer conception of gender may be studied from several perspectives. For example, Sherry Ortner and Harriet Whitehead (1984) provide two useful overarching methodological approaches: the "culturalist" approach, which emphasizes the larger cultural context for gender symbolism; and the "sociological" approach, which considers how particular perceptions of gender reflect and are created by particular kinds of social organizations. The unifying thread of these two approaches is their relationship to prestige structures, or the "social value" assigned to the gender categories and symbols. The prestige structure is an important part of the legitimating ideology and perpetuates society and gender beliefs.

Considering gender domains in terms of prestige structures frequently underlies scholarly work with gender and ideas of power in several disciplines. For example, scholars interested in gender and power investigate the role gender plays in the division of labor, reproduction, and control over basic material and ideological resources (Connell 1987; Bookman and Morgan 1988).

Several recent elaborations include the way gender attribution may be related to cognitive styles and how gender conceptions may affect philosophical and scientific thought (Harding 1986, 1987; Harding and Hintikka 1983 [1982]; Harding and O'Barr 1987; Hartsock 1983; Keller 1985). Other scholars are interested in how gender is created and perpetuated in traditional and contemporary models in social science (Archer and Lloyd 1987 [1982]). Judith Shapiro's (1988) excellent survey of recent feminist literature extends these discussions and explores how traditional gender ideology has influenced particular trends in feminist scholarship.

These numerous, prolific, and exciting explorations of gender have led directly to this volume. Continuing the streams of contemporary discussion, we wish to go beyond the boundaries constraining both gender conceptualization and the subsequent repercussions on social behavior and intellectual discourse. Specifically, we examine the interrelationship between gender constructions and ideology from a variety of disciplinary perspectives and critique the role that gender beliefs play in disciplinary assumptions and structures of authority and power.

The volume's chapters are arranged so that disciplines and themes interrelate; one chapter enhances the previous work and introduces the next. However, we also see the chapters logically grouped into three systematic approaches to gender studies.

For example, the chapters by Susan Jaret McKinstry, Maryann E. Brink, Pamela R. Frese, and Margaret Ford explore the way expressive culture (art, literature, ritual) reflects gender beliefs and acts as vehicles for their reinvention through time. McKinstry's chapter explores the power of literature through the genre of the romance novel as both a reflection of ideal gender roles and (more explicitly) as a vehicle for their subversion and reinvention. Brink examines the nature of images of the Virgin Mary in medieval texts and the subsequent role of gender in the maintenance and transmission of literacy in the Middle Ages. Frese's chapter on the gender symbolism in American wedding ritual explores how images of gender and ideal social roles expressed through cultural vehicles come alive in ritual and are perpetuated through time. The pictorial chapter by Ford includes a short discussion on the imagery of gender by an artist and how gender is reflected in her work. She then lets her images speak for themselves as her sculpture is interpreted by each reader, in the way John Berger (1987 [1972]) argues in his important contribution to feminist art criticism.

A second grouping of contributors are more explicitly interested in the power that ideology has in recreating gender and associated beliefs and practices, emphasizing that both women and men must be viewed as products of their culture. Karen Taylor's chapter on nineteenth-century patriarchy joins scholarly work in a discipline that has only begun to investigate the historical relationship between power, ideology, and gender. She is concerned with the impact of ideology on appropriate social roles, and she argues that the power of ideology and institutional mechanisms forced men to adopt positions of dominance even if this were contrary to their inclinations. John M. Coggeshall discusses the power of gender dichotomy to create male and female where only one biological sex actually exists. He also finds that the creation of gender in male inmate culture reflects gender inequalities in American culture.

While all contributors are concerned with the social and cultural creation of gender, the third grouping of chapters in this collection deals with gender and prestige or power structures as they have influenced the intellectual development of various disciplines and the individuals who are products of that disciplinary training. The chapter by Mark Weaver, Claudia Thompson, and Susan Newton provides a unique multidisciplinary approach to the presuppositions of gender and science by a political scientist, a psychologist, and a sociologist. The authors examine the relationship between gender and science on three levels: the potential of male bias in empirical research; feminist critiques of the structure of cognitive authority in science; and how science, as a product of a particular gendered ideology, perpetuates gender in a patriarchal society. Barbara S. Burnell's chapter explores the neoclassical economic approach and the lack of gender studies in mainstream economics. She raises important questions on methodology while examining the way that economic knowledge is acquired and the effect that economic methodology and analysis has on shaping gender roles. Elizabeth Castelli and James McBride present an analysis of the rapidly growing literature on gender in religious studies using heuristic categories which distinguish the hermeneutical approaches of respective feminist scholars. The scope of the analysis covers not only feminist theological issues in contemporary cultures but also historical studies of religious documents, deemed important in the life of First-, Second-, and Third-World societies. Finally, N. Jane Hurt considers the viewpoints of contemporary female architects for their perspectives on gender and cultural space. She is interested in how women perceive their design work and how their experiences as design students and later as practicing professionals reflect the gendered perspectives of their field.

Of course, the chapters may be read in any order and with any thematic arrangement. We view the chapters as springboards for further discussion of gender, both within the particular disciplines represented by the authors and of the ideas represented in their writings. It is indeed difficult to transcend boundaries, not only those of disciplinary constrictions on gender, but also structural constraints of the disciplines themselves. These became apparent early, as we anthropologists began editing work outside of our own discipline's "authority" on knowledge. Not only does every discipline assume different kinds of knowledge from the reader, but each also provides different kinds of information for the reader, for example, alternate methods of indicating citations and ancillary comments. Moreover, the more artistic contributors, Hurt and Ford, usually present their ideas as two-dimensional drawings or three-dimensional projects and found the restrictions of our scholarly discourse style at first awkward and constraining. By the end we realized the multidisciplinary perspectives on gender were reflected in the multidisciplinary perspectives on structuring and expression of knowledge. Our task became that of a conductor—to prevent a cacophony of sound from a chorus of scholarly singers and to meld them instead into a harmonious symphony. While we hope we have established a unified sound, we also hope each voice remains clear and distinct. Our ultimate goal is that the authors' viewpoints enhance the rapidly growing field of gender studies by enabling the reader to explore the cultural boundaries and social consequences of gender constructs from a variety of intellectual perspectives.

REFERENCES

Archer, John, and Barbara Lloyd (editors). 1987 [1982]. *Sex and Gender*. Cambridge: Cambridge University Press.

Ardener, Edwin. 1972. "Belief and the problem of women." Pp. 135–158 in *The Interpretation of Ritual*, edited by J. S. La Fontaine. London: Tavistock.

Berger, John. 1987 [1972]. *Ways of Seeing*. London: Penguin Press.

Bookman, Ann, and Sandra Morgan (editors). 1988. *Women and the Politics of Empowerment*. Philadelphia: Temple University Press.

Connell, R. W. 1987. *Gender and Power: Society, the Person and Sexual Politics*. Stanford: Stanford University Press.

Harding, Sandra. 1987. *Feminism and Methodology: Social Science Issues*. Bloomington: Indiana University Press.

———. 1986. *The Science Question in Feminism*. Ithaca, NY: Cornell University Press.

Harding, Sandra, and M. B. Hintikka (editors). 1983 [1982]. *Discovering Reality: Feminist Perspective on Epistemology, Metaphysics, Methodology, and Philosophy of Science*. Boston: D. Reidel.

Harding, Sandra, and Jean F. O'Barr. 1987. *Science and Scientific Inquiry*. Chicago: University of Chicago Press.

Hartsock, Nancy. 1983. "The feminist standpoint: developing the ground for a specifically feminist historical materialism." Pp. 283–310 in *Discovering Reality*, edited by S. Harding and M. B. Hintikka. Boston: D. Reidel.

Keller, Evelyn Fox. 1985. *Reflections on Gender and Science*. New Haven: Yale University Press.

La Fontaine, Jean S. (editor). 1972. *The Interpretation of Ritual*. London: Tavistock.

Moore, Henrietta A. 1988. *Feminism and Anthropology*. Minneapolis: University of Minnesota Press.

Ortner, Sherry, and Harriet Whitehead (editors). 1984. *Sexual Meanings: The Cultural Construction of Gender and Sexuality.* Cambridge: Cambridge University Press.

Pilgrim, David (editor). 1989. *On Being Black: An In-group Analysis.* Bristol, IN: Wyndham Hall Press.

Randolph, Richard, David Schneider, and Mary Diaz (editors). 1988. *Dialectics and Gender: Anthropological Approaches.* Boulder and London: Westview Press.

Rosaldo, Michelle Z., and Louis Lamphere (editors). 1974. *Woman, Culture, and Society.* Stanford: Stanford University Press.

Shapiro, Judith. 1988. "Gender totemism." Pp. 1–19 in *Dialectics and Gender: Anthropological Approaches,* edited by R. Randolph, D. Schneider, and M. Diaz. Boulder and London: Westview Press.

———. 1981. "Anthropology and the study of gender." Pp. 110–129 in *A Feminist Perspective in the Academy,* edited by E. Langland and W. Gove. Chicago: University of Chicago Press.

Showalter, E. (editor). 1989. *Speaking of Gender.* New York: Routledge.

Spector, Judith. 1986. *Gender Studies: New Directions in Feminist Criticism.* Bowling Green, OH: Bowling Green University.

Gender Constructions in Science

Mark Weaver, Claudia Thompson, and Susan Newton

HISTORICAL CONTEXTUALIZATION OF GENDER CONSTRUCTIONS AND SCIENCE

For more than a decade, feminist perspectives on a variety of disciplines have helped to broaden and change our understanding of the history, development, and nature of the presuppositions and assumptions of those disciplines. This has been true particularly for the humanities, where genuine transformations have affected our definitions of what counts as literature, storytelling, and art. These themes are addressed in other chapters in this volume. Castelli and McBride, for example, discuss ways in which a feminist perspective in religious studies encourages a reexamination of religious ideology and of women's stories and histories in religion. To a lesser extent, transformations have also occurred in the social sciences, where our understanding of human behavior and development has been altered by reconceptualizations of what is "the norm" (e.g., Chodorow 1978; Gilligan 1982). Burnell's chapter in this volume shows that, even in the highly quantitative field of economics, an examination of gender roles and metaphors reveals the constructed nature of theory and methodology.

The natural or physical sciences, however, have not undergone similar revolutionizing developments and have seemed to many, scientists among them, somehow different and less in need of reexaminations of method and epistemology. This undoubtedly has to do with the history of science and its special status in Western society as a channel to knowledge singularly characterized by objectivity, neutrality, and the unbiased collection and examination of empirical evidence. Indeed, these are the hallmarks of what we commonly call the scientific method, and our confidence in modern science rests largely on this set of suppositions about how science is practiced and how evidence is scrutinized and accumulated. So it is especially problematic to consider the ways in which the scientific enterprise may reflect biases and assumptions that are present in the larger society and that actually lead to claims of knowledge that are not objective, independent of the observer, and "just the plain facts." Given the traditions and great successes in science, how can this be so?

To answer this question, we need to examine how constructions of gender in Western society became tied to historical conceptualizations of what science should be and how it should be practiced. A number of extensive reviews have been written on this subject (e.g., Bordo 1986; Keller 1985; Merchant 1983). They share an emphasis on the ways in which sexual metaphors and gender stereotypes that developed in Western culture influenced the growth of modern science and how present-day concepts of what constitutes good scientific method are inextricably linked with concepts of the stereotypically masculine.

Evelyn Fox Keller (1985), Susan Bordo (1986), and Carolyn Merchant (1983) discuss the pointed sexual metaphors that characterize philosophical writings about nature and the aims of scientific understanding in the sixteenth and seventeenth centuries, the period of the Scientific Revolution. During this period, images of mechanization, control, and domination of nature became powerful conceptualizations and driving metaphors for scientific method. Merchant (1983) argues that these images developed in contrast to older, nurturing images of nature associated with a female earth, and that these changes were necessary because they provided societal sanctions for the domination and mastery of nature characteristic of increasing commercial and industrial development in the West. Images of the nurturing Mother Earth were supplanted by images of a dead, inanimate, physical system; the Earth could thus be mined, plumbed, and exploited without moral censure. Bordo reviews the model of knowledge bequeathed to modern science by Descartes as one characterized by objectivity, clarity, dispassion, and detachment and charges that this view, fraught with some measure of anxiety reflected in Descartes's meditations, is an expression of uneasiness with the "organic female universe of the Middle Ages and the Renaissance" (1986:441), a "flight from the feminine" that contributed to the larger masculinization of scientific thought and model of knowing.

Keller (1985) extensively examines how the language of sex and gender is deeply imbedded in the development of modern science in the writings of Francis Bacon. Bacon's view, according to Keller, is one of "sovereignty, dominion, and mastery of man over nature" (1985:34), and this vision is reflected in explicit sexual metaphors found in Bacon's writings, where Nature is to be married, tamed, and subdued: "I am come in very truth leading to you Nature with all her children to bind her to your service and make her your slave" (1985:36).

Keller further argues that Bacon saw the development of a new, active, "purified'' science as directly related to a cleansing and opening of the mind to God:

Men are to be entreated again and again . . . that they should humbly and with a certain reverence draw near to the book of Creation . . . that on it they should meditate, and that then washed and clean they should in chastity and integrity turn them from opinion. (1985:38)

This association with purity and chastity represents for Keller another powerful sexual metaphor and reinforces the separation of men and their new, pure science from the dark, passionate, and feminine.

All of these authors reveal the historical development of modern science in its larger social context and show that constructions of what is masculine and feminine have interacted with social, economic, and political developments that have in turn influenced modern conceptions of scientific knowledge and practice. The legacy of these historical developments, in which stereotypical characteristics of masculinity (objective, rational, detached, impersonal) are also stereotyped characteristics of science, is today very much a subject for reexamination from alternative perspectives, including feminist perspectives. Although far from unified, these feminist critiques suggest that the perceived immunity of the natural sciences to biases resulting from gender constructions is questionable. The precise ways in which gender biases might influence scientific research and theory are matters of extensive hypothesizing and philosophical debate and reflect questions about who does science, what are important scientific problems, and how science should be done. These issues are complicated by the fact, sometimes oversimplified by feminist critics, that ''science'' is not a uniform entity. Questions about theory, method, and practice differ among scientific disciplines, and issues related to the biases of individual scientists are much different from those pertaining to biases in science when it is viewed as a social institution.

Despite these complexities, examinations of bias in contemporary science have tended to focus on three main areas: gender bias in empirical research, gender bias in the education, training, and employment of scientists, and gender bias reflected in the presuppositions of the underlying ideology of modern science. Each of these three areas is reviewed.

GENDER BIAS IN EMPIRICAL RESEARCH

The most intensive reviews of gender bias in empirical research have concentrated, not surprisingly, on biological and psychological research related to sex and gender differences in behavior. As is clear in the reviews of such research by Anne Fausto-Sterling (1985), Stephen J. Gould (1981), and Ruth Bleier (1986a), among others, the basic issue in this research is that of biological determinism; that is, the extent to which certain behaviors in males and females differ in significant ways because of biology (genetics, evolution, physiology)—in short, by nature. The critiques concentrate on questions about what sorts of meaningful differences actually exist, whether the real differences are explained best by biological effects, why similarities are emphasized much less than differences, and why differences are ranked consistently in favor of white, Western males. All of these questions suggest that traditional scientific research on sex and gender differences has not been totally objective, dispassionate, and impartial and that cultural constructions of gender have influenced the kind of questions scientists ask and the answers they expect to find. According to these critiques, such research is not simply a case of "the facts speaking for themselves."

Empirical Research on Sex Differences in Hormones and Aggression

Fausto-Sterling (1985) critiques a number of areas of biological research on sex differences. For example, her review of research on the relationship between sex hormones and aggressive behavior criticizes claims (e.g., Barash 1979; Goldberg 1973; Hutt 1972) that male strength, domination, and aggression are controlled mainly by male hormone levels, supplying men with a physiological edge over females. In turn this supposedly makes men more suitable for positions requiring ambition and drive or competitive striving—including political and civil positions, according to Steven Goldberg, and, significantly, science, according to Corinne Hutt. Fausto-Sterling argues that the common tendency to link aggression, violence, crime, riots, and war with hormone levels is grossly oversimplistic and illogical (1985:126). She carefully reviews a large body of experimental literature on the relationship between hormones and aggression and concludes that there are actually remarkably few studies measuring a direct correlation between aggressive or hostile behavior in humans and testosterone levels in the blood at the same time, and the correlational results produced have been equivocal. Moreover, even when a positive correlation has been found between hormone levels and aggressive behavior, this is not sufficient to assume a causal relationship between hormone levels and aggression (i.e., that higher levels of testosterone produce more aggressive behavior), since it is just as likely that elevated testosterone levels result from aggressive behavior. Thirdly, "aggression" is defined and measured in various ways in different studies, making the results difficult to compare or generalize. Finally, research on the relationship between sex hormones and aggression has been conducted almost exclusively with male subjects, so that inferences about different levels of aggressive behavior in males and females and their relationship to sex hormone levels are clearly unwarranted.

Fausto-Sterling also reviews research on human fetal hormonal levels and hypotheses linking these levels to subsequent behaviors. For example, research on higher than normal exposure to prenatal androgen has led to the hypothesis

that such exposure results in masculinization of female fetuses and related behavioral effects, such as "competitive energy expenditure" and "tomboyism"
(Money and Ehrhardt 1972). Whereas the physically masculinizing effects of
such exposure of female fetuses to prenatal androgens are clearly documented,
Fausto-Sterling argues that the evidence for masculinizing behavioral effects is
not clear. Also, a number of methodological weaknesses in John Money and
Anke Ehrhardt's study, and in subsequent research with other colleagues, make
the interpretation of their findings extremely problematic. These methodological difficulties include relying on self-report data of the patients, or on reports
of the patients' mothers about past behavior, and, in particular, the researchers'
virtual neglect of the psychological and behavioral effects of total clitoridec-
tomy on female children exposed to excessive levels of prenatal androgen. Fausto-
Sterling argues that these researchers propose a straightforward biological explanation for a set of behaviors that must surely be influenced by environmental
and socialization experiences as well, or at least that such influences cannot be
dismissed or overlooked without further careful scrutiny.

Bleier (1986a) has further criticized the hypothesis that causally links "tomboyism" to androgen effects on the developing fetal brain of Money and Ehrhardt's patients. Bleier notes that this causal link was not emphasized in earlier
papers by Ehrhardt and Money. In subsequent papers, however, the hypothesis
was proposed less cautiously, and anecdotal reports were manipulated so as to
minimize the socialization effects revealed by some of the mothers of the an-
drogenized female children. Both Bleier and Fausto-Sterling conclude that cultural constructions of "tomboyism" as an index of masculinity have influenced
the judgment of researchers about the behavioral effects of prenatal hormones.
Further, "tomboyism" is a culturally, not a biologically, constructed attribute
(Bleier 1986a:150), and any conclusions that fetal hormones directly produce
significant behavioral differences between male and female children are, at best,
premature. The readiness with which scientists (and nonscientists) search for
such conclusions and promote them is an indication that research on such questions is not impartial and objective but instead reflects a set of cultural values
and beliefs, related to gender and gender roles, that predispose them to find
some explanations of behavior more acceptable than others.

Research on Sex Differences in Cognitive Abilities

A second major area of research on sex differences has involved comparisons
of males and females on a variety of intellectual or cognitive tasks. Gould
(1981) has reviewed in detail the development of mental measurement tests in
the United States in the nineteenth and twentieth centuries. Although Gould's
analysis deals more with racial and ethnic biases in testing procedures and the
interpretation of scientific evidence, he does address the issue of male–female
comparisons in several places. He notes, for example, that the size of the brain
was for a time persistently though incorrectly associated with intellectual abil-

ities, and that "comfortable white males" were found by Paul Broca and others to "have larger brains than women, poor people, and lower races" (Gould 1981:88). Gould reviews the deftness with which various researchers in the nineteenth century proposed a series of "correction factors" whenever the empirical evidence contradicted or threatened their own presuppositions about how races, ethnic groups, and the sexes should be ranked for intellectual ability. Indeed, some researchers, including Broca on at least one occasion, saw no need for actual empirical measurement at all. They simply "knew" that females were intellectually inferior to males and saw no real need to verify that "fact":

We might ask if the small size of the female brain depends exclusively upon the small size of her body. Tiedemann has proposed this explanation. But we must not forget that women are, on the average, a little less intelligent than men, a difference which we should not exaggerate but which is, nonetheless, real. We are therefore permitted to suppose that the relatively small size of the female brain depends in part upon her physical inferiority and in part upon her intellectual inferiority. (Broca, quoted in Gould 1981:104)

Although one might dismiss the claims of nineteenth century scientists as quaintly outdated, more recent claims that perpetuate stereotypes of male and female intellectual differences are not so easily dismissed. A great deal of debate has been generated, for example, over the question of visuospatial and mathematical abilities in boys and girls and whether these putative sex differences (with males showing superiority in performance) are biologically determined. Although a great deal has been written and a variety of claims made, few clear reviews of the empirical evidence have been provided. One such review is provided by Fausto-Sterling (1985), who shows on a number of counts that conclusions about innate male superiority in math skills (or female superiority in verbal skills), the existence of a "math gene," or brain hemispheric specialization effects are clearly unwarranted. Her review of the experimental literature points out both methodological and interpretive difficulties that make such conclusions inappropriate.

First, statistical interpretations of the data regarding differences in mathematical skills (e.g., Benbow and Stanley 1980) have emphasized small, though statistically significant, between-group differences (i.e., the difference in performance between girls and boys), but have in general failed to acknowledge that such between-group differences are much smaller than within-group differences in ability (i.e., differences among boys in their own group or girls in their own group). Such high within-group variability makes the psychological meaningfulness of small differences between males and females questionable. Fausto-Sterling further points out that studies of visuospatial and analytical abilities have defined these skills in different ways and that nearly half (five out of twelve) of the studies comparing males and females on such tasks report no sex differences (although in no study did females surpass males in performance). In addition, as is the case for mathematical abilities, the differences, while statistically significant, are so small (accounting for no more than five percent of the variance) that the overwhelming message from the data is that performance variability has mostly to do with individual differences unrelated to whether the subject is male or female. As was the case with research on hormones and aggression, Fausto-Sterling argues strongly that, where visuo-spatial or mathematical differences do exist, they are at least the result of the interaction of cultural, environmental, and biological factors and not related in any direct or simplistic way to biologically determined sex differences.

Fausto-Sterling summarizes her review of this research on sex-related intellectual differences by asserting that the attempts "to derive biological explanations for alleged sex differences in cognition" have been "extensive but futile" because they "both oversimplify biological development and downplay the interactions between an organism and its environment" (1985:60). Bleier, in another review of research on sex-related cognitive differences, reaches a similar conclusion:

It is because learning and environment are inextricable from the structure of neurons and because we have the property of mind, each mind the unique product of our individual, complex histories of development and experience, that I view as futile efforts to reduce human behaviors to biological parameters. Rather than biology, it is the cultures that our brains have created that most severely limit our visions and the potentials for the fullest possible development of each individual. (1986a:162)

In general, the whole area of sex differences in biological and psychological research has come under intense scrutiny, and questions about why it has been so important to search for sex differences and why it has been so important to rank differences when they are found, with males almost always ranked superior, have been the special concerns of feminist critics of such empirical research. The biases in the collection and interpretation of data in these fields have now been brought to light, but the issue of biological determinism and its powerful hold on theoretical explanations and interpretations of data is still of great concern, as is evident in current controversies related to contemporary sociobiological theory (Barash 1979; Wilson 1975; Gould 1981; Haraway 1986). Whatever the resolutions of these controversies are, it is clear that culturally constructed concepts of gender have strongly influenced scientific research in a number of areas, and that presuppositions about gender-appropriate behaviors have influenced the explanations that scientists find in the raw data. In turn, once given scientific verification and sanction, these conclusions have perpetuated gender constructs in societal values and beliefs. Rather than being independent of gender bias, science has thus been affected by and has influenced biased conceptions of behavior in males and females.

Bias in Empirical Research in the Physical Sciences

One would logically suppose that research on sex differences in biology and psychology would be likely candidates for gender bias, but what about research in other fields of biology or psychology, or research in physics, chemistry, or mathematics? Feminist critics are mistaken when they assume, for example, that "attempts to show how Newton's and Einstein's laws of nature might participate in gender symbolization . . . need not be undertaken in order to convince us that modern science is androcentric" (Harding 1986:47–48), because it is precisely science's success in these areas of research that have led scientists to demand demonstration of gender bias there. Although the justification for Sandra Harding's position rests on philosophical and ideological bases (to be discussed later in this chapter) rather than empirical ones, for scientists the question of empirical bias in the science they practice day to day is often the most important. From the perspective of scientists, the contributions to knowledge about the natural world (e.g., the nature of matter, the structure of the universe) and the practical applications of science (e.g., electricity, suspension bridges) suggest not only that a great deal of empirical research is free of gender bias but also that such gender bias is difficult to imagine in their particular fields of research. Therefore the question of gender bias in empirical research outside of the areas dealing directly with sex differences is a crucial one.

In fact there are very few such examples described in critiques of science that deal with gender bias. Keller (1985) has attempted perhaps the most diverse account in a series of chapters describing how research in quantum mechanics, slime mold aggregation, and genetics (specifically Barbara McClintock's work on maize genetics) has been influenced by presuppositions and assumptions that led scientists to construct certain theories and hypotheses and exclude others. Of course, it is typical of scientific theories to follow certain paradigmatic lines of reasoning (Kuhn 1970), to overlook others, and to be constrained by certain assumptions consistent with earlier research and hypothesis testing. But Keller's specific assertion is that the constraints in these cases are related to gender constructions that have influenced the historical development of science (as discussed in the introduction) and that have biased the sorts of theoretical models that emerge as explanations for scientific findings.

For example, according to Keller, confusion and controversy in contemporary theoretical research in quantum mechanics results in large part from a "strong positivist ethos" (1985:147) that derives from classical physics and assumes the objectivity and knowability of nature as distinct from the observer. Keller argues that these conventional tenets are related to masculinist conceptions of objectivity, omniscience, and independence of the knower and the known, which were influential in the development of concepts of science and scientific method in the Renaissance. But, Keller argues, these tenets provide an inadequate cognitive paradigm in modern quantum mechanics; what is needed is a "paradigm that . . . acknowledges the inevitable interaction between knower and known" (1985:139). The newer paradigm would thus move away from masculinist constructions of objectivity and knowability and instead recognize that the observer is not independent of the observed and that our perceived "perfect congruence between us as knowers and an objective reality" (Keller 1985:148) is an implicit but unwarranted assumption.

In her discussion of slime mold research, Keller examines the concept of a central organizing cell called the founder cell or pacemaker cell hypothesized to direct aggregation of single slime mold cells (*Dictyostelium discoideum*) into a multicellular organism. Keller's critique concentrates on the theoretical models proposed to explain the aggregation and subsequent differentiation of cells in the multicellular form. In particular, she challenges the view that aggregation and differentiation result from signals from a central pacemaker cell that are relayed through the medium by the rest of the cells in a unidirectional, sequential fashion (Shaffer 1962). Keller argues that, despite evidence to the contrary (Keller and Segel 1970), the pacemaker concept seemed so natural that "the word pacemaker crept into the literature as a fait accompli" (Keller 1985:153). Keller asserts that the pacemaker concept is an example of the "predisposition to kinds of explanation that posit a single central governor" (1985:155) and that we need to ask ourselves why such models seem so compelling in science. She warns that simple causal explanations may often be inadequate for complexly interactive systems, that our predispositions may lead us to overlook alternative explanations of natural phenomena, and that masculinist conceptions of "master molecules" that govern natural processes in a hierarchical, unidirectional way (1985:154) enter into our predispositions and play an important role in the development of scientific theories.

Keller is a particular authority on Barbara McClintock's work on maize genetics, having written not only several related book chapters and articles (e.g., Keller 1985) but also a biography of McClintock (Keller 1983). Keller's central thesis is that McClintock's research in maize genetics met a number of obstacles over the course of some 50 years. First of all, her work was undervalued or ignored due to her maverick position as a woman scientist. But more importantly, McClintock's difficulties in being recognized and understood for her work on transposition of genetic material and other genetic determinants of variability in maize development can be partly attributed to the different approach that she took in her research. Specifically, McClintock contradicted the "central dogma theory" that became dominant in molecular genetics by the 1950s. The central dogma resulted from the work of James Watson and Francis Crick (1953) on DNA and described genetic prescriptions of cell differentiation and development as a unidirectional sequence of commands from DNA to RNA to protein synthesis. McClintock's work on transposition indicated that development and differentiation were more complex and interactive processes, in which the cellular environment could influence DNA and its instructions to the cell. This challenge to the hierarchical, master molecule concepts of the central dogma has similar implications to those articulated by Keller for cellular slime mold aggregation: that masculinist constructions of control, dominance, and hierarchical chains of command influenced biological theories of DNA's influence on cellular events and that alternative conceptions (such as McClintock's), even when supported by the evidence, were underrated or misunderstood.

From these examples, it is evident that gender bias is not restricted to research about sex differences, although the number of specific examples outside of this particular field is still small. For the present, the examples of gender bias in empirical research remain heavily concentrated in the life sciences, where biological determinism has been the basis for many arguments about the nature of sex differences. But biological determinism is not the pertinent argument in the physical sciences, and it is entirely possible that gender bias in empirical research in the physical sciences is not prevalent or that generalizations cannot easily be made about the types of bias that occur in the life sciences and the physical sciences. As noted earlier, critiques of science need to be more careful about taking into account what kind of science and which scientists are the subject of scrutiny. Nevertheless, there seems ample reason to pursue the examination of the theory and practice of science on a variety of levels, with the objective of evaluating how gender constructions influence science at each level.

SCIENCE AS A SOCIAL INSTITUTION

Recent trends in sociology of science, history of science, and philosophy of science have demolished the image of science as a neutral, value-free body of knowledge that is completely detached from social, historical, and institutional contexts. Although mainstream developments in these fields have largely ignored the role of gender in the construction of science, the emergent view of scientific knowledge as a construction rather than a revelation of natural laws has significantly influenced feminist reexaminations of the role of gender in science. In particular, Thomas Kuhn's work (1970) on the nature of scientific progress, the role of paradigms in the construction of scientific knowledge, and the cognitive authority of the scientific community has been utilized in feminist analyses of how gender functions in science as a social institution.

While Kuhn focused on science as an activity rather than a body of existing knowledge, he treated incompletely the specific social arrangements which influence scientific practice (Addelson 1983). Post-Kuhnian and feminist analyses, however, have paid attention to such arrangements. A central focus in these analyses has been the role of "cognitive authority" in the practice of science. Cognitive authority grants to individual specialists the possession of definitive understanding; it "assume[s] that because there is one reality, there can only be one correct understanding of it" (Addelson 1983:169). As Kathryn Pyne Addelson (1983) suggests, the operation of cognitive authority in science intersects with gender in several ways. First, the granting of cognitive authority depends very much on the power and prestige of individual specialists (and specialties). In patriarchal society, where women have little or no power or prestige, cognitive authority is denied to them and their full participation in science is precluded. Secondly, because cognitive authority assumes only one reality and one understanding of it, the importance of diversity among practicing scientists is discounted. However, according to this analysis, understanding cognitive authority as socially conditioned points to the problems with male hegemony in science. Women have different realities from men, structured by their different material positions and the ideological supports for those positions. Moreover, their absence as practicing scientists affects the practice of science and the very content of scientific knowledge.

Women in Science as Vocation

An overview of the participation of women in science may be attained by examining three interrelated phenomena: educational attainment, employment rates, and salary levels. The extent to which women have made progress along these three dimensions may be evaluated by focusing on change over time as well as on rates relative to men. When these comparisons are made, we find that "despite progress, there is persistent inequality of opportunity for women in science and engineering" (Vetter 1987).

Although women earned 47.8 percent of all science and engineering doctorates awarded in the United States in 1985, only 8.5 percent of these degrees were in the physical sciences, mathematics and computing sciences, and engineering (Vetter 1987). Thus, women are still grossly underrepresented in what are often termed the "hard" sciences (Keller 1985:77 for a discussion of the gendered metaphors implied by the terms "hard" and "soft" sciences). Moreover, despite some small increases in the percentage of undergraduate science degrees earned by women over the last 15 years, the situation is less encouraging in the case of advanced degrees. There have been only modest gains in the percentage of doctorates awarded to women in the social and life sciences (Vetter 1987), and the situation is even worse in the physical and math and computing sciences where there have been proportionate declines in the number of women earning advanced degrees. Whereas in 1970 the percentage of women receiving doctorates was 6.1 percent in the physical sciences and 1.9 percent in the math and computing sciences, by 1985 these percentages had declined to 5.4 percent and 1.3 percent respectively (Vetter 1987). Only engineering exhibited a slightly different pattern: the percentage of doctorates awarded to women increased from 0.4 percent in 1970 to 1.9 percent in 1985 (Vetter 1987). In short, the available data on educational attainment at the higher degree levels, which is today an essential prerequisite to real participation in science, indicate that women continue to be underrepresented in the physical sciences, mathematics, and engineering.

In terms of employment in science and engineering fields, women have made significant gains since 1970 (National Science Foundation 1984)—to the point that in 1980 they constituted about 25 percent of the science labor force (Vetter 1987). However, despite such progress, women still experience much higher rates of unemployment and underemployment across the sciences (Vetter 1987:6). For example, the unemployment rate for women scientists and engineers was about twice that for men in 1982 (4.3 percent vs. 2.0 percent), and underemployment for women in 1984 was three times as high as for men (National Science Foundation 1984).

In terms of the final quantitative indicator of women's participation in science, salary levels, there is further evidence of differentiation by gender. Annual salaries for women doctoral scientists and engineers in 1985 averaged 77.2 percent of those for men (Vetter 1987). This wage gap is lower than that between men and women in the work force as a whole, which averaged about 62 percent in 1984 (U.S. Bureau of the Census 1986), but has shown relatively little change since the early 1970s (Vetter 1987). The wage gap remains after controlling for the differences in science and engineering field distributions between men and women (National Science Foundation 1984). Salaries are most equal for beginning men and women bachelor-degree graduates and diverge increasingly with degree level and additional years of experience (Vetter 1987).

In sum, the overall pattern of women's participation in science as measured by educational attainment, employment rates, and salary levels is essentially the same. Despite the fact that women have made measurable gains in science during the past decade and a half, there is still a considerable "gender gap," particularly in the physical sciences, mathematics, and engineering. Moreover, there are other indicators which reveal that the problem may be even more severe than these data indicate.

First of all, sexual segregation in the sciences is extreme. Margaret Rossiter (1982) describes two forms that this segregation takes. The first is what she calls territorial segregation and involves women being segregated in certain disciplines (e.g., psychology, nutrition, etc.). The second form is hierarchical segregation, where women are segregated within disciplines by their placement in less prestigious institutions or as poorly paid lab assistants. Harding (1986) refers to this distinction as horizontal and vertical segregation, respectively. To the extent that women are currently entering science in larger numbers, the impact of this progress is diminished by their continued separation and devaluation as scientific practitioners. Continued segregation is certain to discourage women from entering or remaining in science (Murphy 1980).

Another reason for mitigated enthusiasm is the fact that the increased entrance of women in science appears to be leveling off (Vetter 1987). Many factors have been suggested as central to the increased number of women scientists in recent years—the women's liberation movement, which encouraged women to defy traditional sex role stereotypes and urged the passage of antidiscrimination legislation (Schiebinger 1987); the increased funding and need for personnel which accompanied the Cold War arms buildup (Haraway 1984); and the general increase in the number of degrees earned by all women and men following World War II (Vetter 1987). However, the tightening of money in the economy and a societal backlash against women's rights and affirmative action portend harder times for women wishing to enter science. Betty Vetter (1987) notes that a number of programs designed to encourage and attract women to science have already been dropped by funding agencies and institutional sponsors. Furthermore, it is unlikely that female science rosters will be bolstered by the increasing entrance of women into college, since women now represent more than 50 percent of college entrants and graduates (Finkbeiner 1987). Some projections indicate as much as a 22 percent drop between 1985 and 1989 for women earning bachelor's degrees in engineering and the physical, math, and computing sciences (Vetter 1987). Because of the more narrow pipeline for women pursuing degrees beyond the bachelor's (Finkbeiner 1987), growing inequality between practicing male and female scientists might be expected to grow. As Vetter suggests:

The rapid increases in number and proportion of these degree awards to women that have marked the past decade appear to be ending well before women's participation in these fields matches their proportion of the population. Bachelor's degree awards to women in several science and engineering fields already are leveling off, and recent surveys of freshman-class women indicate a decrease in interest in these fields. Although some continuing increases in the participation of women in science at the graduate level are probable, future increases are not assured, and some gains of the past decade may not last. (1987:2)

Barriers to Women's Participation in Science

A central issue in examining women in science as vocation concerns the barriers which have inhibited or prevented women's participation in science. The factors which condition sexism in scientific employment are complex, dynamic, and interrelated, and cannot be easily compartmentalized. However, for the sake of clarity and organization of discussion, three categories of barriers which stand in the way of women's entrance into science may be distinguished: 1) socialization and developmental differences between boys and girls; 2) overt and covert discrimination; and 3) social structural factors.

Socialization and Developmental Differences between Boys and Girls

In 1965 Alice Rossi published a now classic paper entitled "Why So Few?" In it, she explored the subtle (and sometimes not so subtle) socialization practices which encouraged boys and girls to follow divergent paths on the way to a science career. As Rossi (1965) notes, the gender stereotypes and expectations of boys as intelligent, hard-working, and independent encourage them to engage in mental and physical labor compatible with scientific work and predispose them to a career in science. The gender stereotypes and expectations of girls as passive, nurturing, and dependent train them for a maternal role which is often incompatible with the demands of a scientific career.

The effects of these gender stereotypes and expectations are cumulative (Harding 1986) and begin to show up dramatically in high school when girls begin to "fall behind" in science, particularly in math. While there is little difference in assessment scores for males and females at a younger age—in fact, females outscore males at age 9 on math assessment exams, males score significantly higher by age 17 (National Science Foundation 1984). Feminist researchers point to the social bases for this transformation, particularly the different curricula for males and females in high school (Fausto-Sterling 1985). Specifically, male students take significantly more math courses (including honors courses) in high school than do female students (National Science Foundation 1984). By the time high school seniors take the Scholastic Aptitude Test (SAT) for college admission, average scores for females on the math component are well below those for males—443 versus 493 (National Science Foundation 1984). The lack of preparation and lower SAT scores for females represent a significant "filter" which prevents them from majoring in scientific disciplines in college (Sells 1980).

These explanations for the absence of women in science suggest that the elimination of different socialization patterns for males and females will solve the "woman problem" in science. Rossi thus notes:

If girls are to develop the analytic and mathematical abilities science requires, parents and teachers must encourage in them independence and self-reliance instead of pleasing feminine submission; stimulate and reward girls' efforts to satisfy their curiosity about the world as they do those of boys; encourage in girls not unthinking conformity but alert intelligence that asks why and rejects the easy answers. (1965:1201)

Certainly, such a change in early socialization patterns remains a necessary prerequisite to women's progress in scientific education and careers. However, we must also understand these socialization patterns and the possibilities of altering them not at the individual level, but rather in terms of more basic structural and institutional forces at work in science and in society at large. .

Overt and Covert Discrimination

Discrimination exists when groups of individuals are denied equal access to socially valued rewards. Organizations often evidence discrimination when they erect barriers to the entrance and full participation of individuals in their ranks. These barriers may be quite overt (obvious and intentional) or they may be, either intentionally or unintentionally, hidden or covert (Namenwirth 1986). Although overt discrimination against women in science has a long and malevolent history (Alic 1986; Rossiter 1982), organizations involved in training and employing female scientists today are more likely to exhibit covert discrimination (Smith 1978).

As one group of women scientists note, "[t]hose few women who manage to transcend . . . socialization and choose scientific careers, encounter a vicious circle of exploitation" (Women's Group from Science for the People 1980:284). At virtually every stage of a woman's scientific career, she will encounter attitudes, behaviors, and structures which reduce the likelihood for success. According to some critics, quotas for women (often not written or even spoken) are sometimes placed on graduate-school admissions, particularly at the more prestigious universities where later successful placements for graduates are almost assured (Women's Group from Science for the People 1980). Women entering graduate school are slightly more likely than men to receive teaching assistantships, which are generally more time-consuming and have fewer payoffs for a woman's own research; men are much more likely to receive research assistantships, which are more prestigious and conducive to publishable work (Matyas 1985). Interactions with (mostly male) professors are characterized by everything from benign neglect to sexual harassment (Dziech and Weiner 1984). Research has shown that male professors typically expect female students to perform most tasks more poorly than men, often resulting in a "self-fulfilling prophecy." When women students do perform well, professors are often likely to attribute their success to good luck or special effort rather than ability (Frieze 1978). Some female scientists note that graduate colleagues often offer little support for women, as they are usually male and often feel suspicious or even hostile toward female competitors (Keller 1977; Project on the Status & Education of Women 1982; Gornick 1983).

Women who make it through the graduate-science pipeline also experience extreme discrimination. As suggested earlier, employment for women scientists is more uncertain than for men, even though affirmative-action programs are often assumed to give women an advantage in the hiring process (Ramaley 1978). When women scientists are hired by either industry or academia, it often means only part-time or temporary (e.g., non-tenure track) employment or employment in less prestigious institutions or positions. Women are usually excluded from the informal networks so important to the sharing of results and the growth of collegiality (Reskin 1978; Cole 1981; Weisstein 1982). While a larger proportion of female than male scientists remain unmarried, the (often temporary) decline in productivity associated with childbirth is rarely tolerated in most research programs or departments.

One might wonder why discrimination against women is so persistent in scientific organizations. After all, if science represents a neutral body of methods and knowledge, it would seem to make little difference who the doer of science is. As noted earlier, however, the cultural stereotype of science as tough and rigorous and rational is intertwined with issues of men's gender identities (Harding 1986; Keller 1985). Consequently, some feminist critics have argued that "we should expect that in science more than any other occupation (except, perhaps, making war) it will take the presence of very few women to raise in men's minds the threat of feminization and thus of challenges to their own gender identity'' (Harding 1986:61–62).

"Proving" discrimination against women in science is a difficult thing to do. While most women scientists (and those who never made it through the pipeline) can relate stories of both overt and covert discrimination, the impact of these as barriers to the full participation of women is hard to quantify. A number of studies have shown that, even when controlling for differences in such factors as education, experience, and productivity, the gaps in average salaries and rank between men and women persist (e.g., Cole 1979; National Science Foundation 1984). However, when discrimination can only be quantified as "unexplained variance," critics are quick to argue that many other unknown variables besides discrimination could lead to the wage and rank gap between male and female scientists.

It is important to understand that discrimination against women by male scientists and scientific organizations need not be practiced in order to insure that women fail. Jo Freeman (1979:221) suggests the "null environment hypothesis," which states that a situation which neither encourages nor discourages males or females "is inherently discriminatory against women because it fails to take into account the differentiating external environments from which women and men . . . come." Hence scientists need not make it a point to discourage female students and colleagues—society will do that for them. As Freeman (1979) notes, all male scientists have to do to insure the absence of women in science is fail to encourage them.

Social Structural Factors

Many feminists have argued that cultural stereotyping and discriminatory practices play less of a role in the relative absence of women from science than the political and economic relations embedded in patriarchal and capitalist societies. For example, Hilary Rose (1986:66) sees the predominantly male scientific work force as "the particular example of a general division of knowledge between men and women in the world, which allocates characteristically different forms of work to men and to women." In other words, the division of mental and manual labor under capitalism parallels the division of public and private labor (i.e., production and reproduction) under patriarchy. An understanding of the operation of dual labor markets for men and women in patriarchal capitalist societies goes a long way toward explaining continuing inequalities between male and female scientists.

Despite recent progress by women in the sciences, contemporary social structure provides less room for women scientists than in the past. The development of the public versus private spheres with industrialization separated women from science much like it separated them from other economic and political production. The movement of science from a "purely intellectual pursuit to a source for industrialization" (Jacob 1988:259) paralleled and exacerbated this separation, for as science and technology have become increasingly valued by patriarchal societies, the scientific work of women has become increasingly devalued (Alic 1986).

Focusing on social structural factors as barriers to women's participation in science makes it clear their complete integration depends not simply on individual change and the elimination of prejudice but the development of alternative institutions and societies. In turn, these alternatives depend on the revision of our epistemologies and ideologies of science. We now turn to a set of issues concerning the relationship between gender and science at this most fundamental and abstract level.

SCIENCE AS IDEOLOGY

Feminist Critiques of Scientific Epistemology

As seen, the feminist critiques of science which focus on the social structure of science do not simply raise issues concerning job discrimination or the division of labor in science, but also pose more fundamental questions concerning the role of gender in the production of scientific knowledge. Essentially, these critiques proceed from the observation that "science is a socially produced body of knowledge and a cultural institution" (Bleier 1986b:2). Thus, since science evolved in a patriarchal society, "it took on a decidedly masculine tone and became burdened and distorted by a pervasive male bias" (Namenwirth 1986:19). In part this means that because practicing scientists cannot completely step outside their embeddedness in a particular cultural and social environment, the gender of scientists and the dominant cultural assumptions concerning gender do affect the kinds of questions which are asked and not asked, the perceptions and interpretations of available data, and other fundamental components of the research process. It is precisely this type of gender bias in the production of scientific knowledge which was examined in the first section on empirical critiques.

There is consensus among feminist critics that a review of this form of cultural bias requires reassessment of dominant assumptions concerning scientific method and knowledge. Thus feminist critiques of science challenge the positivist model which once dominated analytic philosophy of science because it focuses on science as a body of knowledge and the task of a rational reconstruction of the logical structure of scientific explanations and of scientific methodology. Feminist discussions of gender and science generally follow recent currents in philosophy of science, sociology of science, and history of science in focusing on analysis of science as an activity or process and the task of critically examining the sources of bias in the social arrangements which determine cognitive authority in science (Addelson 1983).

In addition, feminist critiques of scientific rationality question standard accounts of scientific method and activity which are based not on philosophical reformulations but rather on the reflections of practicing scientists. For example, feminist criticisms problematize the accounts of the scientific process and the treatment of bias offered in Peter Medawar's *Advice to a Young Scientist* (1979) not because he ignores scientific practice but because he fails to include consideration of the institutional and cultural influences on such practice. Thus his treatment of such topics as racism and sexism in science is confined to such issues as "the sexist illusion that women are more intuitive in character," "hard luck on spouses?," and the possibility of "husband and wife teams" in the contemporary laboratory. He does not even raise the issue of potential gender bias in scientific research or discuss the specific bodies of research where charges of such bias have been made (Medawar 1979:20–27).

Moderate Critiques

Although feminist critics agree in rejecting as incomplete the pictures of scientific methodology presented in positivist philosophy of science and in the accounts of mainstream scientists, there is disagreement concerning how far this critique must be pressed and to what extent scientific method and rationality, and the epistemological and ontological foundations which support them, must be changed. On the one hand, there are those "moderates" (Gornick 1983; Hrdy 1986; Namenwirth 1986) who acknowledge the extent to which masculine bias has infected the production of scientific knowledge but tend to see very little necessity for changing existing scientific goals, principles, and values as part of the process of correcting for such bias. Thus for example, Marion Namenwirth (1986:19) defends "science as a system of procedures for gathering, verifying, and systematizing information about reality." She sees "little in scientific thinking or in the objectives of science that is alien to working women scientists" and expects "moderate, rather than radical, differences between a science influenced by feminism and patriarchal science" (1986:32). In short, this perspective holds that although extensive masculinist bias has marked scientific knowledge in the past, science itself is not "inherently masculine" in that such bias can be eliminated without questioning the most basic standards of scientific method and scientific rationality.

Among the numerous commitments and positions which demarcate this moderate account of the connections between gender and scientific knowledge, two are especially important. First, the moderate feminist critics tend to stress the success of science, perceiving such success as critical to the feminist project of liberation. Namenwirth (1986:37) thematizes this success in terms of three reasons for the "great influence" of science: scientific knowledge is translated into "technological and medical advances that are widely desired"; science "exemplifies some important societal values such as intelligence, rationality, dispassionate objectivity, perseverance, dominance, and control of nature"; and science provides a general "worldview" for understanding ourselves and our environment. Although not all advocates of this moderate position would endorse every value on this list, they do tend to emphasize such achievements and to treat the feminist modification of science as yet another attempt to revitalize science in such a way that its success and achievements are preserved and furthered.

The other fundamental assumption which typifies this moderate account of the relationship between gender and scientific rationality is an ontological commitment to "sameness." As Namenwirth explicitly argues: "Women and men share virtually all abilities, characteristics, and attitudes. The differences between men and women are matters of emphasis and concentration, not a question of absence versus presence" (1986:37–38). Thus the moderate position is characterized by an analysis of gender which is typical of what Hester Eisenstein (1983) calls the first phase of contemporary feminist theory and analysis. This first-phase analysis emphasizes the distinction between sex and gender and the ways in which socially and historically constructed gender roles have oppressed women. The moderate feminist critique is essentially an extension of this type of analysis to science.

Although these moderate critiques have made important contributions to the understanding of the connections between gender and science, particularly in their careful examination of specific bodies of scientific research and knowledge, there are fundamental tensions at work in these moderate critiques of scientific methodology. On the one hand, these critiques do challenge all conceptions of science in which methodological rigor is thought to guarantee forms of neutrality, rationality, and objectivity that are free from political and cultural influences. Namenwirth, for example, argues that "in truth, scientists are no more protected from political and cultural influence than other citizens" and that the dominant "mind-set" or "science-culture" of neutrality simply allows these cultural and political biases to operate freely at an unconscious level (1986:29). Like other advocates of this moderate perspective, Namenwirth views "gender, culture, and class diversity" as the only corrective to this problem of cultural and political bias at the level of our most basic individual and collective presuppositions and assumptions (1986:32).

Similarly, Sarah Blaffer Hrdy examines the problems of objectivity and neutrality in the field of primate behavior. She maintains that the rejection of male bias in sexual selection theory is not the result of changes in methodology or of "new and better data," but rather must be attributed to a "motivational" factor resulting from the entry of a significant number of women researchers into the field (1986:135–136). Moreover, to acknowledge this feature is simply to move from an idealized view of science to a realistic view of science as actually practiced: "inefficient, biased, frustrating, replete with false starts and red herrings, but nevertheless responsive to criticism and self-correcting, and hence better than any of the more unabashedly ideological programs [including feminist "conscious partiality" programs] currently being advocated" (Hrdy 1986:141).

The problem here centers in the moderates' continued confidence in science as "responsive to criticism" and "self-correcting" as it is, whereas their own

analyses of bias indicate that the dominant understanding of scientific methodology as guaranteeing neutrality and objectivity has been a barrier to criticism
and correction along the lines of gender, class, and race. Thus the tension is
between their own diagnosis of the problem of gender and science, where they
reject mainstream accounts of scientific methodology, and their own conclusions in which they seem to reassert these same standards of objectivity and
neutrality. Of course, the new guarantee of such objectivity would seem to be
a kind of gender, race, and class pluralism in the scientific community, but the
moderates provide no account of how such pluralism is connected to scientific
principles, and they specifically reject the notion that such pluralism would
bring different kinds of characteristics or attitudes into the scientific community.

Radical Critiques

The inadequacies of this moderate analysis of gender and science have led
the majority of feminist critics to a much more radical and far-reaching reassessment of science. It is difficult to generalize about this grouping of critiques
because they are much more diverse than the moderate critiques previously
outlined (e.g., Fee 1986, 1983; Haraway 1984; Merchant 1980; Rose 1986,
1983). However, this more radical analysis of gender and science can be demarcated in very general terms by a critical reevaluation of the role of science
in maintaining a patriarchal structure of power, a challenge to the standards of
scientific method and scientific knowledge as themselves the products of a patriarchal culture, and a series of various proposals to revolutionize or refound
science according to feminist epistemological principles.

According to this more radical critique of "phallocentric science" (Rose
1986:57), the general Western assumption that science has always facilitated
and continues to promote social and human progress must be rejected in favor
of a careful assessment of the actual social and political impact of science.
Thus feminist critics document the specific instances in which science has been
and continues to be used as an ideological weapon to justify existing patriarchal
structures and practices (e.g., Bleier 1984; Fausto-Sterling 1985) and how science, like religion and philosophy before it, has played "the task of assigning
to women their proper place in the social order" (Fee 1983:12; also Fee 1976).
At an even more fundamental level, several radical feminist critics have charged
that masculinist science, founded on a relation of domination of and antagonism toward nature, supports a "culture of death" and a politics of "extermin-
ism" and domination of human subjects (Rose 1986:58, 66; also Rose 1983;
Merchant 1980).

For the most part the radical feminist critics of science have grounded this
challenge in the charge that the epistemological commitments and presuppositions of contemporary science are themselves gender biased. Simply put, the
charge is that "the foundations of our knowledge have been built on the assumptions of male domination and patriarchal power" (Fee 1986:43). In other

words, the production of scientific knowledge occurs within the context not of some set of universal principles of rationality and objectivity but rather of historical, "masculinist" understandings of rationality, objectivity, and knowledge. An important part of the project of this group is thus to expose "the ways in which gender-based dominance relations have been programmed into the production, scope, and structure of natural knowledge, distorting the content, meaning, and uses of that knowledge" (Fee 1986:54).

This radical critique of the epistemological underpinnings of masculinist science has focused on exposing a number of contestable dualisms which are operative in the scientific model of knowledge: male/female, subject/object, subjectivity/objectivity, thought/feeling, rationality/emotionality, passivity/activity, expert/nonexpert, the production of knowledge/the uses of knowledge, and culture/nature. The radical feminist position holds that these dualisms are historical rather than universal, gender based rather than gender neutral, and artificial and superficial rather than natural and necessary. Their project is to expose the masculinist biases at work in the dualistic categories of this epistemology and to construct an alternative, feminist epistemology which overcomes these dualisms.

Thus at a fundamental epistemological level, the exclusion of women from the production of scientific knowledge has resulted in a deficient, masculinist science. Radical critics of science, drawing on recent work in feminist theory such as Carol Gilligan (1982) and Mary Field Belenky et al. (1986), point to the explicit or implicit alternatives to masculine epistemologies which provide the basis for constructing an alternative feminist science: "the alternative epistemological assumptions making up women's world view remain subversive possibilities" (Fee 1986:47). Given that this radical critique of science explicitly draws on what Eisenstein (1983) labels a second-phase of contemporary feminist theory which is demarcated by the express rejection of androgyny and the conscious formulation of a woman-centered perspective, it is hardly surprising that it shares with such second-phase feminist theory an emphasis on differences between men and women and on reclaiming the positive in women's experience and perspective.

Certainly, none of the radical critics of science attempt to ground women's access to this alternative way of knowing in biological difference. At the same time, there is presently no consensus concerning how this alternative epistemology is to be theoretically grounded in women's different experiences. The alternative which seemed to be most attractive and useful in early attempts to accomplish this has been post-Freudian psychoanalytic object relations theory. Put simply, this account, drawing on Nancy Chodorow (1978) and Dorothy Dinnerstein (1976), critiques dominant masculine epistemological assumptions and attempts to articulate a feminist alternative in terms of gender differences in "the psychodynamics of cognitive, emotional and sexual development" (Keller 1985:70).

However, more recent attempts to provide the theoretical underpinnings for a critique of mainstream epistemological assumptions and for the construction of a feminist epistemology and science seem to have moved away from such psychological theories. For example, Elizabeth Fee argues that such theories are inadequate to these tasks because they tend to make universal psychological claims on the basis of a particular social form (the nuclear family in a modern Western, capitalist setting), they place too much emphasis on altering the structure of family relationships while ignoring other social constraints and limits, and they can explain only how particular forms of power and domination are reproduced and cannot account for their genesis (1986:48–50). Thus by reducing a complex set of sociological and psychological phenomena to a single psychoanalytic narrative, such theories "lead to systematic difficulties in accounting for or even seeing major aspects of the construction of gender and gendered social life" (Haraway 1985:76). Moreover, such psychoanalytic accounts are inadequate in that they completely ignore or misrepresent important historical, political, and cultural factors at work in the rise of modern science and in the construction of scientific knowledge.

Such problems have led several radical feminist critics to attempt to adopt more sociologically oriented theory to the examination of the connections between gender and science. The theoretical range of these analyses is as wide as the range of social and political theory which has influenced contemporary feminism: Marxism, critical theory, radical feminism, feminist materialism, deconstruction, and so on. Since examination of this body of work is well beyond the scope of this article, we will simply attempt to summarize briefly one particularly powerful example of such applications of social theory to the feminist critique of the epistemological underpinnings of modern science.

Hilary Rose (1983, 1986) analyzes the "oppressive dichotomies" inherent in the dominant epistemology of science in terms of a feminist materialism in which the production of knowledge is understood as other forms of production, namely in terms of a theoretical understanding of the division of labor. Put simply, she contends that contemporary scientific knowledge is partial, biased, abstract, and alienated because it is produced under the conditions of a class division of labor and a gender division of labor. Focusing on the connections between gender and science, Rose states: "We have to begin by seeing scientific work as the particular example of a general division of knowledge between men and women in the world, which allocates characteristically different forms of work to men and to women" (1986:66). Since the "labour of love" and the experiential knowledge which emerges from such labor are systematically relegated to women, and women have been historically excluded from the production of scientific knowledge, scientific knowledge has taken a specific historical form, reflecting the artificial divisions of labor and knowledge characteristic of the patriarchical and capitalist society in which it emerged and evolved.

Rose claims that "women's labour constitutes a material reality that structures a distinctive understanding of the social and natural worlds" (1986:72). It is this distinctive understanding which provides the basis for an alternative feminist epistemology and in turn "a distinctly feminist science and technology" (Rose 1986:73). Rose insists that this feminist epistemology does not represent simply the displacement of one form of partial and gender-specific knowledge with another partial and gender-specific form. Rather, this feminist epistemology represents a "more complete materialism, a truer knowledge" (Rose 1986:72). At the core of Rose's defense of this feminist epistemology and feminist science is the claim that this epistemology has completely eliminated the series of dualisms which dominated the masculinist epistemology: "It transcends dichotomies, insists on the scientific validity of the subjective, on the need to unite cognitive and affective domains; it emphasizes holism, harmony, and complexity rather than reductionism, domination, and linearity" (1986:72). This new feminist epistemology thus ensures a new science which ends the domination of nature and establishes harmonious, pacific relationships between humanity and nature.

Certainly, Rose and other radical feminist critics of modern science have succeeded in opening new questions concerning the relationships between gender and science at the level of epistemology. However, there remain a number of difficulties with such analyses which have already become an important part of the agenda for those now exploring the connections between gender and science. First, as Rose and several other radical feminist critics expressly acknowledge, their analyses and proposals do have a utopian dimension. This acknowledgment is meant to underline that their own projects are designed to explore future possibilities and alternatives and to reject all versions of "realism" in which existing social divisions and inequalities are rationalized as unchangeable.

At the same time, this utopian element can become incompatible with the desire to "sustain the feminist successor science project" (Rose 1986:74): the radical feminist claim that they are articulating a conception of science and of nature, a "truer picture of reality," than contemporary science can provide. This claim is utopian if feminist critics believe that any philosophical critique and alternative vision, no matter how powerful and comprehensive, will revolutionize science. Rose and other critics acknowledge this in part when they insist that this feminist project "builds on traditions that have always been present in science" (1986:72; also Fee 1986). However, one of the most problematic aspects of Rose's analysis in particular and of these radical epistemological critiques in general is that they fail to demonstrate that their own work does connect with submerged traditions within science. Indeed, their critiques tend to generalize about scientific knowledge and scientific method at a very abstract level removed from any specific body of scientific knowledge, specific set of research problems, or specific research communities or traditions.

Toward a Feminist Science

It is particularly in relation to this weakness that Evelyn Fox Keller's work constitutes one of the most significant contributions to the examination of the connections between gender and science. Keller has utilized a number of different theoretical approaches, including psychoanalytic and historical, in her ongoing attempts to explore the relationship between gender and science at the epistemological level (see in particular the collection of essays in Keller 1985). However, her strongest contributions are made by her attempts to integrate these epistemological issues with specific scientific research, especially in her analysis of the work of Barbara McClintock (Keller 1983; Keller 1985:158– 179).

Although Keller refuses to present McClintock's vision of science as a model of "a feminist science," she does attempt to use McClintock as a case study in "the role of gender in the construction of science" (1985:173–174). Keller claims that McClintock, in order to maintain her integrity and identity as a scientist and as a woman practicing science, had to formulate alternative accounts of mind, of nature, and of the relationship between mind and nature. More specifically, Keller maintains that McClintock's alternative views on these abstract philosophical issues were directly connected to major components of her scientific research: her understanding of difference and complexity as alternatives to dichotomization and hierarchy as organizing principles for ordering the world around us and viewing our relation to that world; her conception of scientific cognition in terms of a "feeling for the organism" which aims not at prediction and power over nature but rather at understanding and a form of empowerment centering in our connection to the world; and her emphasis on function and organization rather than mechanism and structure as constituting the basic elements of a model scientific explanation (1985:162–169). Moreover, Keller (1983) does examine the connections between McClintock's alternative approach to her research and earlier research traditions well established within her field, and she does explore the problems as well as the possibilities posed by the differences between McClintock and the majority of her colleagues.

It is simply too early to assess this very promising inquiry which attempts to link the concern with epistemological issues with specific examples of scientific research in ways that may begin to bridge the presently existing chasm between feminist critics of science and the overwhelming majority of practicing scientists. One theoretical obstacle which clearly remains is the continuing absence of systematic work which explicates elements of gender bias in the philosophical underpinnings of the physical as opposed to the biological and life sciences (Harding 1986 for discussion of these issues). Moreover, Keller's own career moves away from active research in the sciences in order to pursue her feminist projects are indicative of the kind of real practical obstacles which this task must necessarily face.

Finally, there is one additional development which cannot be adequately assessed at present. Some radical feminist critics of science (Haraway 1985; Flax 1987) are beginning to utilize elements of "postmodernist" theory to question the claims and the goal of a feminist epistemology and a feminist science. Donna Haraway, for example, challenges the production of theories of experience and the attempt to formulate a feminist standpoint epistemology as simply new versions of the totalizing theories of the past. She contends that such artificial theoretical unities are produced only at the cost of expelling or delegitimizing important differences which are part of the feminist political struggle (Haraway 1985:76–77). Defenders of the successor science project (Rose 1986; Harding 1986) reply that this would be to relegate feminist epistemology to the oblivion of the plurality of discourses which constitute the postmodernist world and that it is possible to ground claims concerning truth, reason, and objectivity without returning to Enlightenment models of them (Rose 1986:72–74).

Whatever the outcome of this series of discussions and debates (Harding 1986 for a more detailed presentation), it is clear that much of the future work on feminist critiques of the philosophical underpinnings of science will be preoccupied with these very abstract, difficult epistemological and ontological issues. The likely prospect is that feminist discussions of gender and science will become increasingly removed from any realm of discourse which is accessible to the majority of researchers working within the natural sciences. If Keller is correct in identifying the ultimate task of these critiques as "the reclamation, from within science, of science as a human instead of a masculine project" (1985:178), this prospect presents a significant danger which future analyses of gender and science must address.

REFERENCES

Addelson, Kathryn Pyne. 1983. "The man of professional wisdom." Pp. 165–186 in *Discovering Reality,* edited by S. Harding and M. B. Hintikka. Boston: D. Reidel.

Alic, Margaret. 1986. *Hypatia's Heritage: A History of Women in Science from Antiquity to the Nineteenth Century.* Boston: Beacon Press.

Barash, David. 1979. *The Whispering Within.* New York: Harper and Row.

Belenky, Mary Field, et al. 1986. *Women's Ways of Knowing.* New York: Basic Books.

Benbow, Camilla Persson, and Julian Stanley. 1980. "Sex differences in mathematical ability: fact or artifact?" *Science* 210:1262–1264.

Bleier, Ruth. 1986a. "Sex differences in research: science or belief?" Pp. 147–164 in *Feminist Approaches to Science,* edited by R. Bleier. Elmsford, NY: Pergamon Press.

———. 1984. *Science and Gender: A Critique of Biology and Its Theories on Women.* Elmsford, NY: Pergamon Press.

Bleier, Ruth (editor). 1986b. *Feminist Approaches to Science.* Elmsford, NY: Pergamon Press.

Bordo, Susan. 1986. "The Cartesian masculinization of thought." *Signs* 11:439–456.

Chodorow, Nancy. 1978. *The Reproduction of Mothering.* Berkeley: University of California.

Cole, Jonathan R. 1981. "Women in science." *American Scientist* 69:385–91.

———. 1979. *Fair Science.* New York: Free Press.

Dinnerstein, Dorothy. 1976. *The Mermaid and the Minotaur.* New York: Harper and Row.

Dziech, Billie W., and L. Weiner. 1984. *The Lecherous Professor: Sexual Harassment on Campus.* Boston: Beacon Press.

Eisenstein, Hester. 1983. *Contemporary Feminist Thought.* Boston: G. K. Hall.

Fausto-Sterling, Anne. 1985. *Myths of Gender.* New York: Basic Books.

Fee, Elizabeth. 1986. "Critiques of modern science." Pp. 42–56 in *Feminist Approaches to Science,* edited by R. Bleier. Elmsford, NY: Pergamon Press.

———. 1983. "Women's nature and scientific objectivity." Pp. 9–27 in *Woman's Nature: Rationalizations of Inequality,* edited by M. Lowe and R. Hubbard. Elmsford, NY: Pergamon Press.

———. 1976. "Science and the woman problem: historical perspectives." Pp. 175–223 in *Sex Differences: Social and Biological Perspectives,* edited by M. Teitelbaum. New York: Doubleday.

Finkbeiner, A. K. 1987. "Demographics or market forces?" *Mosaic* 18 (10): 10–17.

Flax, Jane. 1987. "Postmodernism and gender relations in feminist theory." *Signs* 12:621–643.

Freeman, Jo. 1979. "How to discriminate against women without really trying." Pp. 217–232 in *Women: A Feminist Perspective.* 2nd ed. Edited by Jo. Freeman. Palo Alto, CA: Mayfield.

Frieze, Irene. 1978. "Psychological barriers for women in sciences: internal and external." Pp. 65–95 in *Covert Discrimination and Women in the Sciences,* edited by J. Ramaley. Boulder: Westview Press.

Gilligan, Carol. 1982. *In a Different Voice.* Cambridge: Harvard University Press.

Goldberg, Steven. 1973. *The Inevitability of Patriarchy.* New York: Morrow.

Gornick, Vivian. 1983. *Women in Science.* New York: Simon and Schuster.

Gould, Stephen J. 1981. *The Mismeasure of Man.* New York: W. W. Norton.

Haraway, Donna. 1986. "Primatology is politics by other means." Pp. 77–78 in *Feminist Approaches to Science,* edited by R. Bleier. New York: Pergamon Press.

———. 1985. "A manifesto for cyborgs: science, technology, and socialist feminism in the 1980s." *Socialist Review* 80:65–105.

———. 1984. "Class, race, sex, scientific objects of knowledge." Pp. 212–229 in *Women in Scientific and Engineering Professions,* edited by C. Perrucci and V. Haas. Ann Arbor: University of Michigan Press.

Harding, Sandra. 1986. *The Science Question in Feminism.* Ithaca, NY: Cornell University Press.

Hrdy, Sarah Blaffer. 1986. "Empathy, polyandry, and the myth of the coy female." Pp. 119–146 in *Feminist Approaches to Science,* edited by R. Bleier. Elmsford, NY: Pergamon Press.

Hutt, Corinne. 1972. *Males and Females.* Harmundsworth, Middlesex: Penguin.

Jacob, Margaret. 1988. *The Cultural Roots of Science.* Philadelphia: Temple University Press.

Keller, Evelyn Fox. 1985. *Reflections on Gender and Science.* New Haven: Yale University Press.

———. 1983. *A Feeling for the Organism: The Life and Work of Barbara McClintock.* San Francisco: Freeman.

———. 1977. "The anomaly of a woman in physics." Pp. 77–91 in *Working It Out,* edited by S. Ruddick and P. Daniels. New York: Pantheon.

Keller, Evelyn Fox, and Lee Aaron Segal. 1970. "Initiation of slime mold aggregation viewed as an instability." *Journal of Theoretical Biology* 26:399–415.

Kuhn, Thomas S. 1970. *The Structure of Scientific Revolutions*. Chicago: University of Chicago.

Matyas, Marsha. 1985. "Obstacles and constraints on women in science: preparation and participation in the scientific community." Pp. 77–101 in *Women in Science: A Report from the Field*, edited by J. Kahle. Philadelphia: Falmer Press.

Medawar, Peter. 1979. *Advice to a Young Scientist*. New York: Harper and Row.

Merchant, Carolyn. 1983. "Mining the earth's womb." Pp. 99–117 in *Machina ex Dea: Feminist Perspectives on Technology*, edited by J. Rothschild. New York: Pergamon Press.

———. 1980. *The Death of Nature: Women, Ecology and the Scientific Revolution*. New York: Harper and Row.

Money, John, and Anke Ehrhardt. 1972. *Man and Woman, Boy and Girl*. Baltimore: Johns Hopkins University Press.

Murphy, Angela. 1980. " 'Ladies' in the lab." Pp. 18–41 in *Science and Liberation*, edited by R. Arditti et al. Boston: South End Press.

Namenwirth, M. 1986. "Science seen through a feminist prism." Pp. 18–41 in *Feminist Approaches to Science*, edited by R. Bleier. Elmsford, NY: Pergamon Press.

National Science Foundation. 1984. *Women and Minorities in Science and Engineering*. Washington, DC: U.S. Government Printing Office.

Project on the Status and Education of Women. 1982. *The Classroom Climate: A Chilly One For Women?* Washington, DC: Association of American Colleges.

Ramaley, Judith. 1978. "Introduction and overview." Pp. 1–6 in *Covert Discrimination and Women in the Sciences*, edited by J. Ramaley. Boulder: Westview Press.

Reskin, Barbara. 1978. "Sex differentiation and the social organization of science." *Sociological Inquiry* 48 (3–4): 6–37.

Rose, Hilary. 1986. "Beyond masculinist realities: a feminist epistemology for the sciences." Pp. 57–76 in *Feminist Approaches to Science*, edited by R. Bleier. Elmsford, NY: Pergamon Press.

———. 1983. "Hand, brain and heart: a feminist epistemology for the natural sciences." *Signs* 9 (2): 73–90.

Rossi, Alice. 1965. "Why so few?" *Science* 148:1196–1202.

Rossiter, Margaret. 1982. *Women Scientists in America*. Baltimore: John Hopkins University Press.

Schiebinger, Londa. 1987. "The history and philosophy of women in science: a review essay." *Signs* 12 (2): 305–332.

Sells, Lucy. 1980. "The mathematics filter and the education of women and minorities." Pp. 66–75 in *Women and the Mathematical Mystique*, edited by L. Fox et al. Baltimore: Johns Hopkins University Press.

Shaffer, Blaine. 1962. "The Acrasina." *Advances in Morphogenesis* 2:109–182.

Smith, Elske. 1978. "The individual and the institution." Pp. 7–35 in *Covert Discrimination and Women in the Sciences*, edited by J. Ramaley. Boulder: Westview Press.

U.S. Bureau of the Census. 1986. *Current Population Reports*. Series P-60, no. 151.

Vetter, B. 1987. "Women's progress." *Mosaic* 18 (1): 2–9.

Watson, James, and Francis Crick. 1953. "Genetical implications of the structure of deoxyribonucleic acid." *Nature* 171:964–967.

Weisstein, Naomi. 1982. "The adventures of a woman in science." Pp. 265–281 in

Biological Woman—The Convenient Myth, edited by R. Hubbard, M. Henefin, and B. Fried. Boston: Schenkman.

Wilson, Edward O. 1975. *Sociobiology: The New Synthesis.* Cambridge: Harvard University Press.

Women's Group from Science for the People. 1980. "Declaration: equality for women in science." Pp. 283–286 in *Science and Liberation,* edited by R. Arditti et al. Boston: South End Press.

2

The Plot of Gender: The How-To Romance of *Pride and Prejudice*

Susan Jaret McKinstry

> Now, of course, I know that it was as difficult being a girl as it was a boy, if not more so. While I stood paralyzed at one end of a dance floor trying to find the courage to ask a girl for a dance, most of the girls waited in terror at the other, afraid that no one, not even I, would ask them. . . . No, it wasn't easy for any of us, girls and boys, as we forced our beautiful, free-flowing child-selves into those narrow, constricting cubicles labeled *female and male*.
>
> Lester 1973:112–113

> Perhaps . . . "woman" is not a determinable identity. Perhaps woman is not a thing which announces itself from a distance, at a distance from some other thing. . . . Perhaps woman—a non-identity, non-figure, a simulacrum—is distance's very chasm, the out-distancing of distance, the interval's cadence, distance itself.
>
> Derrida 1977:49

Literature is often read as a template for gender definition, a guide to social dictates and utopian alternatives for maleness and femaleness in any given period. The subject of much literature is sexual relationships, from the bawdy tales of Chaucer to the seventeenth-century *carpe diem* love poetry of Andrew Marvell to the queasy contemporary divorces of John Updike or Ann Beattie. As Nancy Armstrong claims, "The novel, together with all manner of printed material, helped to redefine what men were supposed to desire in women and what women, in turn, were supposed to desire to be" (1987:251). Initially written for a predominantly female audience, the novel was conceived as a forum for vicarious excitement *and* moral illustration: after their Gothic escapades, heroines renounce adventure and marry the hero (while unsuccessful heroines die as a warning to readers). Foregrounding romantic ideology and sexual difference, the romance plot presents marriage as the capstone of success: good men (rich) marry good girls (obedient).

After constructing gender by demarcating the rules of behavior for the male and the female, the romance plot unites the sexes; but it also unites the private self with the public demands of gender, as A. O. J. Cockshut comments:

This double character of love, private and public at the same time, makes general thinking about it peculiarly difficult. It is easy enough to think of love in personal terms, romantic, sensual, faithful, inconstant, predatory or sacrificial. It is easy to think of moral duties, marriage laws and courting customs. But it is extremely difficult to think and write accurately about the strange, shifting no-man's-land between the two. (1978:10)

That shifting area is the site of fiction, where invented individuals follow *and* flaunt the gender customs demanded by their world. By reading characters' lives, and vicariously experiencing them, readers learn the rules of gender: in romance plot and cultural ideology, the reward for proper gender differentiation is marriage. But the definition of male and female, the way in which that marriage is achieved, and the options available to the gendered character all change as the cultural and literary rules change. Examining the impact of gender on the writer, the character, and the reader, feminist literary theory questions how we use language—or it uses us—and how male and female speech and writing differ (Abel 1980; Bauer 1988; Flynn and Schweickart 1986; Lakoff 1975; Spender 1980). In addition, feminist literary theory demonstrates how authorial gender influences the choice of literary genres and how plots reflect (and distort) social and sexual dictates in their quest to divide and define male and female and, ultimately, unite them.

The central problem here, of course, is how to define man and woman in a post-structural, post-feminist age, when we recognize that gender is constructed out of a need to define and predict human behaviors and options. Further, any definition that defines biologically determined sex as a single category—such as Woman—erases the essential differences of race, class, experience, (sub)culture, sexual orientation, and politics (de Lauretis 1986; Marks and de Courtivron 1981). The binary opposition between male/female (and its related pairs: reason/emotion, active/passive, independent/dependent) are questioned and deconstructed. Linguistic, psychological, and developmental studies indicate that there are *potentially* as many differences between woman and woman or man and man, as between men and women (Rosaldo and Lamphere 1974; Williams 1979; Jaggar and Rothenberg Struhl 1978; Chodorow 1978; Eisenstein 1983; Ortner and Whitehead 1981). Instead of an absolute, gender appears to be a spectrum of behavior with social labels of "maleness" and "femaleness" applied to traits that either sex can exhibit.

Over the last few decades, feminist literary theory has tried to understand the connection between language, gender, and genre in an effort to define woman (Miller 1986; Showalter 1985; Meese 1986). Many French feminist critics study the nature of female language *(l'ecriture feminin)* and psychology (Marks and de Courtivron 1981; Jardine and Eisenstein 1980; Jardine 1985; Moi 1985), while many American critics focus on examinations of female experience (Eisenstein 1983; Chodorow 1978; Frye 1986; Gilligan 1982; Fetterley 1978). All feminist critics, however, ask questions about women's situation in the world as reader, author, or character. I would divide feminist literary inquiry into four basic areas: questions of omission (questioning the dearth of female authors in the literary canon of great works), suppression (examining why women did not write), revision (understanding how literary history constructs the world, and feminist revision reconstructs it), and expression (exploring textual commentary, omissions, and subversions; the ways that writing and speaking are gendered and judged).

The problem of defining gender affects all of these areas, particularly in terms of exploring the connection between literature and life, plot expectations and human experience. Feminist literary scholarship highlights gender in the relation between experience, characters, texts, and textuality, wondering, for example, why women tell the stories they tell—or why specific stories are told about women—with such little variation. In fiction, plot often tells us what the culture believes gender should be; gender and genre are related means of constructing assumptions about maleness and femaleness through plot. Joanna Russ (1972:9) asks, "What can a heroine do?" The "Love Story" gives three options: falling in love, dying, or going mad (Russ 1972:9). Nancy K. Miller (1981) argues that the need for "plausibility" binds women to the erotic plot (romance, celebrating community, and marriage) while men are capable of the ambitious plot (the self-directed quest, celebrating individuality, and personal success), for autonomy is an implausible end to female emplotment.

Although real women presumably have broader options than fictional characters, these critics recognize the dual function of narrative as an expression of the cultural ideology that coerces the writer into using received plots and as an expression of resistance to that coercion. We tell stories to order (and sometimes disorder, or defamiliarize) the world as we perceive it. Joanne Frye argues that "experience cannot be absolutely separated from language but that language and experience are not fully coextensive either" (1986:17). Telling a story about an experience transforms it into narrative, and clearly, living and telling stories are not identical acts. Yet the distinction is complicated, since we relate (and relate to) experience through narrative, with its options and coercions. Narrated experience is both personal *and* political, indeed. Frye notes the problems inherent in such retellings: "Can available language elucidate women's lives or is it inescapably patriarchal? Can women interpret their own experience or is experience itself always already interpreted?'' (1986:15).

If woman is traditionally defined by her familial place in the culture—hence her named role as daughter, wife, or mother—it is difficult to perceive her as separate from her (love) story. Individual experience is already interpreted by the culture. Unmarried men are not denigrated, but unmarried women are spinsters or ''old maids'' (also the term for unpopped—useless—popcorn), and in the Victorian era these women were called ''surplus'' or ''redundant.'' Yet clearly many women choose not to marry or bear children; some women do choose the ambitious text—and some choose both the ambitious and the erotic texts. And fiction, in the conventional form of the romance plot, defines and refines our understanding of gender through judgments about these choices on the level of the surface text and its subversive voice. A genre can be examined for its restrictions, its gender system that makes certain stories ''plausible'' and others ''implausible'' for women. The textual language can be examined for its innate gendering, and the specific narrative voice can be studied for its response to the cultural assumptions of the genre and language through which it speaks. Given the rule of the ''Love Story'' for women—marriage, tragedy, or madness—how does a text create an ending that opens new possibilities for heroines?

In plot and purpose, the novel centers around traditional definitions of gender. Nancy Armstrong claims that the romance plot creates and articulates the rules of gender: ''narratives which seemed to be concerned solely with matters of courtship and marriage in fact seized the authority to say what was female'' (1987:5–6). Successfully differentiating male and female behavior, ''narratives in which a woman's virtue alone overcomes sexual aggression and transforms male desire into middle-class love'' reinforce gender expectations: ''to coax and nudge sexual desire in conformity with the norms of heterosexual monogamy affords a fine way of closing a novel and provides a satisfactory goal for a text to achieve'' (Armstrong 1987:5–6).

Ironically, romance must first reinforce the opposition between male and female and then unite them in marriage. Jane Austen's famous *Pride and Prejudice* (1966 [1813]) begins with the sentence that sums up the literary—and literal—plot of gender: ''It is a truth universally acknowledged, that a single man in possession of a good fortune, must be in want of a wife'' (Ibid.:1). Many novels illustrate that universal truth through the dangers and rewards of the romantic plot. For example, Clarissa inevitably dies after Lovelace (presumably) rapes her (Richardson 1985 [1747]); ''Reader, I married him'' (Bronte 1971 [1847]: 395) boasts Jane Eyre after previously escaping bigamy with the now-widowed Rochester. One of Italo Calvino's characters in *If on a Winter's Night a Traveler* argues that ''a story could only end in two ways: having passed all the tests, the hero and heroine married, or else they died'' (1979:159), to which the narrator responds, ''in a flash, you decide you want to marry Ludmilla'' (Ibid.:159). Not every hero or heroine ends up married or dead, certainly—but a good number do, and enough to indicate a pattern in the genre that emplots gender training as essential to social success.

The ideology of romance triumphs: gender training is plotted, male and female are divided, and plots reward obedience to the rules of gender with marriage. Yet variations in that pattern indicate the complicated ideology of such social dictates, the literary convention that reinforces them, and the text that rebels against them. In fact, the romantic plot is often seen as dangerous to women, either corrupting them into sexual fantasy (in the nineteenth century) or tranquilizing them into domestic acceptance (in the twentieth century). In George Gissing's *The Odd Women,* a feminist claims:

If every novelist could be strangled and thrown into the sea, we should have some chance of reforming women. . . . What is more vulgar than the ideal of novelists? They won't represent the actual world; it would be too dull for their readers. In real life, how many men and women *fall in love?* Not one in every ten thousand have felt for each other as two or three couples do in every novel. (1977 [1893]:58).

Austen's *Pride and Prejudice* (the original model for Harlequin romances) provides the rules of male and female behavior and the predictability of a romantic novel. At the same time, the novel's subtle rebellions against ideology indicate that fiction does not merely mirror the socially prescribed gender roles but creates artfully described alternatives, subversions, and revisions. Within the limits of decorum prescribed by culture and genre, Jane Austen's novels allow men and women who bend the rules to marry. *Pride and Prejudice* both reinforces and challenges some of our assumptions about gender, genre, and the ideology of romance.

The opening line of *Pride and Prejudice,* "It is a truth universally acknowledged, that a single man in possession of a good fortune, must be in want of a wife" (1966 [1813]:1) sets up a number of the gender assumptions of the romance plot. The "truth" is "universal," the man is "single" while the woman is "a wife," and the man possesses a "good fortune" but wants a wife—therefore the wife is a purchasable commodity that any single man with money can have (Levi-Strauss 1968). Desire—"want"—is born out of a context of cash; having money means wanting a wife. Wives (women) do not want, nor do they possess anything, while men both possess *and* want. This omniscient narrative voice is expressing the traditional ideology of romance, and feminist critics could be outraged by its assumptions about woman's place.

The text continues: "However little known the feelings or views of such a man may be, this truth is so well fixed in the minds of the surrounding families, that he is considered as the rightful property of some one or other of their daughters" (1966 [1813]:1). Suddenly the text broadens the gender definitions: males are *also* "property," are "rightful" objects of desire by families with "some one or other" daughters, despite any man's "feelings or views" to the contrary. (We still know nothing about any daughter's feelings). A woman is known relationally as "a wife" or "some one or other of [her family's] daughters"; a man by his "good fortune" and lack of relation ("single"). Both men and women are objectified, are made pawns in the "universal truth" of marriage without regard to any individuality. But romance demands a balance of very precise public expectations ("First comes love, then comes marriage" claims the children's rhyme) and equally strong private desires ("It had to be *you*," argues the song). So when the novel moves to the individual level, we read to find the balance of public expectations and private expressions in the story.

Jane Bennet and Charles Bingley seem to fulfill the novel's opening: her mother, with five daughters, "is thinking of his marrying one of them," (Ibid:1) and Bingley has "four or five thousand a year" (Ibid.:1), and is "fond of dancing, . . . a certain step towards falling in love" (Ibid.:5). Instead, however, Elizabeth becomes the heroine of the text, though she is not singled out until Chapter 5, when her sister Jane leaves and we as readers stay behind with Elizabeth. Likewise, Bingley's friend Darcy, the richest man in the novel, becomes the hero, though his prideful manners disqualify him for some time. And despite the novel's opening, their individual feelings seem to deny that universal truth: Darcy considers Elizabeth "tolerable, but not handsome enough to tempt *me*" (Ibid.:7), and Elizabeth claims that "I could easily forgive *his* pride, if he had not mortified *mine*" (Ibid.:12). "If I were determined to get a rich husband, or any husband" (Ibid.:14), she admits she might behave more selflessly, more appropriately (Chapter 6). He does not want a wife; she does not want a husband. Hence the novel sets up rules for gender and provides the perfect couple, Jane and Bingley; then undercuts them by presenting an alternate, imperfect hero and heroine, Elizabeth and Darcy, who must both redefine personal opinions and bad "first impressions" (the first title of the novel) in order to marry.

The power of gender is most evident in the proposal scenes. Marriage is, after all, the "universal truth" of the novel, the "business" of Mrs. Bennet, the reward for obedience to the rules of gender, and the goal of romance. And Elizabeth receives three proposals. She is seen as a potential wife throughout the novel—by Miss Bingley, who teases Darcy about Elizabeth's "fine eyes" (Ibid.:18); by Darcy himself, who struggles against his feelings for her; and by Collins, her cousin who will inherit her father's estate.

Collins is the perfect fulfillment of the novel's opening. Coming to town "with the design of selecting a wife," wishing "to set the example of matrimony" to his parishioners, and anxious to "chuse a wife from among [Bennet's] daughters" (Ibid.:74) to offset the financial damage his inheritance will cause the family, Collins arbitrarily selects Elizabeth and makes his "declaration in form" (Ibid.:73). She refuses.

"I am not now to learn," replied Mr Collins with a formal wave of the hand, "that it is *usual* with young ladies to reject the addresses of the man they *secretly* mean to accept, when he first applies for their favor; and that sometimes the refusal is *repeated* a second or even a third time. I am therefore by no means discouraged by what you have just said, and shall hope to lead you to the altar ere long.

"Upon my *word,* Sir," cried Elizabeth, "your hope is rather an extraordinary one after my declaration. I do assure you that I am not one of those young ladies (if such young ladies there are) who are so daring as to risk their happiness on the chance of being asked a second time. I am perfectly *serious* in my refusal." (my emphases, Ibid.:75)

Gender overcomes individuality here. Elizabeth's "word" is meaningless in the face of Collins' knowledge of "usual" behavior for young ladies who "secretly" mean yes when they say no (how does he know that?—perhaps he has been reading romances!), and her "serious" refusal will not be believed even if she repeats it, for his romance plot includes those repetitions.

Calling Elizabeth's language "the established custom of your sex" (Ibid.:76) and "consistent with the true delicacy of the female character" (Ibid.:76), Collins ignores her individual desires. Elizabeth's language fails to overcome his gender assumptions: "I know not how to express my refusal in such a way as may convince you of its being one" (Ibid.:76), she cries. He defines her refusal as "merely words of course" (Ibid.:76)—ironically, they are only words (what other form of expression does she have?), and words that he can fit into his script for a marriage proposal. The male/female differences between them are clear and deny her even the power of refusal. He points out that he has money and connections, but she has no money, no family connections, and may get no other offers:

"As I must therefore conclude that you are not serious in your rejection of me, I shall chuse to attribute it to your wish of increasing my love by suspense, according to the usual practice of elegant females."

"[T]o accept [your proposal] is absolutely impossible. My feelings in every respect forbid it. Can I speak plainer? Do not consider me now as an elegant female intending to plague you, but as a rational creature speaking the truth from her heart." (Ibid.:76)

Elizabeth's language increases in strength, in honesty, in opinion; Collins is uniformly deaf to her meaning because he sees her as an "elegant female," as the fulfillment of the "universal truth" of the novel. Seeking definition "as a rational creature speaking the truth from her heart" (Ibid.:76), Elizabeth overlooks the law of gender. As a female, she is not rational; her speech is silenced by male meanings. The "truth" is that she will say yes; her heart is, finally, irrelevant to the discussion. Unable to translate her feelings into words that will be understood by Collins, Elizabeth retreats "in silence" (Ibid.:76) to get her father's aid in the refusal, since his "negative might be uttered in such a manner as must be decisive" (Ibid.:77). The proposal scene sets out the fixed expectations of female behavior and demonstrates Elizabeth's individual (female) inability to overrule them.

Despite Collins's warning, Elizabeth receives two more marriage proposals in the novel—both from Darcy, who embodies perfect maleness: he is rich and single. And although the townspeople recognize his rudeness, he is still a public object of desire because he can transform a daughter into a wife. "In spite of her deeply-rooted dislike, [Elizabeth] could not be insensible to the compliment of such a man's affection" (Ibid.:131). His proposal differs from Collins's in that it is based on love: Darcy cries, "My feelings will not be repressed. You must allow me to tell you how ardently I admire and love you" (Ibid.:130). This is the stuff of romance, we think. He has individually chosen her above all others. But he goes on to cite Elizabeth's financial and familial disadvantages, "his sense of her inferiority—of its being a degradation" (Ibid.: 131), and his struggle "to conquer" his unreasonable desire. He may individualize her, but only as the recipient of his emotions without concern for hers. As the narrative voice comments, his rude honesty "was very unlikely to recommend his suit" (Ibid.: 131).

But he is not concerned by any danger in his rudeness. Darcy trusts the rules of gender and assumes that his position as "a single man in possession of a good fortune" (Ibid.:1) must make him "the property" (Ibid.:1) of any woman he chooses, and that she has no power of refusal. When Darcy concludes his proposal with "the hope" that "it would now be rewarded by her acceptance" (Ibid.:131) Elizabeth "could easily see that he had no doubt of a favourable answer. He *spoke* of apprehension and anxiety, but his countenance expressed real security" (Ibid.:131). She believes his words expressing the doubt and anxiety appropriate to the context are "mere words of course" (Ibid.:76), for she reads assurance in his face and it infuriates her. Like Collins, she cites the "usual custom" of behavior in proposals, answering that "it is, *I believe,* the established mode to express a sense of obligation for the sentiments avowed, however unequally they may be returned" (my emphasis, Ibid.:131). Yet she questions that custom. She expresses only belief in "established mode," not acceptance of it, and she emphasizes her personal rejection of "unequally . . . returned" sentiments: "If I could *feel* gratitude, I would now thank you. But I cannot—I have never desired your good opinion, and you have certainly bestowed it most unwillingly" (Ibid.:131). Form must follow feeling. Although the "established mode" dictates her acceptance, she revises that mode to express herself more completely as one who can (or can*not*) desire, and as one who can say no.

Having learned from Collins that her "serious" refusal may not be accepted, Elizabeth rejects Darcy even more rudely when he accuses her of "so little *endeavor* at civility" (Ibid.:131): " 'I might as well enquire,' replied she, 'why with so evident a design of offending and insulting me, you chose to tell me that you liked me against your will, against your reason, and even against your character' " (Ibid.:132). He "catches her words with no less resentment than surprise," then with "mingled incredulity and mortification" (Ibid.:133). When she declares, "I had not known you a month before I felt that you were the last man in the world whom I could ever be prevailed on to marry" (Ibid.:133), he does not accuse her of being "an elegant female" (Ibid.:76). On the contrary. Unlike Collins, Darcy takes her at her word and leaves. Her language has broken the bonds of gender expectations and freed her from being misunderstood.

Collins's "declaration in form" taught Elizabeth how inessential her personal feelings and female language were in the face of male expectations; Darcy's proposal showed her that she could exercise the power of refusal, but at the cost of her civility and, she fears, the loss of her emotional options. For she revises her opinion of him. "She began now to comprehend that he was exactly the man, who, in disposition and talents, would most suit her" (Ibid.:214). "An union that must have been to the advantage of both" (Ibid.:214), their marriage would now fulfill both the public and private needs of romance. But because of her powerful rejections, her refusal to fill the role of accepting female, "no such happy marriage could now teach the admiring multitude what connubial felicity really was" (Ibid.:214). Breaking the model for womanly behavior, she cannot become the model wife.

The third proposal scene revises the lessons of the first two. Darcy proposes again in the language of romance: *"My* affections and wishes are unchanged, but one word from you will silence me on this subject for ever" (Ibid.:252). Suddenly Elizabeth is given the power to refuse with *one* word; her repetitions and revisions with Collins and Darcy are no longer necessary. And unlike the first two occasions, where we as readers were privy to the language of the characters, we get reported speech here. Elizabeth "forced herself to speak" (Ibid.:252) and, "not very fluently, gave him to understand, that her sentiments had undergone so material a change" (Ibid.:252) that she wants to marry him. Suddenly "sentiments" are "material"; the feelings that were irrelevant to Collins and unbelievable to Darcy are primary, and able to overcome even the material disadvantage of her family and fortune. In response, "he expressed himself on the occasion as sensibly and as warmly as a man violently in love can be supposed to do" (Ibid.:252). Suddenly the opposites of male and female, demanded by romance and amply illustrated in Collins's proposal, are united in the language of both characters. Darcy's speech is sensible *and* warm, Elizabeth's material sentiments are expressed (though not fluently) *and* give understanding.

The rules of gender have been broken and, ironically, the result is marriage. The "truth universally acknowledged" (Ibid.:1) becomes a fact; the single men marry, and many of the daughters become wives. Yet the individual variations indicate the inevitable complexity in the progress of the plot of romance which demands initial sexual division and final sexual union. As Elaine Hoffman Baruch notes:

If it is true as Freud said that "some obstacle is necessary to swell the tide of the libido to its height," it may be that romantic love can only thrive in an atmosphere of tension and difference, either that supplied by the prohibitions of the social order, as in adulterous love, or that provided by a polarization of the sexes as in traditional marriage. It is conceivable that the combination of romantic passion and equality cannot exist. (1980:56)

The "polarization of the sexes" provided by the gender assumptions in these proposal scenes paradoxically indicates the power and powerlessness inherent in conventional male and female uses of language (asking/refusing, reason/ emotion) and breaks down any neat division between those binaries. And the result of these initial inequalities is romantic equality, as Baruch claims:

The polarization of the sexes that existed in romantic marriage was seemingly a sign of great inequality. In some ways, however, romantic love was an equalizer in an age of hierarchy. By exalting a chosen individual over all others, it was able to transcend differences of class and sex. (1980:63–64)

For romance is, essentially, a political act. It is the site of the conflict between the social rules of gender and the individual desires that revise those rules, as the happy ending of *Pride and Prejudice* indicates. Seeking to uncover gender inequalities in the world and textual inadequacies in the word, literary critics often see language as both absolute and arbitrary, showing cultural prisons and literary misprisions. And the future of literary explorations of the definition of gender are still balanced between the word and the world. Linda Alcoff (1988) differentiates between cultural feminism, which does not challenge "the defining of woman but only that definition given by men" (Ibid.:407), and post-structuralism's "nominalism," or "the idea that the category 'woman' is a fiction and that feminist efforts must be directed toward dismantling this fiction" (Ibid.:417). While cultural feminism seeks the essential nature of woman, post-structuralism believes that "the politics of gender or sexual difference must be replaced with a plurality of difference where gender loses its position of significance" (Ibid.: 407). Alcoff (1988) argues that both of these positions threaten to dismantle feminism and posits a theory of gender as "positionality," in which "gender is not natural, biological, universal, ahistorical, or essential" (Ibid.:433) yet "gender is relevant because we are taking gender as a position from which to act politically" (Ibid.: 433). Certainly the word has the power to form (and transform) the world. The text's generic conventions and subversions become political acts commenting on the limited options inherent in the rules of gender.

Part of the feminist contribution to theory is a playful awareness of language, using puns and hyphens to reassert the constructions of language as "manmade" rather than natural, as political rather than neutral: *his*tory versus *hers*tory, gyn/ecology, re-vision, *in*valid women writers, and so on. But this playfulness marks a serious challenge to structures of power and meaning in texts and in the world. If women read differently than men, then assumptions about "relevance" and "universal truths" are questionable. If women use language differently than men, then belief in a common language is a myth. And if women experience the world differently, then assumptions about "the human condition" are incorrect. Feminist criticism examines experience (as lived or as represented in texts) and tries to deconstruct the cultural assumptions about man's power and woman's "place" as speaking subjects and linguistic objects. And if Elizabeth Bennet's story is an example, men and women are indeed taught to read, speak, and live differently. But they can also re-learn, revise the rules, and perhaps end happily.

REFERENCES

Abel, Elizabeth (editor). 1980. *Writing and Sexual Difference*. Chicago: University of Chicago Press.

Alcoff, Linda. 1988. "Cultural feminism versus post-structuralism: the identity crisis in feminist theory." *Signs* 13 (3): 406–436.

Armstrong, Nancy. 1987. *Desire and Domestic Fiction: A Political History of the Novel*. New York: Oxford University Press.

Austen, Jane. 1966 [1813]. *Pride and Prejudice*. New York: W. W. Norton.

Baruch, Elaine Hoffman. 1980. "Women and love: some dying myths." Pp. 51–65 in *The Analysis of Literary Texts*, edited by R. Pope. New York: Bilingual Press.

Bauer, Dale. 1988. *Feminist Dialogics: A Theory of Failed Community*. Albany: SUNY Press.

Bronte, Charlotte. 1971 [1847]. *Jane Eyre*. New York: W. W. Norton.

Calvino, Italo. 1979. *If on a Winter's Night a Traveler*. New York: Harcourt Brace.

Chodorow, Nancy. 1978. *The Reproduction of Mothering: Psychoanalysis and the Sociology of Gender*. Berkeley: University of California Press.

Cockshut, A. O. J. 1978. *Man and Woman: A Study of Love in the Novel 1740–1940*. New York: Oxford University Press.

de Lauretis, Teresa (editor). 1986. *Feminist Studies/Critical Studies*. Bloomington: Indiana University Press.

Derrida, Jacque. 1977. *Spurs: Nietsche's Styles,* translated by Barbara Harlow. Chicago: University of Chicago Press.

Eisenstein, Hester. 1983. *Contemporary Feminist Theory*. Boston: G. K. Hall.

Fetterley, Judith. 1978. *The Resisting Reader: A Feminist Approach to American Literature*. Bloomington: Indiana University Press.

Flynn, Elizabeth, and Patrocinio Schweickart. 1986. *Gender and Reading*. Baltimore: Johns Hopkins University Press.

Frye, Joanne. 1986. *Living Stories, Telling Lives*. Ann Arbor: University of Michigan Press.

Gilligan, Carol. 1982. *In a Different Voice: Psychological Theory and Women's Development*. Cambridge: Harvard University Press.

Gissing, George. 1977 [1893]. *The Odd Women*. New York: W. W. Norton.

Jaggar, Alison, and Paula Rothenberg Struhl (editors). 1978. *Feminist Frameworks: Alternative Theoretical Accounts of the Relations Between Women and Men*. New York: McGraw-Hill.

Jardine, Alice. 1985. *Gynesis: Configurations of Woman and Modernity*. Ithaca, NY: Cornell University Press.

Jardine, Alice, and Hester Eisenstein (editors). 1980. *The Future of Difference*. Boston: G. K. Hall

Lakoff, Robin. 1975. *Language and Woman's Place*. New York: Harper and Row.

Lester, Julius. 1973. "Men: being a boy." *Ms* 2 (1) : 112–113.

Levi-Strauss, Claude. 1968. *Structural Anthropology*. London: Allen Lane.

Marks, Elaine, and Isabelle de Courtivron (editors). 1981. *New French Feminisms*. New York: Schocken Books.

Meese, Elizabeth. 1986. *Crossing the Double-Cross: The Practice of Feminist Criticism*. Chapel Hill: University of North Carolina Press.

Miller, Nancy K. 1981. "Emphasis added: plots and plausibilities in women's fiction." *PMLA* 96 (1): 36–48.

———. 1986. *Poetics of Gender*. New York: Columbia University Press.

Moi, Toril. 1985. *Sexual/Textual Politics*. London: Metheun.

Ortner, Sherry, and Harriet Whitehead. 1981. *Sexual Meanings: The Cultural Construction of Gender and Sexuality*. Cambridge: Cambridge University Press.

Richardson, Samuel. 1985 [1747]. *Clarissa or the History of a Young Lady*. New York: Viking Press.

Rosaldo, Michelle Zimbalist, and Louise Lamphere (editors). 1974. *Woman, Culture and Society*. Stanford: Stanford University Press.

Russ, Joanna. 1972. "What can a heroine do? Or why women can't write." Pp. 3–20 in *Images of Women in Fiction,* edited by S. K. Cornillon. Bowling Green, OH: Bowling Green University Press.

Showalter, Elaine (editor). 1985. *The New Feminist Criticism*. New York: Pantheon Books.

Spender, Dale. 1980. *Man Made Language*. London: Routledge and Kegan Paul.

Williams, Juanita (editor). 1979. *Psychology of Woman*. New York: W. W. Norton.

3

The Image of the Word: The Representation of Books in Medieval Iconography

Maryann E. Brink

"For Christ is a sort of book written into the skin of the Virgin."[1]

Medieval think pieces often began with a key text, and Pierre Besuire's metaphor of Christ as a book "written into the skin of the Virgin" serves such a purpose in this study. The imagery of this phrase is intensely medieval; only one whose own days were passed laboriously copying books into the skins of sheep would have thought of it.[2] Besuire's choice of terms suggests that Christ is one among a number of *sorts* of "books" possible in this context. Medieval people were preoccupied with the creation of categories, and images such as Besuire's sorts of books allowed them to impose order on the chaos of the period. The creation of categories, while useful in the pursuit of medieval order, naturally left interstices of thought, experience, and knowledge unaccounted for. This chapter examines two sets of interstices, that between literacy and its representation and that between secular and sacred knowledge, for insight into the workings of the medieval conceptualization of the relationship of gender and knowledge. In particular, this chapter concerns itself with representations in medieval art of the Virgin and other women as literally the keepers of the book.

In Western society today books are so commonplace as to escape notice. Only occasionally does even the content of a book attract attention; we concern ourselves with what is concretely conveyed from its pages to our consciousness. In former times this was not the case, for during the Middle Ages books were less common than the precious stones used to encrust their covers. So rare indeed, that the very *object* of the book became sacred, mysterious. The object could be revered by all, but its content was reserved for contemplation by the few. Thus could Besuire's sorts of books provide yet another image: Christ as a book, worshipped by all yet comprehended by few.

For medieval people, the Bible was the most powerful of books. All other books flowed from it, all religious art and iconography referred back to it. Even granting numerous classical, pre-Christian and extra-European influences, medieval Western European art, in whatever form, as well as secular texts, had somehow to reconcile themselves to Christian influence. To take upon oneself the writing of other books was a sacred task and an enormous responsibility. The social and theological pitfalls were numerous. One need note only that while heresy trials for writers are legion, hardly ever does one encounter similar proceedings against painters and sculptors. Medieval authors occupied a position directly analogous to that of God at Creation. As God's word created the universe, so did an author's words create a new universe.[3] From the end of the Roman Empire until about the year AD 1000, medieval books concerned themselves primarily with issues of religion and morality. Even transcriptions of classical works and the various law codes redacted in this period had as their goal the living of a morally exemplary life or the containment of the evil that medieval people fervently believed was abroad in their world. Little was written in Western Europe in this period that had a truly secular content. Beginning about the eleventh century, however, the revitalization of cities and with them the appearance of a middle class grown ever more dependent upon literacy to conduct its business, increased the number and types of books available. For the first time since the classical period, literacy was put to uses other than the edification of the soul. Only with the development of the printing press and the Reformation, however, did large percentages of the European population gain access to the contents of books.[4]

As sacred objects, books of the early Middle Ages had powerful protectors, particularly the monks who guarded, reproduced, and transmitted them across generations. Discussions of the monks' role in preserving literate culture in the Middle Ages are commonplace and examples of their work, like the Book of Kells and the Lindisfarne Gospels, are well known. Yet an examination of medieval painting and sculpture demonstrates that another category of persons had power similar to that of the monks; they too were keepers and transmitters of the book. These other persons also mediated between the world and the life force, interpreting the message of the book. They were women.

Why women? Given the relatively powerless position of medieval women in politics and the economy, it may at first seem surprising that they should be represented in art as custodians and transmitters of religious knowledge. The beginnings of explanation are to be found in the keeping of book knowledge by monks during the Dark Ages of the sixth through eleventh centuries. The organization of the medieval ecclesiastical hierarchy as a powerful source of paternalism has sometimes obscured the fact that monks and, after the final enforcement of clerical celibacy in the twelfth century, priests, were not mas-culine figures, but self-consciously self-determined non-sexual beings. By re-jecting physical expressions of their sexuality, celibates sought to reaffirm their identity as spiritual beings and to seek closer union with the life of the spirit. The mortal world supported the Church in this regard—in the case of monks and nuns, a person entering the monastery was legally dead to the world. Thus, the monks stood not only as mediators between the world and the creative force that medieval theology described as God, but as the interpreters of the message.

In the case of women, the Christian ideal of eternal virginity, with Mary as model, gradually evolved to encompass the idea of chastity within marriage and without (Atkinson 1983; Gold 1985). In the secular world, women came to play a role analogous to that of the cloistered monks and the priests. Wom-en's existence at a higher spiritual plane—always assuming that they met the requirements of chastity, or else they would slip lower than low in the medieval hierarchy—paralleled and complemented their domestic roles and made them the natural source of religious education outside of the Church. Yet, neither category of person, woman nor male religious, occupied a central role in the secular, masculine world of the Middle Ages. Adalbero of Laon's famous categorization of medieval society into those who prayed, fought, and worked *(oratores, bellatores,* and *laboratores)* did not miss this point.[5] Those who prayed belonged to a category separate from those who worked and fought. Women were accorded no separate role in Adalbero's schema, yet they must have found themselves uneasily occupying the category of *oratores,* for the teaching and transmission of religion were the responsibility of the women of a household, even as they were the responsibility of the pastor of the local parish. How then to achieve access to the interstices of religious education as imparted by the virgin, the chaste, one wishes to say, the innocent?[6]

Victor Turner's description of the ability of liminars to mediate between and operate within transitional phases of ritual passages provides a framework for understanding the role of both monks and women in the transmission and main-tenance of sacred knowledge and of books as both the symbols and sources of that knowledge. As Turner describes them:

[L]iminars are stripped of status and authority, removed from a social structure main-tained and sanctioned by power and force, and leveled to a homogeneous social state through discipline and ordeal. Their secular powerlessness may be compensated for by a sacred power, however—the power of the weak, derived on the one hand from the resurgence of nature when structural power is removed, and on the other from the reception of sacred knowledge. (Turner and Turner 1978:241)

Thus monks, priests, and religious, as well as lay, women occupied, in Turner's sense of the term, a classically liminal position within medieval society. It fell to them to occupy the space between this world and the next (Turner and Turner

1978:247–248), to represent the religious interests of the family (e.g., Swain 1983; Labalme 1980), and to inculcate respect for and understanding of the spiritual. The liminal roles thus played out by both women and monks in the Middle Ages were reinforced by concrete practice: the first, and for centuries only, schools in Europe were found in the monasteries. Within the home (always emphasizing the elite and wealthy nature of the class able to afford books) it was women who acted as teachers. As Joan Ferrante has noted, "among the Christianized Germanic peoples of the early Middle Ages, the women of royal families were usually better educated than the men. In some cases, education was apparently considered effeminate" (1980:10).[7]

Lay men, by contrast, had little or no sacred role to perform. Having acquired knowledge, their role was to enter the world and to act upon it; not for them was careful preservation of knowledge within the monk's cloister or lady's bower. While pictures and sculptures of saints, clerics, and women with books abound, one searches almost in vain for a representation of a medieval knight or king holding other than the occasional scroll of an edict. Even in their role as lawgivers, lay men exercised a sacred, or at least quasi-sacred, function (Bloch 1973; Kantorowicz 1957). Only after the eleventh century's revitalization of cities created a class of merchants and craftsmen whose livelihood depended upon inventories and cash flow did book knowledge for wholly secular purposes become acceptable for laymen. In masculine hands, knowledge could be divorced from its formerly sacred position. No reason any longer existed for the Latin language to be preserved in this secular literature and thus the stage was set for the vernacular prose and poetry of Dante and Petrarch.

Before the book there was the word. In Christian theology, the image of God as Word *(logos)* echoes the Creation and centers around the opening sentences of St. John's Gospel: "In the beginning was the Word. And the Word was with God and that Word was God" (John 1:1). As a medieval religion and in its post-Reformation persona of Catholicism, Christianity perceived of itself, and was perceived by its adherents, as a mystical rather than metaphysical religion. This was particularly true at the level of popular belief. The study of medieval religion by modern scholars still reflects this division. Examinations of the mystical life of the laity abound, especially of medieval women (Bynum 1986; Wilson 1984; Labalme 1980); but metaphysical studies generally confine themselves to medieval theologians whose writings provide a base solid enough to support a metaphysical framework.[8] The mystical side of medieval popular religion was given expression in popular rituals, in the veneration of relics, and also in the artistic expression of religious motifs in painting and sculpture. Within these motifs, the representation of the Bible, itself the concrete representation of God's word, held a central position.

Thus it was that the physical images of books in medieval art came to represent a number of categories of Christian motifs, serially or concomitantly. Books could represent the Bible or God's collected words—both of which taken together could serve to represent Christ as *logos*.[9] Finally, the image of a book could be used as a metaphor for Christian understanding of the Word. In other words, the representation of literacy in the earthly sense could represent literacy in the spiritual sense. In a very real way, during the first part of the Middle Ages, there was no distinction between these two activities. To read was to read God's Word, or some commentary upon it. To understand, to be literate, in the earthly sense *was* to be literate in the spiritual, unearthly sense.

Medieval representations of literate women with books are numerous. How some of these representations might best be catalogued is the subject of a study apart from this chapter. Nevertheless, a description of some of the more general categories of book iconography, as well as reference to a few examples, should help to illuminate women's role as guardians of knowledge. The following examples are drawn from what might best be categorized as public art: church sculpture, painting, and glass. Only a few references will be made to manuscript illuminations and then when they illustrate a specific point. This is to enable the author, in the extended study, to compare the impact of such iconography upon literate and illiterate populations.

In the most general terms, the image of a book or books was used not only to refer to God, or specifically to Christ, but to represent heaven or salvation. In medieval iconography, Synagogue, the personification of Judaism, is often represented as a beautiful but blindfolded woman holding a broken sword or staff—to represent the broken power of Abraham's covenant—and the Torah. Synagogue cannot know the new covenant because *she cannot see it*. The implication is that had Synagogue the ability to see her Torah and her broken staff, she would be convinced of the truth of the new covenant of the New Testament. By contrast, a fourth century Roman mosaic of two early virgin-martyr saints depicts St. Petronilla introducing St. Veneranda to heaven, which is represented as a box of scrolls. Veneranda not only gazes upon the covenant to which Synagogue is blind, but sets as her goal its perpetual contemplation. Thus Veneranda, undeterred by her martyr's death, perhaps even spurred on by it, strides eagerly towards an eternity of study.[10]

The motif of Scripture as the source of salvation and the role of women in its interpretation appears in manuscripts of every medieval period. Two examples from the early sixth century serve to illustrate the point. The canon table of the Rabbula Gospels shows the various prophets and evangelists pursuing their professions in the borders of the page. The canon table, or list of church feast-days, records for the devout the anniversaries of these early services to the cause of the Church. A contemporary canon table from the Syriac Gospels, however, shows Mary of the Annunciation standing on the border, reaching into the canon table proper and pointing directly to specific feasts. Unlike the male prophets and evangelists of the Rabbula tables, whose history is recounted in the eternal cycle of ecclesiastical feasts, Mary of the Syriac Gospels draws the reader into the canon itself. In this context, Mary is not only the recipient of Gabriel's "annunciation" of her role as mother of God, but she herself becomes the announcer of good news. The juxtaposition of word and deed characterizing the Rabbula Gospels does not suffice for the artist of the Syriac canon; it needs an explanation. Thus the illuminator has Mary, in her role of mother of God and of God's people, stand by to "interpret" the meaning of the table to her progeny. Mary's role here is undisputably that of teacher (Graber 1968; plates 231, 232).

The distinction between the female role of religious teacher and the male role of lawgiver may be seen in religious decoration that served a political purpose as well. The thirteenth century Sainte Chapelle in Paris, built by St. Louis IX of France (1226–1270) and his mother, Blanche of Castile, contains two side niches where the royals could sit while hearing Mass. Each niche carries above it a boss of Christ. Louis's shows Christ as ruler of the world with orb and scepter, paralleling the king's role as lawgiver to his people. Blanche's niche, however, depicts a very different Christ, the *Christ bienfaisant* presenting the Scripture, represented as an open book, to his people with one hand raised in benediction. Like her son, Blanche also has Christ as a role model, but in her case, the qualities of teacher and nurturer are highlighted. These variations on the theme of Christ's role in human affairs were appropriate reflections of the ideal roles played by Blanche and Louis. It did not happen, however, that they reflected the political reality of Capetian France in this period, for Blanche was *de facto* ruler of the kingdom throughout her son's minority and much of his adult life until her death in 1254.

Examples of women as teachers of reading or teachers of religion, or both, abound in medieval art (see Illustration 3.1). The royal portal of Chartres, finished in the twelfth century, depicts the liberal art of grammar *(grammatica)* as a woman teaching two small children to read.[11] The use of female figures to represent the liberal arts was widespread in the early Middle Ages, and Michael Evans has argued that the "less allusive personifications [of the *artes*] apparently first employed on the west facade of Chartres cathedral . . . were more widely accepted" (Evans 1978:309–310) beginning in the twelfth century.[12] This representation is echoed in the more explicitly religious iconography of St. Anne instructing the Virgin to read, and the Virgin instructing the Christ Child to read (e.g., Hengsbach 1968) (see Illustration 3.2). In later medieval art, female saints such as Catherine and Ursula are always shown holding, or engrossed in reading, their Scripture.

For all of these women, simply to know about the Word was not enough. One had, unlike Synagogue, to read, to interpret the truth for oneself and one's family. Seen in this context, Marian devotions of the Middle Ages become more than a reflection of feudal hierarchical norms—one appeals to the lord's lady rather than the lord himself—or the supplications of abandoned earthbound children to an ethereal mother. Rather, appeals to the women surrounding Christ, the virgins and martyrs, St. Anne and especially Mary, become crucial to Christianity as experienced by medieval believers. Saintly women, monks, priests, and their own mothers provided medieval people with the interpretation of God's word that was needed to ensure their salvation in this world and the next.[13] As women retreated from the actual role of teachers to their children, their contribution to the process became more symbolic. Later representations of Grammar evolved to underscore a similar, but increasingly allegorical, notion of sustenance: by the fourteenth century, *"grammatica* does not teach children but suckles one" (Evans 1978:310). Only with the onset of the Reformation did the father of a family accede to a central role in familial devotions (e.g., Ozment 1982).

In particular Mary, the Virgin mother of God, alone of all her sex—as Marina Warner (1976) so eloquently put it, played a crucial mediative role between man and God. Without her, God's plan of salvation could not succeed; only with her could it be understood. Devout Christians believed that Mary, as a Virgin mother, provided the most perfect safeguard for God's Word—her own body.[14]

In Western Europe, virtually every Annunciation scene depicts Mary reading her Scripture (examples in Braun 1964 [1943]). God's Word is thus concretely represented, but Mary must be able *to read* to understand. Western European motifs contrast strongly with Byzantine motifs, where Mary of the Annunciation is frequently depicted as spinning a cloth to provide a temple veil.[15] Indeed, book iconography is much more marked in Western European than in Eastern European religious iconography. Thus, in Western iconography, Mary used the medium of her own body to "interpret" the word of God—and the result was the Incarnation. Each time a Christian woman interpreted the Scripture to her family in readings and devotions, she reenacted the mystery of the Incarnation even as the priest's words over the bread and wine could change them into the body and blood of Christ. The essence of Christianity was magical transformation—by chaste women or celibate men. But in order to be effective, the transformation required knowledge, understanding, will, on the part of the interpreters. It required, in a word, literacy.

Nowhere in Western European iconography is the image of Word made Flesh under the protection of women more clearly illuminated than in the multigenerational portraits of Mary, her mother Anne, and the Child, known collectively as "the holy kinship." In one common motif, Anne, holding an open book suggesting the arrival of the Word, sits with her daughter, Mary and grandson, who is, in fact, the personification of the Word she holds in her lap. An immensely powerful image of the same idea is provided by four-generation sculptures depicting Anne, Virgin, and Child with Esmeria, Anne's mother (example in Warner 1976; fig. 41). Esmeria generally holds a pilgrim's staff and open book to guide her—and the rest of her fellow Jews—in search of divine truth. Anne sits with her book closed. The image of the Word is no longer necessary, for her daughter Mary holds in her lap the personification of the Word—the Christ Child, whose hand Anne often holds.

Thus in medieval iconography the sacred symbol of God's Word and its personification were guided and guarded by women who clearly understood and who were literate symbols of divine knowledge. Yet the very power of these

Illustration 3.1
"Grammar Teaching Children to Read"
Chartres Cathedral, 13th century. Photograph by Maryann E. Brink

Illustration 3.2
"St. Emerentia with Virgin and Child and St. Anne" ca. 1515–1530
courtesy of the Metropolitan Museum of Art; gift of J. Pierpont Morgan, 1916 (16.32.208).
Photograph by the Metropolitan Museum of Art

women, like that of their counterparts the monks, derived from their relatively weak position in the secular world. In the four generation kinship sculptures, one sees the whole of Christian theology, as Turner put it, "assigned and arrayed by law, custom, convention and ceremonial" (1977:95). Or, as Pierre Besuire would have it, one sees that "Christ is a sort of book written into the skin of the Virgin" (Gellrich 1985:17). While book knowledge was sacred, it remained in the purview of chaste women and celibate men. Bound by tradition and unable to alter the knowledge they held in trust to transmit to future generations, monks and women were helpless to respond to the revolution in knowledge that accompanied its secularization. But that, as they say, is another story.

NOTES

Thanks are due to Dr. Pamela Frese, who suggested that my observations be transformed into this chapter, and to the College of Wooster for providing financial assistance. At the College of Wooster, Professors Elizabeth Castelli and Gordon Tait gave a helpful critique of an early draft. An earlier version of this chapter was read at the American Anthropological Association in November 1987, and I thank Professors Cynthia Havice and Stanley Brandes for their useful comments.

1. Pierre Besuire, *Repertorium morale* (Gellrich 1985:17). Since this article is intended primarily for an interdisciplinary audience, English has been maintained throughout, including translations of quotations from secondary works. If a translation of a work into English exists, that edition is used.

2. I am indebted to Professor James Turner of the University of Michigan for this observation.

3. "And God said, 'Let there be light,' and there was light" (Genesis 1:3).

4. On the development of literacy in the West and other cultures, see the large volume of work produced by Jack Goody (1987, 1977, 1968). Also, see H. J. Graff (1987); Graff (1981) is a useful starting point for those interested in pursuing this topic. Chartier (1987) has much to offer. Older but still useful is Carlo Cipolla (1969). No such list as this would be complete without reference to Walter Ong (1982, 1967).

5. For an extended discussion of Adalbero's schema of medieval society and its political implications, see Duby (1980). For a different version of this categorization, as well as a discussion of its antecedents, see LeGoff (1980:53–58).

6. Of course, so were the children to whom such information was initially imparted. The paradox of Christianity, that sacred "knowledge" was best understood, best imparted by those "innocent" of the secular world, is worthy of a study of its own.

7. Ferrante cites the case of Theodoric's daughter Amalaswintha, who wished to have her young son educated but was opposed by nobles who believed that reading would turn her son into a woman. See also Ferrante 1975.

8. Examinations of the structure of Peter Lombard's *Book of the Sentences* or St. Thomas Aquinas' *Summa Theologica,* for example.

9. Which may be translated from the Greek as either "word" or "reason." In the case of the former, the utility of book imagery as an appropriate shorthand for this message is apparent.

10. In the Cemetery of Sts. Peter and Marcellus (Diehl 1928; plate II).

11. John Boswell has argued that this figure of a woman as teacher to oblates (children "donated" to God by their parents and sent to monasteries at an early age) was less than realistic and that "[w]omen were oblates as well, but had less opportunity to commemorate their childhoods in art" (1988:fig. 10). Whether women's opportunities were more restricted than men's, it is certain that the royal portal reflects a view of woman as teacher that was widely held in this period and reflected both ideal and practice.

12. Evans also notes that "[w]hen during the twelfth century the *artes* became established as a recognized if occasional element in their iconographic repertory, their appearance was influenced by the formula already established to personify the Virtues: a female figure with an emblematic attribute" (1978:309–310).

13. Carolyn Walker Bynum (1984) has criticized the use of Turner's views of liminality for explaining the various roles played by medieval women, particularly in the religious area. Her remarks were addressed to textual issues, and their utility for the area of representations discussed in this chapter appear limited.

14. "and the Word was made Flesh and dwelt among us" (John 1:14).

15. See for example the Annunciation icon reproduced in H. P. Gerhard (1971). The daughters of rabbis, such as Mary was, would weave the cloth used in the yearly reenactment of the rending of the temple veil. Why this image is rarely used in Western iconography awaits further research. To the extent that one is able to see exactly what Mary is reading in her Scripture in Western art, one is sometimes confronted with a discernible quotation from Isaiah.

REFERENCES

Atkinson, Clarissa. 1983. " 'Precious balsam in a fragile glass: the ideology of virginity in the later Middle Ages." *Journal of Family History* 8 (2): 131–143.

Baker, D. (editor). 1978. *Medieval Women*. Oxford: Basil Blackwell.

Besuire, Pierre. 1985. "Repertorium morale." P. 17 in *The Idea of the Book in the Middle Ages*, edited by J. M. Gellrich. Ithaca, NY: Cornell University Press.

Bezzola, Rato Roberto. 1978. La tradition imperiale de la fin de l'antiquité au XIe siècle. Vol. 1 of *Les origines et la formation de la littérature courtoise en Occident (500–1200)*. Paris: E. Champion.

Bloch, Marc. 1973. *The Royal Touch: Sacred Monarchy and Scrofula in England and France*. London: Routledge and Kegan Paul.

Boswell, John. 1988. *The Kindness of Strangers: The Abandonment of Children in Western Europe from Late Antiquity to the Renaissance*. New York: Pantheon.

Braun, Joseph. 1964 [1943]. *Tracht und Attribute der Heiligen in der deutscher Kunst*. Stuttgart: J. B. Metzlersche Verlagbuchhandlung, rpt. Alfred Druckemüller, Stuttgart.

Bynum, Carolyn Walker. 1986. ". . . 'And woman his humanity': female imagery in the religious writing of the later Middle Ages." Pp. 257–288 in *Gender and Religion: On the Complexity of Symbols,* edited by C. W. Bynum, S. Harrell, and P. Richman. Boston: Beacon Press.

———. 1984. "Women's stories, women's symbols: a critique of Victor Turner's theory of liminality." Pp. 105–125 in *Anthropology and the Study of Religion,* edited by F. Reynolds and R. Moore. Chicago: Center for the Scientific Study of Religion.

Bynum, Carolyn Walker, S. Harrell, and P. Richman (editors). 1986. *Gender and Religion: On the Complexity of Symbols.* Boston: Beacon Press.

Chartier, Roger. 1988. *The Cultural Uses of Print.* Princeton: Princeton University Press.

———. 1987. *Lectures et lecteurs dans la France d'Ancien Régime.* Paris: Sevil.

Cipolla, Carlo. 1969. *Literacy and the Development of the West.* New York: Penguin.

Diehl, Charles. 1928. *L'Art chrétien primitif et l'art Byzantin.* Paris: Les éditions G. van Oest.

Duby, Georges. 1980. *The Three Orders: Feudal Society Imagined.* Chicago: University of Chicago Press.

Evans, Michael. 1978. "Allegorical women and practical men: the iconography of the *artes* reconsidered." Pp. 305–330 in *Medieval Women,* edited by D. Baker. Oxford: Basil Blackwell.

Ferrante, Joan M. 1980. "The education of women in the middle ages in theory, fact and fantasy." Pp. 9–42 in *Beyond Their Sex: Learned Women of the Middle Ages.* New York: New York University Press.

———. 1975. *Woman as Image in Medieval Literature from the Twelfth Century to Dante.* New York: Columbia University Press.

Gellrich, Jesse. 1985. *The Idea of the Book in the Middle Ages: Language Theory, Mythology, and Fiction.* Ithaca, NY: Cornell University Press.

Gerhard, H. P. 1971. *The World of Icons.* New York: Harper and Row.

Gold, Penny Schine. 1985. *The Lady and the Virgin: Image, Attitude and Experience in Twelfth Century France.* Chicago: University of Chicago Press.

Goody, Jack. 1987. *The Interface Between the Written and the Oral.* Cambridge: Cambridge University Press.

———. 1977. *The Logic of Writing and the Origins of Society.* Cambridge: Cambridge University Press.

———. 1968. *Literacy in Traditional Societies.* Cambridge: Cambridge University Press.

Grabar, A. 1968. *Christian Iconography: A Study of its Origins.* Bollingen Series XXXV. Princeton: Princeton University Press.

Graff, Howard J. 1987. *Legacies of Literacy: Continuities and Contradictions in Western Culture and Society.* Bloomington: University of Indiana Press.

———. 1981. *Literacy in History: An Interdisciplinary Research Bibliography.* New York: Garland.

Hengsbach, F. 1968. *Marienbild in Rheinland und Westfalen,* exhibit 14 June–22 September 1968, Villa Hügel, Essen. Essen: Veranstalter der Austellung.

Kantorowicz, Ernst. 1957. *The King's Two Bodies.* Princeton: Princeton University Press.

Labalme, Patricia (editor). 1980. *Beyond Their Sex: Learned Women of the European Past.* New York: New York University Press.

LeGoff, Jacques. 1980. *Time, Work, and Culture in the Middle Ages.* Chicago: University of Chicago Press.

Ong, Walter J. 1982. *Orality and Literacy: The Technologies of the Word.* London: Methuen.

———. 1967. *The Presence of the Word.* New Haven: Yale.

Ozment, Stephen. 1982. *When Fathers Ruled.* Cambridge: Harvard University Press.

Swain, Elizabeth. 1983. "Faith in the family: the practice of religion by the Gonzaga." *Journal of Family History* 8:177–189.

Turner, Victor. 1977. *The Ritual Process*. Ithaca, NY: Cornell University Press.

Turner, Victor, and Edith Turner. 1978. *Image and Pilgrimage in Christian Culture: Anthropological Perspectives*. New York: Columbia University Press.

Warner, Marina. 1976. *Alone of All Her Sex: The Myth and the Cult of the Virgin Mary*. New York: Knopf.

Wilson, Katherine M. (editor). 1984. *Medieval Women Writers*. Athens: University of Georgia Press.

4

Patriarchy and Male Oppression: Suffering the Responsibilities of Manhood

Karen Taylor

Historians have gone to great lengths to demonstrate how women's lives have been constricted and controlled by the mechanisms of institutionalized patriarchy: by governments, courts, medical professions, the churches, didactic writers, and the family. More recently they have begun to examine how women's responses to those mechanisms helped to transform them. But we are only beginning to understand and explore the fact that patriarchal institutions are just the most visible aspects of the gender-based cultural structures which have molded and continue to mold both the past and the future, directing and delimiting both men's and women's lives. One crucial area into which historians must self-consciously focus their attention in order to provide the necessary detail for facilitating our fuller understanding is, ironically, men's history. Although there is no question that women and children have consistently been on the bottom of the social, political, and economic hierarchy, and their lives particularly limited, men have been constrained by their expected roles as well. Like women, they have been limited by what they were not (according to social norm) allowed to do, and also by the duties they were expected to perform as part of the gender identity. If we are to untangle the complexity of how men's coercion into compliance with patriarchy operated to reinforce and perpetuate it, we must look specifically at men's actions, ambitions, and intentions as they sought to fulfill—or transform—the gender expectations society placed on them. We have begun to do this with women's history but we have not yet done it with men, and therefore we are missing some pieces to the puzzle. We do not understand the processes through which ontological assumptions become embodied in actions, or how deviations from culturally privileged assumptions become recast to fit cant or are rejected and therefore disempowered.

The few studies which have focused specifically on men seem to fall more into the category of the history of manhood than a history of men. In a very real sense they began with the men's liberation movement and works by Joseph Pleck (1972), Jack Nichols (1975), and Herb Goldberg (1976). They took up a feminist critique of contemporary maleness, finding that men were imprisoned by dysfunctional social roles, that they were emotionally crippled, that they were unhealthy, and implicitly, that they had grown that way through the same historical mechanism—patriarchy—that had so distorted women's lives.

The works that followed those initial cries of recognition have traced the construction of male responsibility and images. They all take roughly the same approach and arrive at approximately the same conclusions: men's ideal roles changed over time because of changes in the economic, political, and social environment. Virtually the only extensive work has concentrated on nineteenth-century America, though an occasional author (James A. Doyle, *The Male Experience* 1983, for example) has sketched a quick overview of the changes from ancient to modern times.

The general conclusion most studies reached is that men's roles changed over the period of the nineteenth century because of the demise of an exploitable frontier and because of the impact of industrialization and urbanization on the work place and the family. Peter Filene first articulated this interpretation in *Him/Her/Self: Sex Roles in Modern America* in 1974. Through the study of nineteenth-century magazines and newspapers Filene discovered that the ideal man became strenuously manly and physically powerful by the end of the nineteenth century (as opposed to spiritually manly at its beginning) in reaction to the fact that the growth of a corporate world had eliminated individualistic ways to conquer "life." Men's confusion about how to prove their manhood was exacerbated by the nineteenth-century women's movement, which seemed poised on the verge of releasing a flood of pent-up female passions which would drown American society in licentiousness *and* threaten men's control of the public realm. Men, therefore, had to become self-controlled, directing their energies into the perfection and enhancement of their physical health, and therefore able to resist women's interference. Filene's study was followed by several others which elaborated on men's roles in the nineteenth century. For example, Ronald Byars (1979), Joe Dubbert (1979), and James O. Robertson (1979) argued that changes in the work place (e.g., more closely regulated time, poorly lit and ventilated offices, and employee status) transformed frontier-individualist hero images into self-controlled, hard-working hero images. Women also figured prominently in Byars's (1979) study, though in contrast to Filene's interpretation he focused on the impact that women's childrearing responsibilities had on the psychological development of men and therefore on their images of manhood. Byars (1979) suggested that in the last part of the nineteenth century men were in psychological flight from women, which made them overcompensate and become preoccupied with the physical, dominating aspects of their maleness.

More recently David I. Macleod (1983) and Anthony E. Rotundo (1983) have added depth to the argument by looking at specific areas of the nineteenth and early-twentieth centuries. Their findings conform to the basic idea of transformation, emphasizing that men changed from being spiritually and communally focused to being self-interested and bodily centered. Rotundo (1983) also builds the notion that women catalyzed this change: as mothers they were the primary care-givers and created an overpowering female image that boys had to reject in order to become men.

Several studies have brought the argument up to the present. In the thought-provoking *Be A Man* (1979), Peter Stearns examined the difficulties both middle- and working-class men had in continually readjusting to the new roles their American cultures prescribed. He found that working-class men had a slightly easier task in their manual labor and their direct interaction with machines. Middle-class men had the business "jungle" in which to prove their prowess, a role that was more difficult because the ruthlessness it required was viewed by much of society as shameful at the very least, requiring men to retreat to the woman-gentled home for succor.

For both classes the twentieth century required major adjustments. Working-class men found work less and less satisfactory as a fulfillment of their expected roles because machines reduced the range of their action and expertise. While protest became a manly action briefly, increasing bureaucratization of the unions—and more participation by women—decreased its manfulness quickly. Middle-class men found themselves increasingly consumed by their jobs, but only those few who actually succeeded in gaining ascendence over their competitors could expect to live up to the expectations of manhood.

Elizabeth and Joseph Pleck (1980) and James A. Doyle (1983) both present a version of the same scenario for twentieth-century man. The Plecks demonstrated that twentieth-century men have seen their power eroded in the family by the companionate marriage and by three major social movements of the 1960s and 1970s. The women's liberation movement created a crisis in male identity by challenging what it meant to be a woman. The gay liberation movement clarified men's sexual concepts, bringing into question men's inability to display affection openly and also pointing out fallacies in prevalent stereotypes of male homosexuality. The men's movement focused on male-female relationships but also concerned issues affecting the way men related to their roles as fathers.

Doyle (1983) saw the post–World War I American man moving through an era of crumbling sex roles; he could no longer turn to males for companionship because they had become his competitors. Women, increasingly men's equals, became men's source of companionship. While World War II and the postwar economic boom rejuvenated traditional male roles temporarily, the economic upheavals and the women's liberation movement of the 1960s made it obvious that men were going to have to accept the equal status of women and therefore share their power. Men have emerged from this threat to their power angry but not necessarily seeking change.

What is more striking about all these studies is that they portray men as retreating—sometimes desperately—into a more and more narrowly construed range of options for what "being a man" was/is all about. This image is both amusing and perplexing. It is amusing because it seems to confirm an often-repeated (and historically enduring) female adage that male egos are tender (that in fact males are fragile) and must be protected from the knowledge that they are not perfectly capable. It is perplexing because these authors seem intent on proving that men are verging on a profound crisis because they have gradually been losing all the roles which gave them a gender definition. The implication, as Joseph Pleck pointed out as early as 1972, is that much of men's political and social behavior could be understood as a defensive reaction against this "emasculation," arising from their insecurity about their sex roles. The argument is that males have, in fact, no identity left. It seems that, as Pleck (1972) suggests, this is not only an unsatisfactory conclusion, but a con-clusion which might be effectively rethought by asking how the historical char-acteristics of manhood forced men into participating in the replication of the system constraining them. The loss of these characteristics might thereby be demonstrated to be a liberation for men in the same way that the transformation of women's roles has become empowering for them.

The changes in men's roles which these studies have described can be ex-tremely useful to us in understanding the way men interacted with their roles. But to date very little attempt has been made to examine seriously how closely the image fit the reality of men's lives: whether or not the images expressed and reinforced social, economic, or political needs; how men attempted to live up to them and the social and historical ramifications of those attempts; and whether or not social and political institutions had mechanisms to enforce ad-herence to ideal images.

Recently a few studies focusing on other historical problems have revealed the richness such inquiry might uncover. In *Intimacy and Power in the Old South* Steven M. Stowe (1987) weaves a complex picture of the ways in which Southern planter culture's expectations for its men and women gave them a limited number of options through which to express their individual concerns. Stowe (1987) argues that while they perforce used the language and customs available to them in dueling, courtship, and daily life to achieve fulfillment of their life plans, they stretched and remolded the meanings to resemble more closely the lives they wished to lead.

Elaine Tyler May looked at the other side of that process of transformation in her book, *Great Expectations* (1983), deftly illustrating that traditional gen-der roles between 1880 and 1920 failed to alter quickly enough to keep up with the changes the economy forced on them. This lag left late-Victorian men and women in Los Angeles with such impracticable expectations for marriage that few real marriages could fulfill them, resulting in a rising divorce rate.

But neither these nor a growing body of similar studies focus specifically on the relationship between men's lives and actions and their gender roles. In the last ten years anthropologists have started to examine the dialectic between sex roles and the cultures in which they reside by focusing on how the political and social status of males in many societies depends upon their systematic exploitation of the women around them—thus locking men into a variety of behaviors and roles they may not necessarily have chosen for themselves.

In particular, Sherry Ortner and Harriet Whitehead (1982) have argued that power structures are based upon complex systems of prestige which rest on obligations of reciprocal duties which are interactive between every level of a social hierarchy, from the highest to the lowest. These responsibilities invest the entire social structure with a stabilizing legitimacy because that legitimacy is both drawn from and reiterated throughout the hierarchy. In the same vein, Stanley Brandes (1981), Claude Meillassoux (1975), Rayna Rapp Reiter (1977), Gayle Rubin (1975), and others have argued that women's reproductive capacity and/or the goods women produce are used by men as part of the intricate systems of exchange, alliance, and honor through which they bind other families, clans, or groups to their own, and thereby solidify prestige and economic or political power. Because men depend on women's productive or reproductive behavior to solidify their own positions in the prestige structure, it is imperative for them to obtain the appropriate behavior from the women on whom they are mutually (though not equally) dependent. Though men certainly reap the benefits of such a system, they are as much trapped into specific prescribed behaviors—and subjected to as wide (though perhaps not as oppressive) a variety of punishments—as women are.

My own research has turned up some interesting ways in which men were limited and directed by patriarchy in late-nineteenth-century Boston, Massachusetts, and Melbourne, Victoria. The various acts which Boston and Melbourne men were forbidden to do by law and by common social consent included drinking too much, beating members of their families, or committing adultery. Many of the codes of law by which patriarchal America and Australia were regulated concerned such legal sins. But uncodified assumptions about men's duties played an even greater role in listing the ways in which men could live their lives. Two major responsibilities constrained them in particular: men had to be the economic support and the moral regulators of their families.

The first duty has been and continues to be explored by Australian and English historians. Ellen Ross (1982) and Nancy Tomes (1978), for example, have argued that one major source of violence-causing tension between men and women of nineteenth-century London was the fact that men would not—or could not—support their families effectively. The arguments erupting out of this tension caused broken bones, death, and shattered families. Although both

Tomes and Ross concentrated their studies on working-class and poor families, there is ample evidence that both middle- and upper-class families suffered from the same difficulty.

Working with Australian data, Kay Saunders (1984) and Anthea Hislop (1984) have demonstrated that this particular duty, breadwinning, created problems for men both prior to and beyond the nineteenth century. Saunders (1984) explored the domestic world of colonial Queensland and found that men were often forced to leave their homes to satisfy their breadwinning obligation. Hislop (1984) discovered that during the Depression of the 1930s in Australia, the chief source of suicides, intemperance, and family violence and breakup was the tension created by women who demanded of their husbands—and men who demanded of themselves—that they be breadwinners. A very important distinction needs to be made clear here. It was not the fact that these people could not *survive* which was at issue, because often the wives themselves were amply supporting the family. The problem was that both the husband and the wife accepted and operated upon the cultural expectation that the *man* would be the breadwinner. That they often simply could *not* be—or because the woman's income did not have to be—was of no help in allowing these people to understand their dilemma.

The other duty patriarchal Boston and Melbourne expected their men to perform—disciplining their families to keep them virtuous—has yet to be closely examined by historians. Current research suggests that men were expected to force members of their families to obey social rules and were punished if they did not adhere to these rules.

The evidence presents two obvious examples of this duty. The first is fairly unsurprising: men, as heads of their families, had to govern their children as a wise ruler governed his people. Though childrearing advisors did not approve of brutal force, they both recommended and expected fathers to use corporal punishment when necessary. Nineteenth-century childrearing literature is full of examples of fathers gently but firmly chastising their children with stern words and a judiciously applied rod. Parents also were urged to tie their children to bed, fence, or barn posts or in chairs as a means of humane punishment for disobedience.

As the nineteenth century wore on and women became the principal disciplinarians of the family because of the dictates of the cult of domesticity, men were relieved of the bulk of this duty except in those instances when their wives could not or would not perform it. In such cases advisors were very clear. Magazine articles suggested that when a wife and mother disciplined her children incorrectly—by slapping or whipping children in anger, for example—then the husband should demonstrate to her by example the proper method of childrearing: a family prayer followed by a swift caning of the child was preferable. If the parents neglected their duty to rear obedient and respectful children, the courts stepped in to punish the father—as the ultimate government of the family—with public humiliation, fines, or in extreme instances by taking his children away from him (Taylor 1987).

A more complex responsibility was a man's role as guardian to his wife. In this instance the man was to protect his wife from the vices of the world by keeping her away from contact with it as much as possible. But he was also to protect her from herself. According to nineteenth-century definition, women were so innocent that they were ill-equipped to withstand or even understand the temptations of the world, and therefore men had to help them to resist. Often they had to force them to resist. Divorce cases offer particularly reveal-ing evidence.

In an 1862 case in Melbourne, for example, a husband seeking a divorce because of his wife's adultery was informed by the judge that "he had taken the tie of matrimony . . . too lightly" by allowing his wife to go off as she pleased (Miles v. Miles & Bond 1862 in *Wyatt & Webb Reports*). The legal term for the husband's failure to govern his wife's behavior—condonment—became a major mechanism for ensuring that husbands would in fact take an active hand in keeping their wives in their proper places.

Another husband in 1863 came home one evening to find the family tent filled with merrymakers. His wife was seated on their bed with a male neigh-bor, their arms entwined. The husband immediately ordered the group to be gone, only to find that his wife wanted to go as well. His response was, "suit yourself"—at which point she did. The judge was not gentle in his reprimand:

A woman inflamed and excited is allowed to go staggering out of her husband's tent, in the close proximity of the tent of the man with whom she so recently behaved im-properly [i.e., she behaved improperly by sitting on the bed with her arm in his]. She went there and her husband in effect gave her leave. (Roulston v. Roulston & Jones 1862 in *Wyatt & Webb Reports*)

In 1864 a man took the steps he thought necessary to control his errant wife—he deprived her "of such portions of her clothing as he thought neces-sary for her use out of doors, with a view to keeping her at home"—only to discover that even that was legally not enough. The judge declared that the husband had failed in his duty because "when she left his house he took no step to ascertain where she had gone or what she was doing" (Terry v. Terry & Marcutt 1864 in *Wyatt & Webb Reports*).

Many husbands found themselves caught between the duty to support their families and the responsibility to protect their wives from the world. For ex-ample, in 1862 one Melbourne husband was forced to resort to mining, leaving his wife to fend for herself as best she could. In the husband's petition for divorce which followed two years later, the judge ruled that the husband's occupation had deprived him of the ability to live where he wanted to, but that by leaving his wife he had exposed her to temptation. The divorce was not granted (Myles v. Myles & Bond 1862 in *Wyatt & Webb Reports*). A Melbourne judge in an 1886 case summed up the court's stance succinctly: "About 18 months after marriage, when a wife would be . . . particularly requiring the careful consideration and protection of her husband he appears to have determined on abandoning her" to her own resources. (His crime was to let her stay alone in town while he went off to work.) (O'Conner v. O'Conner 1886; in *Wyatt & Webb Reports*). Another husband left his wife so he could find a place to set up a new home for them, and his wife established a boarding house in order to support herself and their children in his absence. She was seduced by one of the boarders. When her husband applied for a divorce he was told that he had taken "no step to control her. . . . A husband is not bound to entertain suspicion, but he ought not to put his wife in a position of temptation" (Bathgate v. Bathgate 1862 in *Wyatt & Webb Reports*).

If they did not fulfill their obligation to control their wives, husbands were punished in a pathetically ironic manner. The almost universal punishment was to force the husband and the wife to remain married. "A husband who has thrown his wife into temptation and exposed her to the address of other men should not be allowed to cast her aside after she has yielded to temptation" (O'Conner v. O'Conner 1886 in *Wyatt & Webb Reports*). At most the court would offer them a judicial separation. The courts thus either granted a potentially miserable life together, or a life apart from which neither could successfully emerge. In the case of a separation, the wife ultimately suffered more profoundly because she could usually neither support herself sufficiently nor obtain another husband to support her.

It is not surprising that husbands aggressively pursued their wives' obedience to social rules. Criminal records as well as divorce records present us with powerful examples. In 1865, for example, a Boston man locked his wife in an outhouse for two days because she insisted on going to visit friends in a neighboring community (Kane v. Kane 1865 in *Wyatt & Webb Reports*). Another husband publicly declared that his wife's pregnancy was the result of incest with her own father because she went to visit her father against her husband's wishes (*Albany Law Review* 1882–1883). Some husbands resorted to physical chastisement. The records are filled with cases in which wives were slapped, kicked, tied up, whipped, or threatened with guns or knives when they refused to conform to their husbands' wishes. The courts *did* punish husbands for this behavior, but often not seriously. An analysis of superior court records in Boston and Supreme Court records in Melbourne reveals that fewer than 3 percent of battering husbands in Melbourne and Boston between 1850 and 1900 received more than a fine for their actions; less than 1 percent of those husbands who killed their wives received a conviction for manslaughter, and of those who did, none received a punishment of more than two years. In one 1856 case a man accidently killed his wife when he knocked her off a stool because she had been drinking. The judge scolded him, declaring that her death was the result of the man's inadequate attention to his role as her "natural guardian."

He was given a sentence of three months in jail (*Boston Herald* 8 June 1867). A doctor in Boston captured the irony in the patriarchal attitude toward male responsibility when one of his own patients was beaten to death by her husband in 1878. He wrote in the Massachusetts General Hospital records (1878) that the husband thus demonstrated that he "clearly had no feeling for the responsibilities of his position."

The implications of the duties forced upon men are multiple. If men chose to allow members of their families to be independent individuals, they ran the risk of being shamed, blamed, *and punished* for their behavior. They therefore had to become their wives' and children's keepers in the strictest sense of that word, confining them to their homes or rooms when necessary and chastising them when all else failed. In that they faced a double bind. When a man's children misbehaved in public he could be construed as neglecting his role as disciplinarian and punished; if his children or his neighbors complained that he was too harsh in his discipline he could lose his children. If a woman chose to run away or commit adultery her husband could be refused a decree of divorce by the courts, but his attempts to inhibit his wife from such behavior could become the grounds for a charge of cruelty or even of criminal prosecution. How was he to judge if hiding her clothes were enough or locking her in an outbuilding were too much? If a child could be punished by being tied to a bedpost, why could not a wife?

In the same way Brink argues in this volume, medieval women were transmitters of God's Word but were essentially unable to claim that power or respond to changes in written culture, men appear to have been assigned the role of enforcers of cultural regulations over which they had little real transformative or directive control. If they attempted to protest the regulations they lost their cultural legitimacy, becoming either "not-men" and punishable through social ostracism and humiliation or becoming objects of the retributions sanctioned by patriarchal institutions. The potential for utilizing our understanding of male gender roles to chart history is both staggering and exciting. As Joan Scott (1988) has demonstrated in her excellent book, history—and thus knowledge, politics, economics, and society itself—is constructed in relation to understandings of gender.

The contradictions in nineteenth-century American and Australian patriarchies compelling men to walk a tightrope between cooperation and coercion, between being protector and jailer, suggest only one of many ways in which we might begin to reacquaint ourselves with the history of men. Women have been invisible in our recorded memory, but men appear to have been transfixed in a monolithic and often monophonic history which forgets all attempts they have made to reconstruct a culture that labels them deviant, or which remembers such attempts in language and images which reconstruct patriarchal orthodoxy. In this instance the evidence offers the stark conclusion that at the heart of the definition of proper nineteenth-century manhood, men sometimes found no border between responsibility and repression.

REFERENCES

Albany Law Review. July 1882–June 1883. "Cruelty: accusing wife of unchastity" 26:83. *Boston Herald* 8 June 1867.

Brandes, Stanley. 1982. "Like wounded stags: male sexual ideology in an Andalusian town," pp. 216–239 in *Sexual Meanings,* edited by S. Ortner and H. Whitehead. Cambridge: Cambridge University Press.

Byars, Ronald. 1979. *The Making of the Self-Made Man: The Development of Masculine Roles and Images in Antebellum America.* Ann Arbor: Michigan State University.

Doyle, James A. 1983. *The Male Experience.* Dubuque, IA: Wm. C. Brown.

Dubbert, Joe. 1979. *A Man's Place: Masculinity in Transition.* Englewood Cliffs, NJ: Prentice Hall.

Filene, Peter. [1974] 1986. *Him/Her/Self: Sex Roles in Modern America.* Baltimore: Johns Hopkins University Press.

Goldberg, Herb. 1976. *The Hazards of Being Male.* New York: New American Library.

Hislop, Anthea. 1984. "Breadwinners and losers." Paper presented at the Australian Historical Association annual conference, Melbourne, Australia.

Macleod, David I. 1983. *Building Character in the American Boy: The Boy Scouts, YMCA, and Their Forerunners, 1870–1920.* Madison: University of Wisconsin Press.

Massachusetts General Hospital Records. 1859–1910. Medical Archives, Harvard University Medical Library. Boston.

May, Elaine Tyler. 1983. *Great Expectations: Marriage and Divorce in Post Victorian America.* Chicago: University of Chicago Press.

Meillassoux, Claude. 1975. *Maidens, Meals, and Money: Capitalism and the Domestic Community.* Cambridge: Cambridge University Press.

Nichols, Jack. 1975. *Men's Liberation.* New York: Penguin Press.

Ortner, Sherry, and Harriet Whitehead. 1982. *Sexual Meanings: The Cultural Construction of Gender and Sexuality.* Cambridge: Cambridge University Press.

Pleck, Elizabeth, and Joseph Pleck. 1980. *The American Man.* Englewood Cliffs, NJ: Prentice Hall.

Pleck, Joseph. 1972. "Psychological frontiers of men." *Rough Times* 6:14–15.

Reiter, Rayna Rapp. 1977. "Gender and class: an archeology of knowledge concerning the origin of the state." *Dialectical Anthropology* 2:309–316.

Robertson, James. 1979. "Horatio Alger, Andrew Carnegie, Abraham Lincoln, and the cowboy." *Midwest Quarterly* 20:241–257.

Ross, Ellen. 1982. "Fierce questions and taunts: married life in working-class London, 1870–1914." *Feminist Studies* 8:575–603.

Rotundo, Anthony E. 1983. "Body and soul: changing ideals of American middle-class manhood, 1770–1920." *Journal of Social History* 16 (4): 23–38.

Rubin, Gayle. 1975. "The traffic in women: notes on the 'political economy' of sex." Pp. 157–210 in *Toward an Anthropology of Women,* edited by Rayna Rapp Reiter. New York: Monthly Review Press.

Saunders, Kay. 1984. "The study of domestic violence in Queensland: sources and problems." *Historical Studies* 21 (2): 68–84.

Scott, Joan. 1988. *Gender and the Politics of History.* New York: Columbia University Press.

Stearns, Peter. 1979. *Be A Man.* New York: Holmes & Meier.

Stowe, Steven M. 1987. *Intimacy and Power in the Old South.* Baltimore: Johns Hopkins University Press.

Superior Court Criminal Records. 1859–1900. Suffolk County Archives, Suffolk County Courthouse. Boston.

Supreme Court Criminal Records. 1850–1900. Victoria State Archives. Melbourne, Australia.

Taylor, Karen. 1987. "Blessing the house: moral motherhood and the suppression of corporal punishment." *Journal of Psychohistory* 14 (2): 256–281.

Tomes, Nancy. 1978. "Torrent of abuse: crimes of violence between working-class men and women in London, 1840–1875." *Journal of Social History* 11:329–345.

Wyatt and Webb Reports: Victorian Law Reports. 1861–1910. Vols. 1–34. Melbourne: Sands and McDougal.

5

Economic Methodology and Gender Roles

Barbara S. Burnell

This chapter examines the ways in which mainstream neoclassical economics contributes to an understanding of gender roles. The relationship between gender and economic thought is explored, with emphasis on the way that economic knowledge is acquired and the effect that economic methodology and analysis has on shaping gender roles. Generally, the fundamental philosophical foundations of neoclassical economic theory and the way in which the theory is used to understand behavior preclude an adequate understanding of the way in which gender roles are shaped and how these roles determine one's position in an economy.

This chapter, like others in this volume, suggests that some of the limitations of the discipline's ability to understand gender-based experience arise from the particular methodology that economists use. Other limitations result from the fact that the socioeconomic and institutional environment within which economists work inevitably affects the nature and scope of economic analysis. To the extent that a given conception of gender roles is a part of this environment, it will be reflected in the conclusions of economic analysis and the uses to which it is put.

LOGICAL POSITIVISM AND NEOCLASSICAL ECONOMICS

Economics can be defined as: "the systematic study of the production, distribution and use of scarce resources of a society so as to satisfy the maximum number of wants. It is the study of choices among alternatives in a situation of scarcity" (Peterson 1973).

   As with all sciences or areas of inquiry, the study of the issues raised in this definition is accomplished using a certain technique or method: logical positivism. Since the methodology of neoclassical economics is based on logical positivism, it is helpful to understand the aspects of positivism that are important elements of the construction and application of economic theory. Logical positivism has as one of its basic premises that the purpose of science is to develop techniques that allow useful and reliable predictions. In fulfilling this purpose, both logical analysis and empirical testing are crucial aspects of scientific discovery.

   More specifically, Homa Katouzian (1980:72–73) identifies several important features of logical positivism: (1) it expects hypotheses to be formulated on the basis of direct observation; (2) statements are considered as scientific if and only if they are verifiable; statements which are not verifiable contribute nothing to scientific understanding; (3) logical positivism requires that theories be verified by empirical tests; (4) logical positivism claims a unique, universal scientific method. These characteristics suggest that it is possible, indeed essential, to distinguish clearly statements of fact from statements of value and that when statements of fact are formulated as hypotheses, their verification or falsification contributes to the advancement of scientific knowledge.

   How does this brief description of logical positivist philosophy shape the methodology of neoclassical economics? In answering this question one must recognize that there is a distinction between what economists preach and what they practice; that is, economists claim a close alliance with logical positivism in principle, but the actual process of developing and testing economic theories involves some important departures from this principle.

   Perhaps the single most important feature of neoclassical economic methodology is the claim that:

positive economics is in principle independent of any particular ethical position or normative judgment. Its task is to provide a system of generalizations that can be used to make correct predictions about the consequences of any changes in circumstances. . . . Positive economics is or can be an objective science in precisely the same sense as any of the physical sciences. (Friedman 1984 [1953]:211)

The primary mechanism for providing the system of generalizations to which Friedman refers is the construction of theories or models of behavior. The construction of an economic model involves making several assumptions about (1) the motivations for behavior and (2) the forces in the real world that are unimportant or held constant for the purpose of focusing on a particular relationship between economic agents.

   It is this process of abstraction that makes economic analysis sufficiently rigorous to make consistent predictions about behavior in different circumstances. According to positivist doctrine, the validity or realism of the assumptions made in this process are unimportant; what matters is whether the theory "works." If the theory works, then the behavior the model purports to explain is "as if" the assumptions were valid; what matters is the plausibility of the hypothesis being tested according to the conformity of its implications with actual behavior (Friedman 1984 [1953]:222–223).

In this sense, theory can be viewed as having two elements. First, theory can be regarded as "a 'language' designed to promote 'systematic and organized methods of reasoning' " (Marshall 1955:164, cited in Friedman 1984 [1953]:213). In this capacity, the importance of theory lies not in its factual content but in its ability to classify or organize information. Second, theory can be regarded as "a body of substantive hypotheses designed to abstract essential features of complex reality" (Friedman 1984 [1953]:213). According to this interpretation of what theory is and why it is important, the assumptions that are made in the process of constructing theory are made on the basis of how they enable the theory in question to perform these two functions.

There are several assumptions common to the majority of neoclassical economic models: maximizing behavior, rationality, and individual self-interest. They are, by implication, important for the ability of economic theory to perform its "filing system" (Friedman 1984 [1953]:213) function and to allow hypotheses about economic phenomena to be deduced. Given their prevalence in economic analysis, it is worthwhile to consider them in some detail. The first of these assumptions is the assumption of maximizing behavior. That is, individuals are assumed to maximize utility, firms to maximize profits, and societies to maximize the total output available to their citizens. The second assumption is the rationality of individual behavior. That is, given the maximizing goal, economic agents will make choices in such a way as to attain it within the constraints they face. Third, economic agents are assumed to be motivated by individual self-interest; they are assumed to behave in isolation from one another, with the only interaction or exchange occurring as a result of voluntary efforts to enhance one's own position.

There are several important implications of these assumptions for economic methodology. First, the use of a standard core of assumptions in economic models is intended to enhance the ability of economic theory to predict and to be either verified or falsified on the basis of empirical testing. By abstracting from complex reality and assuming a particular motivation for behavior, some fundamental principles can be developed and tested against actual experience. Second, according to logical positivism, the construction of theoretical models through the process of abstraction allows an objective description of economic phenomena free from value judgments or moral statements. That is, the use of the scientific method enables economists to separate positive from normative statements. Finally, the use of economic models allows for generalizability to a wide variety of circumstances. By abstracting from social context, individuals become role players, so that their behavior in different situations can be predicted.

PHILOSOPHICAL CRITIQUE OF NEOCLASSICAL ECONOMICS

This brief discussion of neoclassical economic methodology has indicated that, at least in principle, economics claims logical positivism as the foundation for advancing economic knowledge. This foundation has, however, been increasingly questioned in recent years.

Whether neoclassical economics fulfills its claims to a scientific method depends on two factors: whether logical positivism itself forms a firm foundation upon which the development and testing of scientific theories can be based; and whether neoclassical economics in practice actually follows the principles of positivism upon which its methodology is based. Both of these issues will be addressed in this section.

The first line of criticism of logical positivism as a basis for economic methodology rests on whether or not there can be a truly positivistic, objective methodology. Increasingly, the answer to this question has been a negative one for several reasons. The first is that positivism is itself prescriptive or, as Donald McCloskey (1983:490) would claim, "arrogant." Positivism asserts that there is only one correct and universal scientific method, and by this very assertion it is itself normative. By claiming that only certain kinds of information and methods count as valid means of acquiring scientific knowledge, positivism is itself making the value judgments that it purports to disallow as knowledge. Thus, the positivist claim of a unique scientific method appears to be circular and logically inconsistent.

A second reason to question positivism as a basis for economic methodology rests on whether any scientific method can be completely objective and value-free. Critics of economic methodology have argued that objectivity is impossible, and that the distinction economists make between "positive" and "normative" economics is artificial and potentially dangerous. Economists generally define "positive" economics as what is—that is, as a description of economic phenomena—and "normative" economics as what should be, and emphasize that the two must be distinguished from one another. The danger in making this distinction is that positive economics is seen as objective, scientific, and value-free, and predictions made on the basis of positive economic models must therefore be "right" since they are logically derived from a behavioral model. For example, Gordon Tullock and Richard McKenzie claim that:

the approach of the economist is *amoral*. Economics is not so much concerned with what *should be* . . . our analysis is devoid (as much as possible) of our own personal values—we are interested in gaining an understanding of the behavior of others, *given their values*. (my emphases, 1984:7).

The danger in this claim is that values, either of the researcher or society at large, become embedded in a supposedly positive, as opposed to normative, analysis.

It has become increasingly clear to critics of neoclassical economic methodology that it is impossible to develop a completely objective, value-free theory.
Economists, like all scientists, are products of social institutions, and what they
do is inevitably affected by this institutional context. As Katouzian (1980:84)
points out, "scientific activity—as a part of the pursuit of all knowledge—is
not merely a *logical* but also a *social* and *psychological* process. . . . [Men's]
past personal, cultural and social histories are likely to affect their systems of
valuation, their modes of thinking and even their analytical methods." In the
case of economics, much of its methodology has been developed in the context
of capitalist economies, and the characteristics of this system—individualism,
freedom, competition—become imbedded in the structure of the theory. Yet it
is clear that, in addition to being descriptive, these terms have an ideological
or value-laden interpretation. Even methodological terms that are on the surface
neutral often:

have two meanings, one in the sphere of "what is" and another in the sphere of "what
ought to be." The word "principle" for instance, means, on the one hand, theory which
means a certain systematic understanding of objective regularities. But the word "principle" may also mean an "aim of conscious striving" or "chief means of attaining a
postulated end" or a "general rule of action." (Myrdal 1984 [1954]:255)

But this normative dimension is frequently denied or dismissed. The result is
that these values are considered as abstractions that can be incorporated into
theory and asserted as fact, so that "positive and normative economics have
become tightly wedded" (Faulkner 1986:59).

A final problem in developing objective theory arises from the scientific method
as it is applied in economics. Although economists claim positivism as the
basis for their methodology, some critics assert that economic method is more
instrumentalist, particularly with regard to empirical testing of theory, and that
instrumentalism is inconsistent with positivism (Katouzian 1980; Hollis and
Nell 1975). This instrumentalism is based on Friedman's notion, discussed earlier, that if a theory "works," the realism of its assumptions is unimportant.
Economic theory begins with, and its testing proceeds with, observations of
relationships between economic phenomena. Yet, as Katouzian points out,

the observer is *looking for* [facts] even before he succeeds in locating them. In other
words, he uses certain criteria for *selecting* the *relevant* facts, and these criteria are
themselves subjective, *a priori*, prior to the observation. . . . Once selected, such facts
are *processed* by certain procedures . . . that is by analytical or empirical methods
which are entirely products of the human mind . . . the so-called observer would even
have to select the appropriate analytical and empirical methods from a wide range of
possibilities. (1980:139)

The question of values also arises in connection with the types of problems
economics chooses as a focus of study. The emphasis on maximizing behavior

discussed earlier has resulted in a preoccupation with problems related directly
to the efficient allocation of resources. As Katouzian states:

orthodox economic theory is ethically biased because, as a prescriptive science, it is
lopsided and selective: in all its basic theories it addresses itself to one set of objectives
only; that is, the static [and, recently, dynamic] problems of the efficient allocation of
national—and international—resources. And it ignores other important social objectives
by arbitrarily relegating them to the realm of "moral judgements." (1980:146–147)

Questions of equity and fairness, among others, are thus seen as uninteresting
or unsuitable for analysis using economic theory or, at the very least, not "scientific."

There is a final aspect of the practice of economics that warrants discussion
here. It was pointed out earlier that the official methodology of economics often
varies significantly from what economists actually do. Probably the most well-
developed argument on this point is made by McCloskey (1983, 1985), who
summarizes his position by claiming that all information can be categorized as
belonging on either the right- or left-hand side of the following chart:

scientific	humanistic
fact	value
truth	opinion
objective	subjective
positive	normative
rigorous	intuitive
precise	vague
things	words
cognition	feeling
hard	soft
yang	yin
male	female

(*Source:* McCloskey, as cited in Nelson 1987)

According to McCloskey, the goal of science in general, and the "official
rhetoric" of economics in particular, is to separate the good (the left-hand side
of the chart) from the bad (the right-hand side). McCloskey would claim, however, that economists actually incorporate many of the "nonscientific" characteristics on the right side of the chart into their methodology. Indeed, the
previous discussion of values in economics demonstrates that this is inevitable.
The problem is that these characteristics are not explicitly recognized as an
important part of the way economists actually work.

IMPLICATIONS OF ECONOMIC METHODOLOGY FOR
GENDER ROLES

The preceding discussion indicates clearly that the methodology of neoclassical economics has come under much closer scrutiny and criticism in recent

years. Yet most of this criticism has not adopted an explicitly feminist perspective and, for the most part, has been silent on the implications of positivism
for gender roles. This section argues that economic theory provides an inaccurate and incomplete basis for understanding gender. Two issues emerge. The
first is that the scientific method of positivism used as the basis for economic
theory makes it impossible for economics to say very much about how female
and male gender roles evolve and are differentiated. It is clear from the previous discussion that economic method abstracts from social reality, and since
gender roles are for the most part socially constructed, economics simply ex-
cludes many of the factors that are central to this construction. Moreover, what
positivism in general and economics in particular consider to be "good" science is usually described with a set of adjectives that are associated with stereotypical conceptions of male gender roles. This association makes it particularly difficult for neoclassical economics to contribute much to our understanding
of female gender roles. The second issue is related to the assumption of free
and equal participation in market exchange as the fundamental process for resource allocation. The assumed voluntary nature of this exchange and the emphasis on free choice precludes any consideration of power relationships or
coercion that are important aspects of gender roles.

First, it is useful to recall McCloskey's chart presented in the previous section. As he stated, the goal of science is to separate the left side of the chart
from the right side and to admit only those forms of inquiry that can be described using the left side as legitimate scientific knowledge. It is clear from a
comparison of the pairs of terms in the chart that the left side includes those
associated with stereotypical conceptions of male gender roles while those on
the right are typically associated with females. This suggests that most economists' conception of science is "male" and that characteristics generally associated with "female" are devalued and relegated to the realm of "normative"
economics, if they are considered at all. Although the explicit equation of "male
equals good science, female equals bad science, or nonscience" is not frequently stated, it is important to recognize that it can have some major implications for how well economic analysis captures women's experiences. If the
method that is used devalues female characteristics, then the results of analyses
that use the method would seem not to provide an adequate conception of
female gender roles.

A specific economic example may serve to demonstrate this point more
forcefully. The model of pure competition is among the most widely used in
economic theory. The model demonstrates that, under certain assumptions,
competition will result in an efficient allocation of resources. Although the
model is used as a description of economic markets and is thus considered as
a "positive" one, the fact that it logically produces efficiency, or maximization
of total welfare or output, elevates it to an economic ideal or standard of comparison—that is, competition is considered a "good" thing in economic theory.
Yet when we consider the dichotomy "competition-cooperation" in conjunc-

tion with the way in which gender roles are typically dichotomized, the equation of male with competitive and female with cooperative makes it clear that
the female role is devalued.

McCloskey's point in developing the dichotomies between "good" and "bad"
science is to demonstrate that economists do not necessarily practice what they
preach. His claim is that many of the "female" or "nonscientific" elements
are an important part of actual economic methodology and that intuition, subjective reasoning, and opinions play a significant role in the development and
testing of economic models. This is probably true, and economics would, according to McCloskey (1983, 1985), be a better science if this were explicitly
recognized. Nevertheless, the official doctrine is equally important to the extent
that it shapes the direction of the discipline in terms of the questions it asks
and the way in which it answers them. If the official doctrine devalues characteristics associated with the female gender, as this discussion indicates, then
the method itself is simply a mirror of societal gender roles. The dominance of
male characteristics and the subordination of female ones will thus be used to
perpetuate this relationship, and the method itself will contribute little to an
understanding of how these roles evolved or how they may change.

While the method itself may mirror societal conceptions of a gender hierarchy, it does little to explain it. Economics as a science claims to be asexual
or gender-neutral; it is impersonal in the sense that it analyzes individuals only
in their capacity as economic role players—as producers or consumers that
interact to determine resource allocation. As Nancy Barrett says, it is:

instructive to think in the abstract about how gender (sex) might, in and of itself, im-
pinge upon resource allocation in a neo-classical view of the economy. . . . Personal
characteristics become significant *only to the extent* that they affect economic choices or
preferences on the one hand, and economic contributions, or productivities on the other.
(1981:102–103)

Since economists generally ignore or take as given the origins of individuals'
preferences, the significance of gender in economic analysis is usually very
minor. As Carolyn S. Bell points out, "One must inquire how human beings,
people themselves and women among them, enter into the economic calculus.
It turns out that they don't, for the most part" (1974:616–617).

Given the assumptions made about the motivations for individual behavior
and the goal of economic theory—to predict outcomes in a wide variety of
circumstances—it is perhaps not surprising that economics does not have much
to say about individuals as human beings. In order to make theory sufficiently
rigorous to accomplish this goal, economists necessarily assume away important characteristics that make individuals human. As Martin Hollis and Edward
Nell (1975:87) note, models of utility maximization never even mention the
consumer specifically, even though it is consumer behavior that such models
attempt to explain.

It is this process of abstraction, of assuming "other things are equal," in the development of economic theory that results in its inability to explain how gender roles are constructed. By leaving to other social sciences questions of how and why social institutions have developed in a particular way, economics essentially ignores important factors that determine conceptions of male and female. For example, economics does consider individuals' roles as producers and consumers, but it generally does so without reference to the gender of the person who is filling the role. It is simply assumed that people enact these roles with the goal of maximizing their income or utility. In the case of producers, Bell claims "that the woman's choice about her economic role as a producer has been shaped by the social model that portrays the nuclear family as the dominant mode [and] means that the woman does not exercise any independent choice" (1974:622). Yet the economic models that incorporate the roles of individuals as producers completely ignore the social model to which Bell refers, and thus portray women as having the same free choice as do men.

In the case of consumer roles, individuals are assumed to make choices to maximize utility in accordance with their tastes and preferences for goods and services. But: "from an economist's point of view, it does not matter whether these differences in tastes are innate or developed through social conditioning" (Barrett 1981:103). Thus, gender-based differences in individuals' roles as consumers are seen as unimportant and are not explained by economic models of consumer behavior.

Considering more specific examples, one theory that has been extensively used to analyze gender-based differentials in economic status is Gary Becker's (1975) theory of discrimination. Becker's theory has been used to explain both wage differences between males and females and differences in their occupational distributions on the basis of a "taste for discrimination" which exists on the part of employers, co-workers, and/or consumers. Given these tastes for discrimination, the theory predicts that women will be paid less than men and that they will be segregated into different occupations. Both of these predictions fit reality, but the problem with the theory in terms of its ability to explain gender differences is that it takes the discriminatory tastes as given and makes no attempt to explain their origins or bases.

Aside from this neoclassical model of labor market discrimination, most economic analyses of gender-based differences in economic status are premised on the assumption that such differences result from free rational choices made within competitive markets. These assumptions, which to a large extent remove economic actors from their relevant social context, preclude a consideration of the fact that gender differences may result from socially constructed conceptions of gender roles which present men and women with different sets of constraints within which decisions are made. Constance Faulkner has argued that the assumption of individual, rational pursuit of self-interest implies that people are "disconnected from anything larger than self, from anything (including sex, race and social class) that limits their ability to exercise economic freedom'' (1986:59). Cynthia Lloyd and Beth Niemi (1979) are among the authors that recognize that women's secondary economic position is related to women's lack of free choice, yet the majority of neoclassical economic models fail to recognize this. As Lloyd and Niemi point out:

The dominant orthodox approach to labor market analysis assumes that roughly the same wide array of choice lies before each individual. . . . Although each individual engages in maximizing behavior, two people with identical preferences and non-market opportunities may well end up making completely different decisions in the labor market, because they are choosing from different sets of available alternatives. (1979:2–3)

The assumption that all individuals face the same set of choices is gratuitous given that economics has chosen to ignore those factors which may result in gender-based differences in the ability to choose.

The assumption of free rational choice that is characteristic of virtually all neoclassical economic models essentially implies that, as economic actors, everyone starts off from an equal position regardless of gender, unless there are gender-specific differences in innate characteristics. This is simply inaccurate when it comes to the economic dimensions of male and female roles. As Bell notes:

Certainly the assignment of certain roles by society, to both men and women, begins at birth. How much ''free choice'' or ''individual'' preference exists when one's gender dictates so much in life, must be an open question. But that such roles allow less economic freedom to women, as individual producers or consumers, than to men, is irrefutable. (1974:629–630)

While Bell's emphasis clearly concerns the socially imposed constraints on female gender roles, it should be pointed out that there exist constraints on male roles as well. If female gender roles are defined largely on the basis of home responsibilities, it is equally true that male roles are defined in terms of their duty to provide the family with material support. Thus the question of free choice is to some extent an open one for men as well as women. The difference is essentially one of degree; while it is certainly true that both male and female roles as economic actors are circumscribed by societal definitions of gender, these definitions have almost universally placed female roles in a secondary status. Thus, as Barrett says, ''economic status may well be a reflection of social worth or status judgements'' (1981:107).

It is clear from this discussion that economic models ignore these societal judgments on status. Yet it is important to consider them in relation to economic analysis to discuss some of the more problematic implications of such analysis for its failure to understand gender roles and, indeed, to legitimize their hierarchical nature. As has been discussed previously, economic models assume away the institutional context within which economic agents interact.

Yet, as Nancy Hartsock comments: "the most important consequence of the refusal to recognize the impact of social institutions on social relations is a theoretical failure to recognize relationships of domination" (1985:43). It is undeniable that issues of domination and power relationships are an extremely important aspect of gender roles; this is clear both from the standpoint of the methodology itself and of the phenomena that the methodology analyzes.

But economic analysis is not equipped to deal with these power relationships; in fact, given the way in which economic models are constructed, it is almost impossible to see how they could exist. If rational, self-interested behavior is seen as the force motivating economic actors, then any market interaction between individuals will be interpreted in an economic context as a means of furthering one's own interest. Viewed in this way, any market exchange has to be purely voluntary, almost by definition. If it were not, no rational individual would take part in it. Thus it is not possible, given the assumptions underlying the behavior of rational economic agents in a neoclassical economic model, to see any elements of exploitation or coercion influencing the outcome. As Hartsock says,

If one accepts neo-classical assumptions, social relations in market societies are not fundamentally antagonistic, but represent the relations of an "orderly supermarket, where, even if the off customer is shortchanged or the odd item shoplifted, people in the long run get what they pay for and pay for what they get." The operation of the assumption that social relations are fundamentally equitable . . . legitimizes (by obfuscating and concealing) relations of domination, presents coercion as choice, and ultimately legitimizes domination. (1985:49)

The neoclassical belief in the supremacy of the free market system for allocating resources is based on the term "free." Unless it is recognized that institutional factors affect the voluntary nature of market interaction, economic models cannot logically incorporate relations of power. To the extent that males have traditionally held more economic power than females and that this imbalance has had an impact on society's conception of gender roles, economic analysis inhibits our understanding of gender by ignoring this important factor and, in fact, sanctioning it by predicting it as a logical outcome of market interaction.

Three major points can be summarized. First, the values and ideology that underlie neoclassical economic methodology result in the failure of economics to address specifically the definition of gender roles in general and female gender roles in particular. This is true largely because the characteristics associated with the scientific method used by economists and the ideologies of the market system economists analyze are identified with male stereotypes. As Bell says: "we have a sexually neutral economics; its gender is indubitably male" (1974:631). Secondly, the process of abstraction essential to the development of economic theory precludes the consideration of social context and other factors that are essential to an adequate understanding of how gender roles are shaped. Finally, neoclassical economic models, since they are based so heavily on the notion of exchange intended to maximize one's own self-interest, do not address the notions of power and domination that are important aspects of gender roles. This is unfortunate since, as Bell states, "economic choices deal with human life itself [and] who makes these choices and where they are made depends upon the loci of power" (1974:615).

SUMMARY AND CONCLUSIONS

This assessment of the discipline's contribution to our understanding of gender roles may seem unduly pessimistic. The ability of economics to explain the general definition of gender roles is limited, and more specifically, "economic science, as a discipline, has very little to offer in terms of explaining the fundamental reason why a sex-based status differential has been so deeply engrained in all societies" (Barrett 1981:107). The analysis is not meant to imply that economics has ignored women's issues or that it has not made specific comparisons between men's and women's economic positions. These issues have been addressed, and with increasing frequency, but they have been addressed from a particular perspective and with the use of a methodology which ignores many forces important to the shaping of gender roles.

The criticism of economic method should also not be construed to imply that economics can provide us with a complete understanding of gender roles—no single discipline is capable of this task, or should be expected to be, as feminist criticism of the traditional academic disciplines has made clear. In her discussion of women's economic status, Barrett argues that: "economics holds out no solution to the enigma of why women continue to be judged inferior to men in all aspects of life. . . . Women's studies should continue to be an interdisciplinary activity, precisely because the study of women through the perspective of any one discipline is likely to lead squarely into another" (1981:107). Barrett's point is equally applicable to the study of gender role determination in general; just as economics alone does not provide an adequate perspective on this study, sociology, psychology, or anthropology alone is not likely to either. Nevertheless, the analysis in this chapter does provide the basis for two major categories of suggestions as to how economic methodology might be modified so that it could be used to provide a better insight into how gender roles are constructed and how they evolve.

First is the issue of values in economics. If economics is ever to provide a firmer foundation upon which to analyze issues relating to gender, it is essential that the artificial distinction between positive and normative economics be recognized for what it is and be removed as a cornerstone of much of economic methodology. The above discussion has strongly suggested that economists as social scientists are products of the societies within which they work and live, and because of this, it is impossible to have a completely value-free economics. To continue to pretend that it is possible will result in values becoming embedded in "positive," logical economic models, with the predictions of those models being used to perpetuate a particular system of values unconsciously.

For the study of gender roles, this essentially means that, to the extent that roles are considered at all, they will be taken as given and not questioned. In other words, if specific values about "appropriate" gender roles (i.e., roles as they are currently constructed) are built into supposedly positive economic models as assumptions or objective "givens," then such models will tend to make predictions that will reinforce the status quo in terms of how gender roles are assigned. This clearly indicates that economics as it is presently constructed does not say very much about how these gender roles were defined in the first place. In order for the discipline to do so, it will have to broaden its inquiry to include questions of value and normative issues, such as: why might labor market participants have a "taste for discrimination" against certain groups based on gender?, or how have social judgments operated to link the public sphere so closely with male gender roles and the private sphere with female ones?, instead of simply taking these issues as given.

The second major category of suggestions concerns the question of the scientific method in economics. For example, much can be learned from the feminist critique of method in the hard sciences (Weaver, Thompson, and Newton in this volume) or, in slightly different terms, from applying a feminist perspective to the work of McCloskey (1983, 1985) cited previously. As discussed earlier, McCloskey calls for economists to abandon their formal ties to the scientific method and to "accept and consciously examine the intuitive and subjective elements already present in economic discourse" (Nelson 1987:3). This recommendation closely parallels that of much of the feminist literature on scientific thought, in which "the modernist or 'objectivist' view of science is rejected in favor of a vision of science in which there is a fruitful integration of reason and emotion, of the abstract and concrete" (Nelson 1987:3). Thus, in science in general as well as economics in particular, there is an emerging consensus that positivism as a basis for the scientific method leaves much to be desired, and that much could be gained from integrating so-called "feminine" characteristics into the scientific method.

In the case of economics, Julie Nelson has referred to these changes as the " 'de-gendering' of economic thought—a move from a distinctly masculine to a more fully human way of understanding" (1987:4). Neither Nelson nor the few other economists who have considered the impact of feminism on economic method (e.g., Bergmann 1983; Faulkner 1986) believe that this "de-gendering" is likely to be easily accomplished. This is because, as has been stressed, the social construction of gender roles has a great deal to do with how we view the world. Moreover, "self-consciousness about the subjectivity of the economists . . . [requires] an examination of how the personal experiences of an economist contribute to and influence the propositions that are propounded" (Nelson 1987:5).

Such an examination reveals the ethical bias toward the free-market system, and an androcentric bias as well. Overcoming these biases may well require dismantling the assumptions upon which neoclassical economics is based, particularly the notion of free, individual choice. This is no easy task, to be sure. But Nelson's proposal for the more human way of understanding that will lead in this direction is essential if economics is to contribute to an understanding of gender-role construction. It is crucial to remember that gender roles are filled by human beings, not one-dimensional economic actors.

REFERENCES

Barrett, Nancy. 1981. "How the study of women has restructured the discipline of economics." Pp. 101–109 in *A Feminist Perspective in the Academy,* edited by E. Langland and W. Gove. Chicago: University of Chicago Press.

Becker, Gary. 1975. *The Economics of Discrimination.* Chicago: University of Chicago Press.

Bell, Carolyn S. 1974. "Economics, sex and gender." *Social Science Quarterly* 55:615–631.

Bergmann, Barbara. 1983. "Feminism and economics." *Academe* 69 (5): 23–28.

Faulkner, Constance. 1986. "The feminist challenge to economics." *Frontiers* 8 (3): 55–61.

Friedman, Milton. 1984 [1953]. "The methodology of positive economics." Pp. 210–245 in *The Philosophy of Economics,* edited by D. Hausman. Cambridge: Cambridge University Press.

Hartsock, Nancy. 1985. *Money, Sex and Power.* Boston: Northeastern University Press.

Hollis, Martin, and Edward Nell. 1975. *Rational Economic Man.* Cambridge: Cambridge University Press.

Katouzian, Homa. 1980. *Ideology and Method in Economics.* New York: New York University Press.

Lloyd, Cynthia, and Beth Niemi. 1979. *The Economics of Sex Differentials.* New York: Columbia University Press.

Marshall, Alfred. 1955. "The present position of economics." P. 164 in *Memorials of Alfred Marshall,* edited by A. C. Pigou. London: Macmillan.

McCloskey, Donald. 1985. *The Rhetoric of Economics.* Madison: University of Wisconsin Press.

———. 1983. "The rhetoric of economics." *Journal of Economic Literature* 21 (2): 481–517.

Myrdal, Gunnar. 1984 [1954]. "Implicit values in economics." Pp. 250–259 in *The Philosophy of Economics,* edited by D. Hausman. Cambridge: Cambridge University Press.

Nelson, Julie. 1987. "Gender and economic thought." Pp. 2–6 in *Newsletter of the Committee on the Status of Women in the Economics Profession.* Nashville: American Economic Association.

Peterson, Wallace. 1973. *Elements of Economics.* New York: W. W. Norton.

Tullock, Gordon, and Richard McKenzie. 1984. *The New World of Economics.* New York: Irwin.

6

Those Who Surrender Are Female: Prisoner Gender Identities as Cultural Mirror

John M. Coggeshall

"You here to see the show?" the inmate leered. The focus of attention was the tall, slim blond then receiving her food in the cafeteria line. The kitchen workers in the medium-security prison served her with polite deference, and as she walked between the tables her fine blond hair bounced over her shoulders. "Make you want to leave home?" a guard teased. His comment clarified the significance of the events the guards, staff, and inmates had just witnessed. The object of interest was genetically a male, but reconstructed as a female according to the perception of gender within prisoner culture. Behind bars, certain males become redefined as females. The process by which this transformation occurs reveals clues about gender perceptions in prisoner culture and also offers reflections of gender inequality in American culture in general.

GENDER IDENTITY, ROLES, AND STATUSES

To understand the gender redefinitions in prisoner culture requires a conception of gender itself as primarily a cultural construct; cultures define male and female (Mukhopadhyay and Higgins 1988:485). This approach follows the contemporary deconstructionist movement in the social sciences and humanities; that is, seeing gender as mutable and malleable, depending on the social context. Moreover, this perspective shifts emphasis from exclusively viewing female studies to highlighting *both* male and female genders, for to understand one requires at least a consideration of the other.

For example, many Western cultures view genders as dichotomous, despite obvious contradictions to these restrictive cultural categories (Grimm 1987:67–

68). The dichotomy further enhances gender identities (Bem 1981, cited in Devor 1987:13–14) because the contrastive elements mutually exclude each other. In Western culture, one is either male or female. The two genders exist in binary opposition, each defining and being defined by the other.

In American culture, the dualistic contrast of gender identities reinforces a contrast in roles as well (Brandes 1980:6 for a European example). Masculine identity embodies role behaviors such as success and status, toughness and independence, aggressiveness and dominance (Herek 1986:568). Moreover, masculinity is defined in contrast to femininity; acting male assumes *not* acting compliant, dependent, or submissive, and not being effeminate in physical appearance or mannerisms (Herek 1986:568). Males who exhibit these behaviors become "unsexed"; that is, no longer males (Read 1980:97). Gender categories remain viable by simply excluding obvious inconsistencies.

Since in American culture gender roles exist in binary opposition, it is often assumed that homosexuals adopt the roles of their genetically opposite sex. However, this situation does not always occur cross-culturally (Davis and Whitten 1987:80–82). Female homosexuality, for example, does not form a "mirror image" of male homosexuality (e.g., Blackwood 1985, cited in Davis and Whitten 1987:81–82), because various cultures place different expectations and roles on heterosexual genders in those societies. Likewise, in social ties between male homosexuals, dyads do not always pair in "male-female" roles (Davis and Whitten 1987:81). While gender identity varies considerably, gender roles also vary cross-culturally.

In American culture, gender dichotomization assumedly leaves little flexibility for gender identity, role behavior, or methods of sexual gratification. Most automatically assign homosexuals to the opposite gender identity and role and infer certain types of sexual activity. However, sexual behavior and gender identity are extremely complex and often separate phenomena. Individuals may classify themselves as homosexual, bisexual, or heterosexual in identity and may adopt the gender roles of masculine, feminine, both, or neither. In addition, individuals may engage in erotic activities with members of their own biological gender (homoerotic behavior) or they may engage in heteroerotic behavior, or both, regardless of their self-perceived gender identity or role. In other words, sexual gratification exists independently of gender identity and gender roles.

In American culture, most heterosexuals assume that males engaging in homoerotic sexual behavior would describe themselves as both homosexual in sexual orientation and "feminine" in gender identity (Read 1980:16). But this assumption is patently false. Jack Weatherford (1986), in a study of an urban red-light district, described numerous instances of homoerotic behavior between males who still identified themselves as heterosexuals. Similarly, in the street life described by Albert Reiss, Jr. (1967), teenagers permit adult males to fellate them for money. However, the "peers" do not equate this homoerotic behavior with a feminine, or even homosexual, identity (Reiss 1967:225, 201).

Although American culture assumes homosexuals adopt and retain dichotomous "masculine" (insertor) or "feminine" (insertee) roles, "the terms active
or passive partners, masculine or feminine role," simply have no meaning for
homosexual dyads (Hooker 1967:182). Nearly all male homosexuals know they
are men, as do their lovers (Read 1980:105, 110). Nevertheless, they sometimes adopt exaggerated female roles, ridiculing women while reaffirming their
masculine identity in binary contrast (Read 1980:98). This denigration of women
by men to enhance or supplement a male identity, even though in jest, requires
closer scrutiny.

As noted, genders in Western cultures frequently exist in binary opposition;
males define themselves in contrast to females. Quite often this juxtapositioning
becomes not just a difference in identities but also a qualitative and quantitative
difference in status between genders. Because of the opposition, and in fact
enhanced by it, one gender comes to dominate and control the other.

While in some cultures males and females retain relative status equality, no
cultures politically or economically elevate women as a group at the expense
of men (Mukhopadhyay and Higgins 1988 for a summary of gender status
research). However, many cultures denigrate and devalue women (Sanday
1981:33–34). Why this occurs is unclear. While gender inequality correlates
strongly with overall social inequality (Mukhopadhyay and Higgins 1988:484)
and male domination appears correlated with overall aggression and socially
approved violence (Mukhopadhyay and Higgins 1988:471), research still seeks
to discover why women as a group always lose status when gender inequality
occurs.

Gender inequality need not necessarily imply sexual antagonism and violence, however (Davis and Whitten 1987:77). Cultures differ in degree, severity, and consequences of the male control of economic and political power
(Mukhopadhyay and Higgins 1988:466–467). The question is, of course, what
factors transform gender inequality (when it does occur) into the degradation,
humiliation, and sexual assault of women.

Some researchers have proposed psychological explanations for the male
domination of females. Early formulations of this idea emanated as a reaction
to Freudian theory. Instead of the androcentric assumption of penis envy as
universal, Karen Horney (1926:330–331) argued that males envied the procrea-
tive powers of women and thus denigrated them. Nancy Chodorow (1974) felt
that insecurity stemmed from difficulties in establishing separate gender identities. More recently, Eva Feder Kittay (1983:95, 121) suggested that because
males cannot reproduce while women can, male "womb envy" led directly to
the oppression and exploitation of women (also Mukhopadhyay and Higgins
(1988:482–483). Thus men humiliate and denigrate women, for they envy and
fear that which they cannot control (Brandes 1980:76 for a European example).

Other researchers have suggested that where a culture's value system con-
dones, or at least does not strongly discourage, male sexual antagonism against
women, then this provides at least implicit acceptance of such brutalization.

Cross-culturally, evidence indicates that the lower the status of women, the greater male sexual aggression (Baron and Strauss 1987:480–481). Many cultures, such as those of Western Christianity, emphasize male domination symbolically through all-powerful male deities, providing a "script" for male control (Sanday 1981:215–216; Castelli and McBride, this volume). In such societies, sexual aggression both reflects the lower status of women and contributes further to the gender inequality (Baron and Strauss 1987:481). The cultural misconception is that women are submissive; therefore, males can dominate them. But, through the process of domination, males perceive women as submissive. The vicious circle of control and violence is completed.

In American culture, physical and sexual violence against women has been directly associated with the cultural devaluation of women (e.g., Scott and Tetreault 1987:379; Silbert and Pines 1984:864; Schur 1984:150). In actuality, rape represents only the tip of a chilling iceberg of male psychological and physical oppression directed against women, a terrible "extension and distortion of . . . the approved patterns of sexual behavior in our society" (Schur 1984:148). For this sexual aggression to decline, dramatic modifications in values and behavior must occur, including the elimination of male perceptions of women as property to be possessed and as conquests to be dominated (Schur 1984:156).

Other researchers suggest that male domination of and hostility toward women ultimately stem from economic inequality (Mukhopadhyay and Higgins 1988:463; Schlegel and Barry 1986:149; Sacks 1974:221–222). Where women lose control over resources, they lose power while men retain or enhance it (Mukhopadhyay and Higgins 1988:463). Where men control women's contributions to subsistence, men also control women's sexuality, including the toleration of sexual aggression and rape (Schlegel and Barry 1986:147). When coupled with a cultural value system emphasizing male domination, the male control of female economic power leads directly and frequently to the oppression and sexual domination of women by men (Sanday 1981:184–187, 210).

GENDER CONCEPTS IN PRISON

Prison provides a microcosmic social situation to observe in horrifyingly clear detail the consequences of gender inequality in American culture. In prison, inmates face antagonism from guards, violence from fellow inmates, and deprivation from incarceration itself. One method by which male inmates retaliate is to humiliate and assault their fellow inmates sexually. However, not all inmates face these attacks. By a complicated cultural process, certain inmates become redefined as women in prison. This metamorphosis allows males engaging in homoerotic behavior to retain a heterosexual identity, and it also justifies the brutality directed to these unfortunate inmates. As will be shown, gender roles and status in prison reflect those in American culture.

Victims of sexual assault in men's prisons "are perceived as those who are (or [who] may be) willing to occupy the passive role" (Nacci and Kane 1984:46–47). According to attackers, victims appear "weak and attractive (i.e. a *logical stand-in for a woman*)" (my emphasis, Nacci and Kane 1984:47; also Wooden and Parker 1982:3). In prison, "the supreme act of humiliation is to be reduced to the status of a woman" (Cardozo-Freeman 1984:400). In turn, the perception of female passivity justifies male domination: victims ask to be raped through "sexually stimulating behavior or appearance or negligence in self defense" (Nacci and Kane 1984:49). In other words, victims of sexual assault become so because they appear to be defenseless, vulnerable females, and forced sexual intercourse becomes the weapon of offense (Nacci and Kane 1984:47; Jackson 1974:377).

Why "female" inmates become "logical" targets reveals much about American culture in general as well as prisoner culture in particular. In the sexual domination of female substitutes, inmate exploiters gain power and self-esteem: "to express your machismo you must have people without it" (Jackson 1974:377; also Nacci and Kane 1984:47; Nacci and Kane 1983:33). The dehumanization of one gender by another enhances the latter's esteem. In prisoner culture, as in American culture in general, men "seek to preserve a threatened identity by retaliating by force" against those without power, that is, women (Sanday 1981:210).

In dramatic contrast, sexual victimization does not occur in women's prisons (Giallombardo 1966:98). Despite the parallel oppression and dehumanization of incarceration, female inmates do not retaliate in exactly the same ways. In women's prisons, homoerotic dyads are extremely common (Burkhart 1973:376), seen by inmates "as a meaningful personal and social relationship" (Giallombardo 1966:98). Frequently, these dyads involve the gender roles of stereotypical American culture; dominant "husbands" often control submissive "wives" (Giallombardo 1966:148–149; Burkhart 1973:371; Williams and Fish 1978:547–548). While economic exploitation occurs (Williams and Fish 1978:549–50), and while jealousies and indiscretions sometimes spark violence (Williams and Fish 1978:551), the ideal relationship is based on romantic love (Giallombardo 1966:125). In fact, couples with a mutually compatible relationship gain the greatest prestige (Giallombardo 1966:149). While in some ways Rose Giallombardo's research has become outdated, more recent examinations of women's prisons have replicated the lack of sexual aggression in those institutions (e.g., Burkhart 1973; Williams and Fish 1978).

Giallombardo (1966:17, 130) suggests that sexual exploitation occurs only in men's prisons because American culture expects men to be aggressive and women passive; prison behavior reflects these American gender roles. More specifically, Wayne S. Wooden and Jay Parker (1982:44) argue that prison sexual aggression replicates "sexual patterns and ethnic differences" among lower-income groups. Inez Cardozo-Freeman (1984:400) feels that male inmates react violently because of the dehumanization of the social situation: "the state 'screws' the prisoner; he, in turn, does the same to his fellow prisoners." Gang rapes become, at least in part, a reflection of displaced antagonism against a repressive society (Cardozo-Freeman 1984:374).

While these researchers approach an explanation of gender redefinition and sexual assault in men's prisons, none completely explains it. As Giallombardo (1966:130) argues, sexual assault by males in prison does reflect differential cultural values, but more fundamentally than simply a contrast between aggression and passivity. Moreover, sexual antagonism is not exclusively a lower-class or "ethnic" phenomenon, as Wooden and Parker (1982:22–23) suggest (also Buffum 1972:9, 16). While it is true that, as Cardozo-Freeman (1984:400) proposes, prison rape represents "a metaphor," it is not as generalized as a symbol of the exploitation of all incarcerated human beings. Instead, prison rape represents a metaphor of male domination over females, reflecting differential gender values in, and the social consequences for, American society in general.

For inmates, the concept of female emerges from the concept of male. To borrow a polysemic metaphor, the rib for Eve's creation is taken from Adam's side, and draws both its cultural significance and social status from the extraction. Woman is defined in contrast to man and takes a lesser place at his side. This juxtaposition explicates the concept and relative status of gender construction and identity in prisoner culture. In prison, males create females in their image, and by doing so, dominate and subjugate them.

GENDER PERCEPTIONS IN MALE PRISONER CULTURE

Overview

Prison culture is extremely complex and deserves much more detailed study by anthropologists (e.g., Goffman 1961; Giallombardo 1966; Davidson 1983; Cardozo-Freeman 1984; Fleisher 1989; also Coggeshall 1988:6 for further research suggestions). This chapter concentrates on prisoner cultural views; that is, on the views of inmates themselves.

The fieldwork for this study was conducted in two medium-security Illinois state prisons between 1984 and 1986. During that time three university-level courses were taught to 44 adult inmates, constituting a range of racial group and criminal record diversity representative of the overall prison population. Student-inmate perceptions provided a portion of the data, supplemented by observations of and conversations with guards, staff, and other inmates. After having received some instruction on data collection, one student-inmate, Eugene Luetkemeyer (now released), volunteered to collect additional information. His nine detailed interviews of various inmates, identified below by pseudonyms, significantly enhanced the scope and detail of the study.

Various estimates exist on the amount of homoerotic activity in prison. As with most research on human sexual activity, "it is difficult to find out just how much activity actually goes on, and impossible to find out who does what to whom" (Jackson 1974:375). Tommy, a self-described homophobe, believes that about 33 percent of prisoners engage in homoerotic activity, while Spankie, a self-described homosexual, suggests about 50 percent (Luetkemeyer 1987; Jackson 1974:375, Buffum 1972, cited in Nacci and Kane 1983:35). Paul and Sandy, homosexual lovers, estimate that about 65 percent engage in homosexual activity, an assumption supported by Doctor B, an incarcerated medical doctor (Luetkemeyer 1987; Davidson 1983:75). While not all inmates accept or condone homoerotic behavior outright, the vast majority see it as at worst an unpleasant necessity and at best an acceptable alternative.

A small percentage of inmates do not condone or participate in homoerotic activity because for them such participation implies a feminine identity, even if one actor occupies the dominant role exclusively. For example, Tommy considers any homosexual act to be reciprocal; that is, both dominant and submissive: "if you pitch, you catch," he feels; "there's none of this 'being a man one day and a freak the next' business" (Luetkemeyer 1987; also Jackson 1974:375).

On the other hand, Spankie estimates that about 96 percent of sexual participants are "bisexual," giving as well as receiving pleasure (Luetkemeyer 1987). In other words, many inmates adopt both an "insertor" and an "insertee" role, at various times, for sexual gratification and emotional bonding (also Jackson 1974:373, 398–403). In such relationships, though, genders remain distinct, differentiated not on methods of sexual gratification, and not necessarily on "active" or "passive" sexual participation, but primarily on the basis of control of the relationship. In fact, domination defines the structure of the relationship which distinguishes the genders.

Gender Perceptions

In prisoner culture, males have a gender identity quite distinct from females. Robert, an inmate, describes "a big . . . macho, weight-lifting, virile, Tom Sellek-type guy" as a typical male (Luetkemeyer 1987). Weight lifters seem to predominate in the category, for strength suggests masculinity. Men vigorously protest sexual advances from other males by exhibiting a willingness to fight. Men also are perceived as those who can keep, satisfy, protect, and control women.

In direct contrast to the male definition of themselves, men see women as passive, subordinate sex objects. Terms from inmate folk vocabulary (Luetkemeyer 1987) support this view. According to male inmates (Luetkemeyer 1987), women exhibit certain typical behaviors and characteristics. As Robert commented, women are "sweet and charming," "fluid of movement," with "seductive gestures." Doctor B believes that he himself exhibits such effeminate qualities as "mild manners" and a "passive demeanor."

Primarily, women are defined by men on the basis of their sexuality. Sandy, a male perceiving herself as female, views promiscuous women as "tramps" or "whores." On the other hand, Sandy equates her distinguished status in prison to that of a well-respected woman on the streets:

If you want to be treated like a lady and get respect, you've got to demand that respect. . . . If you whore around . . . you'll get no respect. But if you are true to your daddy, carry yourself well, have a dignified demeanor, you'll be treated with respect. (Luetkemeyer 1987)

According to the predominant male view, women are sex objects; some respected, others not, defined primarily on the basis of male control of female sexuality and gender identity.

Some genetically female prison employees reinforce these stereotypes, according to inmates. Women work as wardens, guards, staff, and teachers, so that numerous role models exist for typical females for the inmates. Prisoner culture suggests that these women cannot resist being sexually attracted to inmates, due to the diversity of males from which to choose and the relative lack of female competition in prison.

Of course, nearly all female staff resist inmate advances. By inmate definition, then, they must not be women. Such "unsexed" women do not challenge gender constructs but reinforce them further. Female guards, staff, and teachers occupy positions of authority over inmates, decidedly atypical for women from a prisoner's perspective. Moreover, most female employees deliberately dress to deaccentuate anatomical differences for their own professionalism and safety. Because these women control men, dress as non-women, and act in a professional, non-enticing manner, they do not fit the inmate perception of women at all. Thus they cannot be women and must be homosexuals, or "dykes" as the convicts term them. To inmates, this can be the only explanation for women who do not act like women.

Prisoner gender concepts maintain distinct boundaries even when faced with apparent contradictions. In the mutually exclusive dichotomy of gender definitions in prisoner culture, members of one gender who act like those of another are placed into the proper category. Thus women who control men are reclassified as "dykes" (non-women), and men who submit sexually are reclassified as "girls" (non-men). The validity of cultural categories continues uninterrupted as potentially illogical anomalies disappear through recategorization.

Gender Transformation and Reconstruction

However, since the non-men in prisoner culture had been males at one time, this presents "real" men with a gender identity inconsistency: the need to reconcile sexual activity with other males while maintaining a masculine self-concept. This adjustment is accomplished by means of a unique folk explanation of the etiology of gender development and orientation. Basically, dominant males in prison redefine submissive males as incipient females.

In prisoner culture, certain males are believed to have a deep-seated proclivity for being female; they are, in effect, trapped in between male and female,
needing to be released to achieve their true gender identities. Inmate terms for
the metamorphosis reveal this gender ambiguity: males "turn out" these non-
males, transforming them into the cultural equivalent of females. Certain males
become redefined from the dominant male perspective as being females trapped
in male bodies. Such individuals figuratively "turn out" to be females, reconstructed according to the prisoner cultural stereotypes of female. They thus
become their true selves at last.

This transformation creates additional complications in gender identity for
such inmates. Men readjusting sexual orientations face a reassessment similar
to the adjustments Erving Goffman (1961:146–169) had described. These individuals must reconcile past heterosexual behavior and male identity with present
homoerotic behavior and a feminine identity. The newly created female must
convince herself that this had been her true identity all along, and she now has
adopted the normal role befitting her gender identity. As might be expected,
this role acceptance creates difficult psychological problems for such inmates,
and not all easily reconcile themselves to the transition.

Vindication for the transformation comes as those forced to become females
remain so. The inmate's acceptance of her new gender identity and associated
behavior justifies the conversion for the rest of the prison population. If the
new woman had no natural proclivity or had not been submissive and thus by
definition female, she would never have embraced a feminine identity. As inmate culture (illogically) explains (Luetkemeyer 1987), those who surrender
are weak, and females are weak. Therefore, those who surrender must be female by nature.

In fact, the structure of the relationship defines gender identity and role, not
the actions of sexual gratification. "Real" men may engage (surreptitiously) in
either active or passive homoerotic behavior with their "ladies" or "girls."
Nevertheless, the former retain a heterosexual gender identity because they control
their partners, both socially and sexually. Because those controlled *are* controlled, they are by cultural definition female.

Folk conceptions of the etiology of gender support this perspective on gender
transformation. For example, Tommy believed that all humans are "conceived
as female, then either, as fetuses, develop genitalia or not" (Luetkemeyer 1987).
Some perpetuate this ambiguous fetal identity into adulthood. Those who do,
even unconsciously, can be transformed or "turned out" by stronger (i.e.,
male) inmates. Not resisting, or not resisting aggressively enough, merely val-
idates this hidden gender identity. In inmates' views, it is only appropriate that
those trapped in the wrong gender be released, to unfetter their true natures.
The gender conversion, through trickery, coercion, or rape, restores the natural
order.

Once the metamorphosis has taken place, most inmates agree that it can
never be reversed (also Davidson 1983:75). In effect, individuals have been

restored to their true feminine natures. In prisoner culture, most retain that identity throughout their incarceration.

Homosexual Categories, Roles and Statuses

First, a note about inmate terminology is in order. As discussed earlier, homosexual identity and homoerotic behavior are not always correlated, and homosexuals are not passive or effeminate. However, gender identity in prison replicates the dichotomy in American culture: masculine or feminine. By necessity, though, sexual gratification becomes primarily homoerotic. Thus, in prisoner culture, inmates designate males engaging in homoerotic but primarily dominant sexual relationships as heterosexuals, while males in homoerotic but primarily passive relationships are termed homosexuals. This preserves the gender dichotomy in American culture (also Nacci and Kane 1983:35). Hereafter, the term "homosexual" refers to the inmates' category of male transformed to female. As noted earlier, social control, not gender identity or sexual gratification *per se,* defines gender categories and their status relationships in prisoner culture.

Prisoner culture divides homosexuals into several types (also Jackson 1974:373–374; Jackson 1978:260; Cardozo-Freeman 1984:369–403), each defined on the basis of degree of sexual promiscuity, amount of self-conceptual pride, and severity of coercion used in transformation. Generally, status declines as promiscuity increases, self-concept decreases, and the intensity of coercion used in the conversion process increases.

The highest status category of homosexuals in prison contains "queens" or "ladies," those who had come out both voluntarily and willingly. Spankie defines queens as having self-concepts as women and thus they behave as such (Luetkemeyer 1987). Prisoner cultural belief suggests that these individuals had been homosexual before incarceration but had not felt comfortable in "coming out." Prison provides them with the freedom to do so. Such individuals maintain a high status by ostensibly remaining in control of their own lives and of their own gender identity.

For example, Sandy had been a female impersonator before imprisonment and had voluntarily turned out immediately upon entering prison (Luetkemeyer 1987). She feels that she has a certain amount of class and thus a high status. She always has and always will select her own lovers. Granted, she admits, she draws part of her status from Paul, her current lover and a well-respected but retired gang leader. But Sandy feels she also has her own status, determined by her "dignified demeanor." Her self-confidence has allowed her to maintain a secure and stable identity and status in prisoner culture.

While other inmates volunteer to be females (in effect selling their male identities for rare or contraband goods), many are forced to become homosexuals against their initial will. According to an inmate, "everyone is tested. The weak—of personality, personal power, willingness to fight, physical frailty, timidity—are especially susceptible. . . . Respect is given to one who can control the life of another" he adds (Luetkemeyer 1987). Those unwilling or unable to control others are thus themselves controlled. According to inmate cultural rules of gender identity, those who dominate, by natural inclination, are males, and those who submit, by natural temperament, are females.

According to Doctor B, some homosexuals actually prefer to be dominated (Luetkemeyer 1987). The prevalent value system in prison suggests that those who resist sexual attacks vicariously enjoy being dominated physically and sexually by more powerful inmates. The more resistance, the greater the challenge, especially if the victim is youthful, naive, weak, and thus "effeminate."

Individuals forced to adopt a female role have the lowest status and are termed "girls," "kids," "gumps," or "punks" (also Reiss 1967:218). These individuals are kept in virtual servitude, as a sign of the owner's power and prestige (Luetkemeyer 1987). A gump may also have been tricked into surrendering his male identity by initially trusting an older "friend" who gradually draws the novice into a debtor situation where the only repayment is through submissive sex. A punk, most agree, initially hesitates, and is turned out by forcible rape and continued domination.

However created, homosexuals perform numerous functions. Generally, the higher the status, the more control one has over one's activities. High-status individuals such as Sandy select their own lovers and live as wives and husbands in what Jackson (1974:373) termed a "parody" of heterosexual relationships. In these situations the submissive partner provides stereotypical female services such as laundry, cell cleaning, grooming, and sexual gratification for her dominant "daddy" (Luetkemeyer 1987).

Those with less status perform the same tasks but less voluntarily and with less consideration from their daddies. For example, Robert had forced his kid to perform "certain menial functions" such as cleaning his cell. This established Robert's prestige *vis a vis* other inmates (Luetkemeyer 1987). As one of Cardozo-Freeman's (1984:370) informants commented, "a punk in the bunk is like a crack in the shack [a woman at home]. . . . They wash your clothes, they clean the house, [and] make your bed."

Once an inmate has been forced to adopt a submissive lifestyle, the more intense the nightmare of domination becomes. For example (Luetkemeyer 1987), in a maximum-security prison one inmate had been forced to fellate an entire row of inmates in the prison theater. Another inmate recalled the capture of a first offender by a convict in a county jail, who then forced the "girl" to submit to sex with anyone he sent. Gumps might be forced to pleasure a gang chief and then be passed down to a trusted lieutenant or to gang members for their enjoyment. A particularly attractive kid might be put "on the stroll," forced to be a prostitute for the financial benefit of the gang.

As valuable profit-making enterprises, kids might be sold to gangs by specialists who had trained or recruited them (Luetkemeyer 1987). Particularly attractive or submissive individuals bring high prices, as much as $100 in a cash-poor prisoner economy where money cannot be easily acquired. Economically productive kids might also be won or lost through gambling or traded from owner to owner like property. "Gumps are bought and sold and traded between gangs like baseball players under contract," an inmate observed (Luetkemeyer 1987).

The Cultural Significance of "Males as Females"

Hated and abused, desired and adored, males as females in prison occupy an important niche: they are the women of that society, constructed as such by the male-based perception of gender identities. In prison, actual females are termed "holes" and "bitches," reflecting the contempt of what Doctor B believes to be characteristic of society's view of lower-class women in general (Luetkemeyer 1987). In prison, he adds, a homosexual "is likely to receive much of the contempt [and] pent-up hostility that would otherwise be directed at women." Herein lies the key to unlocking the deeper significance of gender construction and maintenance in prisoner culture.

Recall the general inmate perception of gender in prisoner culture. As Cardozo-Freeman (1984:394) noted, submissive homosexuals "are seduced, raped, beaten, forced to please men, often in degrading ways and against their will, [and] assigned the usual drudgeries real women have always been assigned." Even such a high-status individual as Sandy commented that homosexuals in prison have "far less respect; [you are] kept in your place, have no rights, your opinions and viewpoints are not acknowledged." Eloquently symbolic of Sandy's perceptions, her lover Paul interrupted and forced her to rescind her opinion (Luetkemeyer 1987).

In prisoner culture, homosexuals are owned and protected by daddies. In exchange, homosexuals provide sexual gratification and menial labor upon demand. Many are forced to sell their bodies for material objects or for protection from physical harm. Homosexuals are viewed as being emotional, helpless, and timid. Best suited for certain tasks, homosexuals provide domestic and personal services for their daddies, serving their every whim.

Most fundamentally, homosexuals in prison are seen as sexual objects to be used, abused, and discarded whenever necessary. Passive recipients of male power, they are believed to enjoy being dominated and controlled. In fact, males do them favors by releasing their female identities through rape. In prisoner culture, "no" means "yes," and resistance to sexual advances can be ignored as merely teasing taunts or further exemplification of weakness. A homosexual's wants and self-concept matter little, for in prison sexuality equals power. Males have power, females do not, and thus males dominate and exploit the weaker sex.

Ultimately, in whose image and likeness are these "males as females" created? Genetically female staff and administrators do not fit the stereotypical gender view, and thus provide no role models for "real" males to fashion

females from other males in prison. The female role models for prison homosexuals are not women but male perceptions of women. Males themselves sculpt
the image of female in prison, forming her from the clay of their own impressions. Males turned out as females perform the cultural role allotted to them
by "real" males, a role of submission and passivity. In actuality, males produce, direct, cast, and write the script for the cultural expression of gender
identity behind bars.

IMPLICATIONS FOR AMERICAN CULTURE

In prison, woman is made in contrast to the image and likeness of man; men
establish their own identity from the juxtapositioning. In prisoner culture genders are reflexive; each pole draws meaning from a negation of the other. As
discussed earlier, this dichotomy parallels the value system in many cultures,
enhancing and reinforcing maleness at the expense of femaleness and the powerful at the expense of the powerless. Gender differences in many cultures
come to be gender inequalities. By means of male domination, women remain
in a culturally defined place of servitude and submission. In turn, males interpret women's powerless position as justification for the continued exploitation
of females.

It is precisely this concept of gender identity and status inequality that has
proven most disquieting about the position of "males as females" in prison.
Granted, prisoner culture presents a terribly distorted view of American culture.
Nevertheless, one sees in the mirror of inmate culture a shadowy reflection
which remains hauntingly familiar. As "males as females" are viewed by males
in prisoner culture, so are females perceived by many males in American culture. Gender roles and attitudes in prison do not contradict American gender
concepts, they merely exaggerate the domination and exploitation already present.

Thus the gender status of "males as females" in prison presents not an
anomaly but a caricature. Although aberrant and grotesque, the relationship
between girls and their daddies in prisoner culture unfortunately provides a
reflexive discourse on gender relationships in American culture today.

NOTE

A much shorter version of this article was read at the 1987 American Anthropological
Association annual meeting in Chicago. The paper was later published in *Anthropology
Today* 4(August 1988):6–8. I would like to thank the editor of *Anthropology Today* for
permission to reprint portions of the paper.

I would also like to thank the participants at the 1987 meeting for their helpful comments on the first draft. Dr. Pamela R. Frese (College of Wooster) and Dr. Joan Gero
(University of South Carolina) added welcome editorial suggestions and bibliographic
sources. The views expressed in the paper, however, are mine.

REFERENCES

Baron, Larry, and Murray Straus. 1987. "Four theories of rape: a macrosociological analysis." *Social Problems*. 34:467–489.

Bem, Sandra. 1981. "Gender schema theory: a cognitive account of sex typing." *Psychological Review* 88:354–364.

Blackwood, Evelyn (editor). 1985. "Cross cultural perspectives of homosexuality." *Journal of Homosexuality* 11(3–4).

Brandes, Stanley. 1980. *Metaphors of Masculinity: Sex and Status in Andalusian Folklore*. Publications of the American Folklore Society (n.s.). Vol. 1. Philadelphia: University of Pennsylvania Press.

Buffum, Peter C. 1972. *Homosexuality in Prison*. Washington, DC: U.S. Department of Justice.

Burkhart, Kathryn. 1973. *Women in Prison*. Garden City, NY: Doubleday.

Cardozo-Freeman, Inez. 1984. *The Joint: Language and Culture in a Maximum-Security Prison*. Springfield, IL: Charles C. Thomas.

Chodorow, Nancy. 1974. "Family structure and feminine personality." Pp. 43–66 in *Women, Culture, and Society*, edited by M. Z. Rosaldo and L. Lamphere. Stanford: Stanford University Press.

Coggeshall, John M. 1988. "Behind bars: transformations in prison culture." Paper presented at the American Anthropological Association annual meeting, Phoenix.

Davidson, R. Theodore. 1983. *Chicano Prisoners: The Key to San Quentin*. Prospect Heights, IL: Waveland Press.

Davis, D. L., and R. G. Whitten. 1987. "The cross-cultural study of human sexuality." Pp. 69–98 in *Annual Review of Anthropology*, edited by B. Siegel, A. Beals, and S. Tyler. Palo Alto, CA: Annual Reviews.

Devor, Holly. 1987. "Gender blending females: women and sometimes men." *American Behavioral Scientist* 31 (1): 12–40.

Fleisher, Mark. 1989. *Warehousing Violence*. Frontiers of Anthropology. Vol. 3. Newbury Park, CA: Sage.

Giallombardo, Rose. 1966. *Society of Women: A Study of a Women's Prison*. New York: John Wiley and Sons.

Goffman, Erving. 1961. *Asylums: Essays on the Social Situation of Mental Patients and Other Inmates*. Garden City, NY: Anchor Books.

Grimm, David. 1987. "Towards a theory of gender: transsexualism, gender, sexuality, and relationships." *American Behavioral Scientist* 31 (1): 66–85.

Herek, Gregory. 1986. "On heterosexual masculinity: some psychical consequences of the social construction of gender and sexuality." *American Behavioral Scientist* 295:563–577.

Hooker, Evelyn. 1967. "The homosexual community." Pp. 167–184 in *Sexual Deviance*, edited by J. Gagnon and W. Simon. New York: Harper and Row.

Horney, Karen. 1926. "The flight from womanhood: the masculinity-complex in women, as viewed by men and by women." *International Journal of Psycho-analysis* 7:324–339.

Jackson, Bruce. 1978. "Deviance as success: the double inversion of stigmatized roles." Pp. 258–275 in *The Reversible World: Symbolic Inversion in Art and Society*, edited by B. Babcock. Ithaca, NY: Cornell University Press.

————. 1974. *In the Life: Versions of the Criminal Experience.* New York: New American Library.

Kittay, Eva Feder. 1983. "Womb envy: an explanatory concept." Pp. 94–128 in *Mothering: Essays in Feminist Theory,* edited by J. Trebilcot. Totowa, NJ: Rowman and Allanheld.

Luetkemeyer, Eugene. 1987. "Prison fieldnotes." Personal correspondence.

Mukhopadhyay, Carol, and Patricia Higgins. 1988. "Anthropological studies of women's status revisited: 1977–1987." Pp. 461–495 in *Annual Review of Anthropology,* edited by B. Siegel, A. Beals, and S. Tyler. Palo Alto, CA: Annual Reviews.

Nacci, Peter, and Thomas Kane. 1984. "Sex and sexual aggression in federal prisons: inmate involvement and employee impact." *Federal Probation* 48 (1): 46–53.

————. 1983. "The incidence of sex and sexual aggression in federal prisons." *Federal Probation* 47 (4): 31–36.

Read, Kenneth. 1980. *Other Voices: The Style of a Male Homosexual Tavern.* Novato, CA: Chandler and Sharp.

Reiss, Albert, Jr. 1967. "The social integration of queers and peers." Pp. 197–228 in *Sexual Deviance,* edited by J. Gagnon and W. Simon. New York: Harper and Row.

Sacks, Karen. 1974. "Engels revisited: women, the organization of production, and private property." Pp. 207–222 in *Women, Culture, and Society,* edited by M. Z. Rosaldo and L. Lamphere. Stanford: Stanford University Press.

Sanday, Peggy Reeves. 1981. *Female Power and Male Dominance: On the Origins of Sexual Inequality.* Cambridge: Cambridge University Press.

Schlegel, Alice, and Herbert Barry III. 1986. "The cultural consequences of female contribution to subsistence." *American Anthropologist* 88:142–150.

Schur, Edwin. 1984. *Labeling Women Deviant: Gender, Stigma, and Social Control.* New York: Random House.

Scott, Ronald, and Laurie Tetreault. 1987. "Attitudes of rapists and other violent offenders toward women." *Journal of Social Psychology* 127:375–380.

Silbert, Mimi, and Ayala Pines. 1984. "Pornography and sexual abuse of women." *Sex Roles* 10:857–868.

Weatherford, Jack M. 1986. *Porn Row.* New York: Arbor House.

Williams, Vergil, and Mary Fish. 1978. "Women's prison families." Pp 541–552 in *Justice and Corrections,* edited by N. Johnston and L. Savitz. New York: John Wiley and Sons.

Wooden, Wayne S., and Jay Parker. 1982. *Men Behind Bars: Sexual Exploitation in Prison.* New York: Plenum Press.

7

The Union of Nature and Culture: Gender Symbolism in the American Wedding Ritual

Pamela R. Frese

Rituals, like other forms of cultural text, reflect and validate contemporary beliefs and practices and serve as vehicles for their reinvention. As a rite of passage, a ritual provides the powerful motive force to move individuals from one state of being to another, to a new status in society, and to a different stage in the person's life cycle. Ritual can also be described as a formal structure that is given meaning through associated myths and symbols (Myerhoff 1974; Ohnuki-Tierney 1988; Turner 1969; Van Gennep 1960).

The ritual process, the particular actors, and the ritual symbols have been analyzed by anthropologists to reveal aspects of a society's political and economic relations, kinship networks, religious beliefs, and even a society's interrelationship with the environment. While all rituals may implicitly express cultural beliefs about gender as well, few studies have focused explicitly on this element of the ritual process and its symbolism. In this sense, life-cycle rituals are particularly useful for understanding the social and symbolic construction of gender. Based upon fieldwork with participants in over 50 weddings, this chapter analyzes the American wedding ritual and its symbolism as a model of and for cultural beliefs about gender.

RITUAL AND GENDER

Descriptions of life-cycle rituals (those of birth, marriage, and death) have always been a part of a traditional ethnography that included circumcision rites and rites of passage that mark age grades in non-Western societies. But even though these cultural phenomena are essential elements of a society's understanding of sex and gender roles, these traditional studies have only implicitly dealt with gender (Allen 1967; Goodale 1971; Gough 1955; La Fontaine 1972; Ortiz 1969; Richards 1956; Strathern 1970; Turner 1967, 1969).

Ardener's (1972) seminal discussion on the absence of the woman's voice in ethnographic materials and in disciplinary models argues also for the power of ritual and ritual symbolism to reflect both male and female understandings of gender. Anthropologists have begun to explicitly explore the relationship of gender to rites of passage in general (Aschwanden 1982; Boddy 1982; El Guindi 1986; Lewis 1988 [1980]; MacCormack 1982b [1980]) and to emphasize the function of ritual gender celebration in relation to sacred beliefs and myths (Hugh-Jones 1980; Murphy and Murphy 1974; Poole 1984; Reichel-Dolmatoff 1971; Schieffelin 1976). And some studies are concerned with the relationship of ritual and gender to social reproduction, particularly the relationship of production activities to ideas of ownership, procreation, and the life processes (Alland 1988; Herdt 1980, 1987; Lindenbaum 1972; Schloss 1988; Weiner 1976; Werbner 1986; Worley 1988).

The relationship between rites of passage and gender can be examined in many ways but the ritual union of male and female in marriage is a particularly rich context for revealing beliefs about gender. For example, John P. Mason (1975) examines the wedding rite in a Libyan oasis community and explores how patrilineality, ideas of male superiority, and the role of women are reflected in ritual, in the larger society, and through Islam. The marriage ritual is used to explore economic and exchange relationships that indirectly reflect gender domains (Schlegel and Eloul 1988). And D. George Sherman (1987) uses marriage celebrations to question previous assumptions about gender and the nature of kinship and kinship terminology.

Ardener (1972) argued in favor of a symbolic approach to explain how gender beliefs are reflected in society and recreated through ritual. Sherry Ortner and Harriet Whitehead's (1984 [1982]) critical contribution to gender studies also emphasizes the value of a symbolic approach to the study of gender and borrows Victor Turner's (1967, 1969) concept of multivocal symbol. Gender is then viewed as a cultural construct invested with many meanings; constructs that are a part of a much larger cultural system of symbols and meanings that reflect and help to perpetuate social institutions. Adopting this symbolic perspective, Pauline Kolenda (1984) focuses on how the symbolism of woman revealed through marriage rituals is related to different forms of exchange in two regions of India. While arguing that the broader category of social relations and other rituals must be considered to understand the marriage ritual, Melinda A. Moore (1988) examines three rites of the Nayar marriage ceremony as they reveal the symbolic ritual treatment of both genders, the relationship of gender to the prestige of the house and land units of the bride and groom, as well as how these elements relate to the larger society. Nicole Belmont (1982) deals with the symbolism in the spatiotemporal movement of the bride during the marriage ritual and argues that this process reflects the patriarchal structure underlying all Indo-European domains. Sharing these assumptions that the wedding ritual reveals the relationship between gender, religious beliefs, and social organization, John R. Gillis states that the extravagant British weddings are an attempt by a marginal group (women) to "interpret and express symbolically what they cannot control directly" (1985:261). He argues that women have little real public power and the wedding day becomes the major event in their lives, one in which they help perpetuate traditional gender roles as distinct and unequal domains within marriage.

The scholars discussed above treat various aspects of the transformational process inherent in a rite of passage and the rich symbolism that places the ritual in its particular social and cultural context. As Clifford Geertz (1973) argues, cultural texts serve as "models of" and "models for" reality. Rites of passage, especially the marriage ritual and its symbols are cultural texts that reflect and shape particular social institutions and beliefs about gender and are a part of the process involved in perpetuating a society and its culture. Contemporary gender beliefs, reflected through symbol and ritual, are a product of history and current social organization. The contemporary American wedding ritual can be viewed through these lenses as well, with an explicit focus on the gender categories that are validated and reinvented through the symbolism of the ritual process.

THE AMERICAN WEDDING RITUAL

This process and the symbolism of the ritual have roots in America's past and her mythology and reflect the underlying structure of meaning that equates American female with sacred nature and the domestic sphere while male is identified with culture and the public domain. Specifically, the bride and groom are multivocal symbols, representing at the same time several different beliefs about ideal American female and male.

As Annette Kolodny (1975) has so eloquently shown, America has been metaphorized since colonial days as a fertile, sacred paradise on Earth and has been assigned female qualities, especially that of virgin/mother. Kolodny convincingly argues that the necessary counterpart to female/virgin/sacred nature is reflected in metaphors that depict the colonist, frontiersman, and pioneer as male/inseminator/corrupt civilization. The interaction between "male" and "female" explicitly produces the American nation and implicitly the American family. Kolodny presents this dialectic as the underlying and motivating force for contemporary American society and cultural beliefs.

These gendered metaphors were reflected in society and gender roles. Men became associated with the public sphere of influence and women with the domestic. Within the home women were perceived to be spiritually closer to the sacred and were referred to as "angels" on Earth, ethereal creatures in charge of moral and religious values (Welter 1966). Home was perceived as "paradise on earth," a separate, sacred, natural place where children were raised and nurtured, away from the male public sphere of work. It was in the home, within the female sphere, that the life-cycle rituals were held until the turn of the twentieth century. These historic beliefs about gender qualities were embedded in the symbolism of the life-cycle rituals and are still a powerful part of these practices today. The ideal American bride is conceived in three inter-related aspects of female: beautiful seductress associated with nature, virgin, and mother. Each of these vocalities of symbolic female is represented by images derived from Christianity (Eve, Virgin/Mother Mary) and borrowed from the American understanding of Aphrodite and Venus, the Greek and Roman goddesses of love, beauty, and nature. The emphasis of the wedding ritual is the transformation of bride from seductive goddesses of love and beauty associated with the bounty of nature and natural processes (Eve, Aphrodite, Venus) to virgin, yet productive, mother.

The groom, on the other hand, undergoes little change. The members of two patrilines, marked by surnames, are exchanging a woman during the wedding ritual. It is the control over what is perceived as nature and natural cycles that is represented by the groom as ideal male. The symbolism of these male attributes includes the Christian God, the Father and Son, and the Greek and Roman gods of agriculture and time, deities used by American culture to represent the Grim Reaper and Father Time. This gendered dichotomy underlies nineteenth-century American culture and is metaphorized through fictive kin terms (mother nature and mother earth, father time) and through the patriarchal structure of Christianity discussed by Castelli and McBride in this volume.

The oppositions discussed above are perpetuated through all forms of expressive culture (art, architecture, literature, etc.), Christianity, and the rituals of the life cycle. While many of the practices and beliefs associated with the wedding ritual are legacies from British influences on the first American colonies, the "authentic" American wedding (which combined other cultural beliefs as well) arose only after the Civil War. The modern American wedding ritual is invented by borrowing from a variety of sources including etiquette books, contemporary bride's books, and ritual specialists (including caterers, florists, bridal consultants, photographers, clergy, and older female relatives). Each source can echo a different time period and is primarily a reflection of white, Anglo-Saxon middle-class values and beliefs.

Viewing the underlying structure of American gender beliefs as a set of binary oppositions is not without potential problems. Judith Shapiro (1988) summarizes the oppositions between nature/culture and private/public in gender studies in a variety of disciplines. In anthropology Ortner's controversial article (1972) relating these oppositions to gender domains has provoked considerable discussion and debate (Ardener 1972; Barnes 1973; Biersack 1984; Brown and Jordanova 1982; Llewelyn-Davies 1984; MacCormack and Strathern 1982 [1980]; Ortner and Whitehead 1984 [1982]; Shore 1984; Strathern 1980, 1984). Following Ardener (1972), Ortner argued that most cultures relate male with culture and view female as inherently closer to nature and natural processes. Carol

P. MacCormack and Marilyn Strathern took issue with the assumption of uni-versality of these oppositions, arguing rather that Ortner's categories were based in part on her own cultural heritage. As Strathern and MacCormack correctly remind us, "nature" is a cultural category. These authors argue for a different interpretation:

rather than viewing women as metaphorically in nature, they (and men) might better be seen as mediating between nature and culture, in the reciprocity of marriage exchange, socializing children into adults, transforming raw meat and vegetables into cooked food, cultivating, domesticating and making cultural products of all sorts. (MacCormack 1982a [1980]:9)

In a later reflection on this exchange, Ortner and Whitehead conclude that the oppositions (female/nature/domestic and male/culture/public) are certainly universal to the extent that the domain primarily associated with males usually encompasses the female domain and is consistently assigned a higher value (Ortner and Whitehead 1984 [1982]). If, as Strathern and MacCormack (1982 [1980]) argue, these oppositions reflect the categories that underlie Western culture, Ortner's oppositions can be fruitfully explored in terms of American culture and its rituals.

Certainly, the modern American wedding reflects the larger patriarchal soci-ety in many ways. For many women, the wedding day is still viewed as the most important day in their lives. Even for intellectually and socially "liber-ated" men and women, the symbolism involved in the wedding ritual is a powerful force for continuity of tradition. Many women still view the wedding as a test of their managerial abilities, skills that should appropriately be in-vested in the domestic sphere after the ceremony. The bride as future home-maker, mother, and, in contemporary society, even working woman is being evaluated through her management and staging of the wedding ceremony and the reception festivities that follow.

Part of this evaluation stems from the knowledge that the woman has planned most of the wedding celebration herself. The groom is not "officially" in-cluded in much of the wedding planning since the wedding is not perceived to affect him as much as it will the bride, nor does it reflect any of his talents, which are traditionally illustrated within the public sphere where he works. Even when couples elect to work cooperatively to make "their" wedding, most of the responsibility for decisions still falls on the bride and certainly the guests do not expect that the groom had much input into the planning of the celebra-tion. The bride's family still pays for the entire wedding, unless the couple had been living together and acting as a married unit before the ceremony.

The wedding ritual explicitly deals with gender roles and the cultural quali-ties associated with gender through three major types of symbols: the flowers chosen by the bride to be carried by ritual participants or as decoration for the church, the ritual clothing, and, finally, the ritual exchange of gifts. All of these symbolic objects define ideal gender in American culture. But, because the wedding primarily symbolizes the creation of a new domestic unit within the bride's domain, most are explicitly related to the sacred, natural, and nurturing qualities of female.

Wedding Flowers

In American culture, the practices surrounding the ritual use of flowers has remained fairly constant since the early 1800s. A bride may always carry whatever flowers are blooming at the time of the wedding, but the orange blossom is considered as the bridal flower since: "its leaves never wither, and the successive generations, hanging together on the same bough are truly symbolic of an ideally happy and prolific family life" (*A Gift to the Bride* 1937:16). Orange blossoms, baby's breath, white roses, or the madonna lily are most commonly used in modern bridal bouquets as symbols of fertility, purity, and sacredness, since the white rose and madonna lily are symbols for the Virgin Mary. One florist jokingly referred to baby's breath as "the hint that something is going to happen after the wedding." This "promise" of future life is used in every bouquet designed by the florist unless otherwise specified by the bride. Several brides expressed the belief that baby's breath (the promise of fertility) is what really makes the bouquet "feminine."

Flowers are perceived to be female and are used as symbols for the natural, cyclical processes of reproduction being honored on the wedding day. There are three major uses for flowers and floral arrangements at the wedding: the flowers for the altar in the church, the flowers carried by the female members of the wedding party, and those worn by the male ritual participants and honored guests. These arrangements are all carefully chosen by the bride to complement the overall color scheme that usually reflects the season in which the wedding takes place.

The altar flowers are usually moved after the ceremony and used as natural decoration for the food tables at the reception, uniting the sacred repast with the sacred ceremony. Since most weddings occur on Saturdays, these flowers are returned to the church altar for the sacred church service on Sunday. As one florist put it: "Brides would announce this floral dedication in the Sunday church bulletin. This double use is a tradition, a statement about the bride's relationship to God and the church." This movement of the wedding flowers (female nature) from the altar after the wedding to the reception feast and back to the altar for the Sunday church service illustrates the powerful perception of female as sacred and nurturer of spiritual and moral life.

American ideology equates nature with both sacred and fertile qualities, as Kolodny (1975) relates in her discussion of the American land and nature as both sacred virgin and fertile mother. The flowers carried by the flower girl, bridesmaids, and bride are the most explicit symbols of female as fertile nature. Florists and historic and contemporary literature explicitly relate these forms of nature to the bride's potential as fertile mother through the kinds of flowers used and in the particular forms that these symbolic flowers are given for the ritual.

The bridal floral arrangement is commonly of three types: the cascade or shower bouquet, the arm bouquet, or the colonial nosegay. The cascade bouquet is perhaps the most popular and derives from the shower metaphor used repeatedly throughout the wedding celebration. This bouquet is typically a loose arrangement of flowers with ribbon or floral streamers "showering" from the central arrangement. The nosegay is a tight arrangement of flowers rising into a peak in the center. This central part of the bouquet, known as the "climax," may be removed and worn as a corsage by the bride as she leaves for the honeymoon. Both of these bouquets represent fertility and are appropriately carried over the bride's womb, an action that has been practiced during the wedding rehearsal the night before the actual ceremony. The arm bouquet is carried as if the bride were carrying a child; most women who elect to use this type of bouquet express this relationship between flowers and baby. One of my informants consciously elected to carry an arm bouquet for this reason: "My flowers . . . I wanted them so I could carry them down the aisle like a baby almost."

The bride uses a "practice" bouquet made of ribbons threaded onto a paper plate during the wedding rehearsal. These ribbons were taken from shower gifts presented to the bride to help her prepare for her new home. The bride is jokingly reminded at her showers that each ribbon she breaks as she unwraps her shower gifts represents a future child. It is this bouquet, symbolic of potential fertility and future children, that prepares the bride to carry the bridal bouquet during the wedding ceremony that represents her fertility and future motherhood. The bride may elect to replace the bouquet with a prayerbook with flowers attached, fan, muff, or an umbrella with flowers that should be carried like the arm bouquet. These are all historic symbols associated with ideal female; the Bible and flowers especially emphasize the bride's sacred fertility. The umbrella with flowers is carried like an arm bouquet and elicits the same "feelings" about carrying a child while also reflecting the shower metaphor of future fertility. The bride on her wedding day represents female in "full bloom" (as several informants have phrased it), a woman at the height of her beauty and fertility. Both attributes are represented by her bridal bouquet.

The bridal bouquet also has qualities associated with contagious magic, for whoever catches the bouquet when it is thrown by the bride will be the next to be married and to attain her "full bloom." This rite within the wedding festivities symbolizes the transformation of woman as nature: "the tossing of your bouquet is a symbol of farewell to your maidenhood" (Manning 1978 [1974]:31). So closely is the bridal bouquet associated with a woman's beauty and fertile essence that brides over 30 are urged not to throw their bouquets away (O'Shaughnessy 1961). There is also an explicit relationship of this fertility to what is sacred female. Many Catholic brides will lay their bridal bouquet at the feet of the Virgin's statue as they leave the church after the ceremony, expressing in an important way the association of female fertility with sacred virgin/mother. The wedding flowers are selected by the bride and reflect the sacred fertility being honored as part of the "bride's day." While the bride pays for most of these floral statements, the groom purchases three significant arrangements of flowers: the corsages for the mothers of the bride and groom and the bridal bouquet. Many different explanations are offered for the groom's purchase of the mothers' corsages but his role in providing the bridal bouquet is particularly important for this discussion. The groom's purchase of the floral arrangement carried by the bride is, in essence, his (and his lineage's) control over the bride's fertility and future children.

The groom appropriately wears a flower from the bride's bouquet and the other male members of the wedding party also wear flowers chosen by the bride as compatible with her other flower arrangements. These symbolic gifts of nature from the bride are the only direct relationship that men have to the celebration of natural processes that are occurring during the wedding.

Ritual Dress

The prescribed ritual costumes and their ornamentation for both bride and groom reflect and perpetuate these gender categories. The bride is always "glowing and radiant as if something supernatural were affecting her," according to one bridal consultant. This image of bride as something "otherworldly" is symbolized in a variety of ways that relate the bride and her wedding gown to Virgin/Mother Mary and Venus and Aphrodite. The traditional bridal gown, for those who can afford it, is white, indicating purity and the sacred ethereal qualities historically associated with female. One magazine designed for prospective brides described the wedding dress as the embodiment of seductive, supernatural female: "a gown formed of the crystalline winds, unfurls a gossamer wing of illusion. Woven of satin whispers, inscribed with a tracery of beaded lace then colored in moon beams. Ethereal imagery. A goddess held captive in time" (*Bride's* 1987:121).

The names given to the appropriate colors of a wedding gown and the mythology that surrounds the ornaments of the dress also symbolically link the bride to these goddesses. The primary names for the color of the wedding gown are pearl and oyster or milk white and connect the bride, through her gown, to a sea mollusk (oyster) and its creation (the pearl), as well as to the nurturing fluid produced by lactating women (milk). These symbolic associations are complemented by the primary decorations that embellish most wedding gowns, including silk orange blossoms, pearls, cameos, crystals, and lace.

These objects symbolically connect the bride to her female ancestors as borrowed items or heirlooms as well as relate her to the Virgin Mary or Aphrodite and Venus as myth and bridal literature suggest. Certainly Aphrodite and Venus are symbolically related to the sea and pearls, which are associated with these goddesses in literature and by my informants. One wedding consultant likened a photograph of a bride wearing her ancestral pearls to "Aphrodite rising from the sea." According to religious texts, Mary's name signifies among other things: "star of the sea" (Alberione 1981 [1962]:47). She is also related to natural beauty: "Mary is the garden of delights that God found as pure as Heaven's Angels. She is the source from which springs the stream of water that bathes the earth. She is a paradise adorned by the most beautiful flowers" (Alberione 1981 [1962]:172). Most of my informants also explained that pearls were symbols of the Virgin Mary. And as one source states: "pearls have been revered as symbols of purity, chastity, wisdom, and feminity since 3500 B.C." ("Special Collection: Fine Pearl Jewelry" 1987:30–31). Contemporary wedding advertising explicitly makes this connection through labeling styles of wedding gowns with names like: Madonna, Venus, Aphrodite, and Moonlight (emphasizing the changing natural cycle of woman). Advertising photographs present the bride in her gown with containers of flowers, with the fruits of nature (apples, peaches, or strawberries), arising from the ocean, or posing in ancient Greek and Roman temples. All of these images serve to unite the bride to the goddesses of love, beauty, and sacred, ethereal nature.

The wedding gown and veil are symbols of virginity and purity and also are perceived to connect the bride to the Virgin Mary in oral knowledge and bridal literature. As Miss Manners, a contemporary specialist in female knowledge, points out: "the white dress . . . symbolizes an unopened package" (*Washington Post* 1980:H2) or the bride as virgin. The veil has been equated with "a halo . . . draped like a nun's veil" (*The Bride* 1938:13) and is seen as a symbol of "obedience and chastity" (*Washington Post* 17 May 1981:7). If a veil is worn, it is traditionally lifted either by the bride's father as he presents the bride to the groom or by the groom after the vows are exchanged, symbolizing a passing of the virginal bride from one patrilineage to another. Only since the 1960s has the bride lifted her own veil, and most brides of the 1970s and 1980s do not wear facial veils. Most of the brides in my study who did use a veil (about 20 percent) were in their late teens or early 20s and had not set up a household with the groom before marriage. These brides expressed their desire for a veil as a symbol of their purity and as a separation from their past lives with their parents.

Men may own their wedding tuxedos or borrow them for the occasion, but most commonly all the men of the wedding party will rent their wedding costumes. In a sense, maleness is transferable from male to male through the ability to rent an image. These tuxedos are used for many different public occasions and make the groom's relationship to the wedding event qualitatively different from that of the bride. Grooms may borrow stick pins, cuff links, or, most importantly, watches from male ancestors or friends to ornament their wedding costume. Grooms may also wear a sword, either their own or an heirloom, that ties them to the ideals of the military. But these objects, like the groom's outfit, are prescribed ornaments associated with public events, reflecting male control of public time and are distinctly different from the objects used by women in the ritual sphere to symbolize ethereal, sacred nature. Furthermore, men are instructed by the etiquette books and other ritual specialists to blacken the bottoms of their shoes, which may also be rented, so that no dirt or other parts of nature will be evident if they kneel at the altar. These ritual practices and beliefs illustrate the separate spheres perceived to be associated with distinct gender domains.

Both bride and groom may be loaned objects for their wedding outfits that connect both bride and groom to same-sex family and friends. These objects are borrowed for only a short period of time, with the expectation of return. However, a more formal exchange also occurs. This formal exchange of appropriate and similar gifts reveals much about gender categories as they are represented in the marriage ritual.

Gift Exchange

Appropriate gift-giving events associated with the wedding ritual include bridal showers, gifts to the ushers and bridesmaids at the rehearsal night dinner, the wedding gifts displayed during the wedding reception, and favors from the bride to the guests. There are other, informal gift exchanges, such as those between bride and groom, parents of the bride and groom to the couple, attendants to the couple, etc., but even these gifts reflect the larger, more formal symbolic exchanges and so I will not discuss them here in detail.

Shower gifts are presented at the parties thrown for the bride-to-be by her close friends, relatives, co-workers, and women of her church. These gifts are designed for use in the domestic sphere after marriage and revolve around a number of different shower themes: linen, kitchen, bathroom, sewing needs, garden, pantry, recipe, or lingerie (primarily seductive nightgowns) or miscellaneous showers that combine a variety of domestic needs. The "pounding" party is a form of shower at which the bride receives a pound of any kind of food, usually dry or canned food for use in preparing meals after marriage. These gifts prepare the bride for her ideal role as homemaker and nurturer in the domestic sphere.

Wedding gifts also are primarily designed for the domestic sphere, although they are usually more expensive than those given at showers. Wedding gifts should be addressed to the bride and not the bride and groom unless the gift arrives after the marriage day, since wedding gifts are recognized as appropriately destined for the domestic sphere, the female domain. Most common gifts are those traditionally "listed" by the bride in a department store and are related to maintaining and nurturing a family or entertaining in the home. Examples include crystal, china, silverware, linens and towels, sheets, tablecloths, etc., all those gifts designed for setting up a home that the bride did not receive at her showers. These gifts, like those from the shower, celebrate the beginning of a new home under the bride's management, and therefore perpetuate the traditional opposition of male-public/female-private spheres.

Gifts presented to the attendants by both the bride and groom reflect ideas about gender in much the same way as the loaned items to the couple on the day of their wedding. Women attendants are most frequently presented items of silver jewelry, cameos, pearls, silk flowers in crystal vases, or crystal or silver containers in the shape of a heart or an egg. These gifts reflect images of ideal female in two ways: they echo the symbolism that surrounds the bride as ideal, fertile, female; and they are gifts from the bride and will therefore always be linked with her in memory. As Marcell Mauss (1967) illustrated, objects remain attached and associated with their original owners even when they are passed to others through time. These objects are "gifts" in Mauss's framework and so create a relationship between gift giver and the one who receives. This bond between individuals is created by the passage of a gift/heirloom and:

the thing itself is a person or pertains to a person. Hence it follows that to give something is to give a part of oneself . . . one gives away what is in reality a part of one's nature and substance, while to receive something is to receive a part of someone's spiritual essence. (Mauss 1967:10)

Ushers may receive a variety of gifts from the groom that are for use in the public sphere and signify a special controlling relationship to money, work, and ownership. These gifts include liquor flasks, money clips, key chains, cuff links, pen and pencil sets, and watches.

Gifts or favors to wedding guests from the bride in remembrance of the wedding day and implicitly of the bride as gift giver include a variety of forms of containers: small urns, eggs, umbrellas, and swans. These containers hold silk flowers, bird seed, or small candied almonds that resemble eggs. The powerful metaphor here is of bride as container of future life. Explanations for these almond eggs as gifts include "almonds [eggs] are considered symbolic of wishes for a happy and fertile wedding" (*Elaine's* advertising package 1981:35). Since the 1800s, almonds have been used as metaphors for a woman's ovaries, those organs that produce the eggs that are a woman's contribution to the creation of new life. These favors are also intimately associated with the bride as gift giver, for she has selected and paid for them. Moreover, these favors emphasize the qualities of femaleness associated with the container, eggs, and the "shower" of fertility or rice as the couple leave for the honeymoon. The bride and groom are "showered" with either rice or, more commonly, bird seed as they leave for their honeymoon. This "showering" promises fertility as well as providing food for the birds. These foods used in this rite are provided to the guests by the bride, either in one of the containers mentioned above or in simple netting tied together with ribbons and flowers. These symbols, among others, are what give meaning to the wedding ritual. It is the experience of this ritual that brings these symbols to life.

Rite of Passage

The marriage ritual is designed to move two people and their families from one state of being (unmarried/unrelated) to another (married/in-law relationships). In the process of the ritual, the appropriate gender roles within the patriarchal structure of American society are revealed. These meanings derive from the actual structure of the ritual, particularly, as Belmont (1982) argues, the spatiotemporal movement of the bride. The groom awaits the bride as she proceeds down the aisle on the arm of her father. Most weddings feature this symbolic process, the approach of the bride with a male representative of her patriline to "give her away" to the groom. This transference from one patriline to another is finalized as the new husband and wife return down the aisle after the ceremony. Significantly, contemporary couples who consciously wish to eliminate this transformation may walk down the aisle together without the presence of the bride's father, or the bride may approach the altar alone to meet the groom. While these alternatives apparently eliminate the more traditional statement of patrilineal authority, my research has shown that in the first case the couples had been living together before the wedding and in the second the woman has her own public career and makes this statement by approaching the altar alone; however, she does exit on the arm of the groom. The meaning of the processional structure does not change in spite of the possible transformations.

Another way to discuss the wedding as a rite of passage is to follow the symbolic transformation of female from the beginning of the ceremony to the time at which the couple returns from the honeymoon. The woman is the one who is perceived to be changed in this process, not the man, and her transformation is bound up with the symbolic association of female to fertile, virgin/mother nature.

On the day of the wedding, through the meanings imparted by the wedding gown, veil, and flowers, the bride is symbolically both the Virgin Mary and the sacred figures of seduction, beauty, and love: Eve, Aphrodite, and Venus. Popular wedding photography features double exposures of the bride and groom at the altar with an image of the bride in her veil and holding her flowers looking down on the couple. Informants equate this image (and others like it) with Mary, simultaneously virgin and mother. After the exchange of vows, the bride symbolically becomes mother, through her act of throwing away her maidenhood in her flowers, and leaving for the honeymoon under a "shower" of fertility and the promise of future children.

The honeymoon is ideally a retreat to a natural paradise, whether it is the ocean, mountains, or country in general. Advertising for honeymoon resorts plays on the image of their paradise as the "Garden of Eden." Some even feature the additional symbolism of an apple with a bite out of it superimposed over a kissing couple, symbolically equating the groom and bride with Adam and Eve. When the bride and groom return from the honeymoon, the woman's transformation into "mother" is complete. No longer a virgin, she is potentially fertile mother expected to take over the efficient management of the domestic sphere, children, and even her career.

CONCLUSION

The following dichotomy is validated and reinvented through the wedding ritual: female-nature-domestic/male-culture-public. The symbolism of the wedding equates female with container of life and eternal, cyclical natural processes traditionally associated with the domestic sphere.

Men are not simply representatives of culture, although the ritual symbolism certainly equates them with the public sphere. Men are rather controllers of nature and natural cycles as the custodians of marked or linear time. Male last names mark cycles of people and "father time" demarcates the eternal cycles of "mother nature" and of all life, since "father time" is also the "Grim Reaper" or Death. As Ortner and Whitehead (1984 [1982]) noted, the male domain encompasses the female and is perceived to have a higher value, as reflects a patriarchal society. It may be that both male and female mediate these oppositions, as Strathern and MacCormack (1984 [1980]) argue, but ritual symbolism recreates the oppositions by validating and reassigning gender qualities to these domains. Since most individuals participate in the wedding ritual at least once during their lives, the ritual is a powerful force for the reinvention of traditional gender categories in American culture.

REFERENCES

Alberione, Rev. James, SSP, STD. [1962] 1981. *Mary, Hope of the World.* Boston: Daughters of St. Paul.

Alland, Alexander, Jr. 1988. "Phallic symbolism and reproductive expropriation: sexual politics in cross-cultural perspective." Pp. 20–37 in *Dialectics and Gender: Anthropological Approaches,* edited by R. Randolph, D. Schneider, and M. Diaz. Boulder and London: Westview Press.

Allen, M. R. 1967. *Male Cults and Secret Initiations in Melanesia.* Melbourne: Melbourne University Press.

Ardener, Edwin. 1972. "Belief and the problem of women." Pp. 1–17 in *The Interpretation of Ritual,* edited by J. S. La Fontaine. London: Tavistock.

Aschwanden, H. 1982. *Symbols of Life: An Analysis of the Consciousness of the Karanga,* translated by Ursula Cooper. Shone Heritage Series, 3. Gweru, Zimbabwe: Mambo Press.

Barnes, J. A. 1973. "Genetrix:genitor::nature:culture?" Pp. 61–74 in *The Character of Kinship,* edited by J. Goody. Cambridge: Cambridge University Press.

Belmont, Nicole. 1982. "The symbolic function of the wedding procession in the popular rites of marriage." Pp. 1–7 in *Ritual, Religion, and the Sacred: Selections from the Annales Economies, Societes, Civilisations*. Vol. 7. Edited by R. Forster and O. Ranum , translated by E. Forster and P. Ranum. Baltimore and London: Johns Hopkins University Press.

Biersack, Aletta. 1984 "Paiela 'women-men': the reflexive foundations of gender ideology." *American Ethnologist* 11(1):118–138.

Boddy, Janice. 1982. "Womb as oasis: the symbolic context of Pharaonic circumcision in rural Northern Sudan." *American Ethnologist* 9:682–698.

The Bride. 1938. *Ladies home Journal*. Curtis Publishing.

Bride's. 1987. February/March.

Brown, Penelope, and L. Judith Jordanova. 1982. "Oppressive dichotomies: the nature/culture debate." Pp. 221–241 in *Women in Society*, edited by The Cambridge Women's Studies Group. London: Virago.

El Guindi, F. 1986. *The Myth of Ritual: A Native's Ethnography of Zapotec Life-Crisis Rituals*. Tucson: University of Arizona Press.

Elaine's advertising package. 1981.

Forster, Robert, and Orest Ranum (editors). 1982. *Ritual, Religion, and the Sacred: Selections from the Annales Economies, Societes, Civilisations*. Vol. 7. Translated by E. Forster and P. Ranum. Baltimore and London: Johns Hopkins University Press.

Geertz, Clifford. 1973. *The Interpretation of Cultures*. New York: Basic Books.

A Gift to the Bride. 1937. New York: MacArthur Publications.

Gillis, John R. 1985. *For Better, For Worse: British Marriages, 1600 to the Present*. Oxford and New York: Oxford University Press.

Goodale, Jane. 1971. *Tiwi Wives: A Study of the Women of Melville Island, North Australia*. Seattle: University of Washington Press.

Gough, Kathleen. 1955. "Female initiation rites on the Malabar Coast." *Journal of the Royal Anthropological Institute* 85:45–80.

Herdt, Gilbert H. 1987. *The Sambia: Ritual and Gender in New Guinea*. New York: Holt, Rinehart, and Winston.

————. 1980. *Guardians of the Flutes*. Vol. 1. New York: Macmillan Press.

Hugh-Jones, S. 1980. *The Palm and Pleiades: Initiation and Cosmology in Northwestern Amazonia*. Cambridge: Cambridge University Press.

Kolenda, Pauline. 1984. "Women as tribute, woman as flower: images of 'woman' in weddings in north and south India." *American Ethnologist* 11:98–117.

Kolodny, Annette. 1975. *The Lay of the Land: Metaphor as Experience and History in American Life and Letters*. Chapel Hill: University of North Carolina Press.

La Fontaine, Jean S. 1972. *The Interpretation of Ritual: Essays in Honour of A. I. Richards*. London: Tavistock.

Lewis, Gilbert. 1988 [1980]. *Day of Shining Red: An Essay on Understanding Ritual*. Cambridge: Cambridge University Press.

Lindenbaum, Shirley. 1972. "Sorcerers, ghosts, and polluting women: an analysis of religious belief and population control." *Ethnology* 11:241–253.

Llewelyn-Davies, Melissa. 1984. "Women, warriors, and patriarchs." Pp. 330–358 in *Sexual Meanings: The Cultural Construction of Gender and Sexuality*, edited by S. B. Ortner and H. Whitehead. Cambridge: Cambridge University Press.

MacCormack, Carol P. 1982a. [1980]. "Nature, culture, and gender: a critique."

Pp. 1–24 in *Nature, Culture and Gender,* edited by C. P. MacCormack and M. Strathern. Cambridge: Cambridge University Press.

———. 1982b [1980]. "Proto-social to adult: a Serbro transformation." Pp. 95–118 in *Nature, Culture and Gender,* edited by C. P. MacCormack and M. Strathern. Cambridge: Cambridge University Press.

MacCormack, Carol P., and Marilyn Strathern (editors). 1982 [1980]. *Nature, Culture and Gender.* Cambridge: Cambridge University Press.

Manning, M. 1978 [1974]. *Make Room for the Groom.* Richmond, VA: National Bridal Service.

Mason, John P. 1975. "Sex and symbol in the treatment of women: the wedding rite in a Libyan oasis community." *American Ethnologist:* 2:649–661.

Mauss, Marcell. 1967. *The Gift: Forms and Functions of Exchange in Archaic Societies,* translated by Ian Cunnison. New York: W. W. Norton.

"Miss Manners." 1980. *The Washington Post,* April 2:H2.

Moore, Melinda A. 1988. "Symbol and meaning in Nayar marriage ritual." *American Ethnologist* 15:254–273.

Murphy, Robert F. and Y. Murphy. 1974. *Women of the Forest.* New York: Columbia University Press.

Myerhoff, Barbara. 1974. *The Peyote Hunt.* Ithaca, NY: Cornell University Press.

Ohnuki-Tierney, Emiko. 1988. *The Monkey as Mirror: Symbolic Transformations in Japanese History and Ritual.* Princeton: Princeton University Press.

Ortiz, Alphonso. 1969. *The Tewa World: Space, Time, and Becoming in a Pueblo Society.* Chicago: University of Chicago Press.

Ortner, Sherry. 1972. "Is female to male as nature is to culture." Pp. 67–88 in *Women, Culture and Society,* edited by M. Z. Rosaldo and L. Lamphere. Stanford: Stanford University Press.

Ortner, Sherry, and Harriet Whitehead (editors). 1984 [1982]. *Sexual Meanings. The Cultural Construction of Gender and Sexuality.* Cambridge: Cambridge University Press.

O'Shaughnessy, M. 1961. *How to Plan and Have a Beautiful Wedding.* New York: Marjorie O'Shaughnessy.

Poole, F. J. P. 1984. "Female ritual leaders among Bimin-Kuskusmin." Pp. 116–165 in *Sexual Meanings: The Cultural Construction of Gender and Sexuality,* edited by S. Ortner and H. Whitehead. Cambridge: Cambridge University Press.

Randolph, Richard R., David M. Schneider, and Mary N. Diaz (editors). 1988. *Dialectics and Gender: Anthropological Approaches.* Boulder and London: Westview Press.

Reichel-Dolmatoff, Gerardo. 1971. *Amazon Cosmos: The Sexual and Religious Symbolism of the Turkano Indians.* Chicago: University of Chicago Press.

Richards, Audrey. 1956. *Chisungu: A Girls' Initiation Ceremony among the Bemba of Northern Rhodesia.* London: Faber and Faber.

Schieffelin, Edward L. 1976. *The Sorrow of the Lonely and the Burning of the Dancers.* New York: St. Martins.

Schlegel, Alice, and Rohn Eloul. 1988. "Marriage transactions: labor, property, status." *American Anthropologist* 90:291–309.

Schloss, Marc. 1988. *The Hatchet's Blood: Separation, Power, and Gender in Ehing Social Life.* Tucson: University of Arizona Press.

Shapiro, Judith. 1988. "Gender totemism." Pp. 1–19 in *Dialectics and Gender: An-*

thropological Approaches, edited by R. Randolph, D. Schneider, and M. Diaz. Boulder and London: Westview Press.

Sherman, D. George. 1987. "Men who are called 'women' in Toba-Batak: marriage, fundamental sex-role differences, and the suitability of the gloss "wife-receiver." *American Anthropologist* 89:867–878.

Shore, Bradd. 1984. "Sexuality and gender in Samoa: conceptions and missed conceptions." Pp. 192–215 in *Sexual Meanings: The Cultural Construction of Gender and Sexuality,* edited by S. B. Ortner and H. Whitehead. Cambridge: Cambridge University Press.

"Special collection: fine pearl jewelry." 1987. *USAA Aide Magazine* (March/April): 30–31.

Strathern, Andrew J. 1970. "Male initiation in the New Guinea highlands." *Ethnology* 9:373–379.

Strathern, Marilyn. 1984. "Self-interest and the social good: some implications of Hagen gender imagery." Pp. 166–191 in *Sexual Meanings: The Cultural Construction of Gender and Sexuality,* edited by S. Ortner and H. Whitehead. Cambridge: Cambridge University Press.

———. 1980. "No nature, no culture: the Hagen case." Pp. 174–222 in *Nature, Culture and Gender,* edited by C. MacCormack and M. Strathern. Cambridge: Cambridge University Press.

Strathern, Marilyn, and Carol MacCormack (editors). 1984 [1980]. *Sexual Meanings: The Cultural Construction of Gender and Sexuality.* Cambridge: Cambridge University Press.

Turner, Victor. 1969. *The Ritual Process: Structure and Anti-Structure.* Chicago: Aldine.

———. 1967. *The Forest of Symbols: Aspects of Ndembu Ritual.* Ithaca, NY: Cornell University Press.

Van Gennep, Arnold. 1960. *The Rites of Passage,* translated by M. B. Vizedom and G. L. Caffee. Chicago: University of Chicago Press.

Washington Post. 17 May 1981. p. 7.

Weiner, Annette. 1976. *Women of Value, Men of Renown.* Austin: University of Texas Press.

Welter, Barbara. 1966. "The cult of true womanhood, 1820–1860." *American Quarterly* 18 (2): 151–174.

Werbner, Pnina. 1986. "The virgin and the clown: ritual elaboration in Pakistani migrants." *Man* (N.S.) 21:27–50.

Worley, Barbara A. 1988. "Bed posts and broad swords: Twareg women's work parties and the dialectics of sexual conflict." Pp. 273–287 in *Dialectics and Gender: Anthropological Approaches,* edited by R. Randolph, D. Schneider, and M. Diaz. Boulder and London: Westview Press.

8

Beyond the Language and Memory of the Fathers: Feminist Perspectives in Religious Studies

Elizabeth Castelli and James McBride

This chapter outlines the rich variety of positions that have been taken as feminist thinkers have engaged in critical commentaries on the texts of masculinist culture and the patriarchal religious traditions that interact with that discourse. Focusing on religious discourse and practice is particularly important because, as many scholars have pointed out, religions have had a special legitimizing role in patriarchy. Religious discourse performs a didactic function and is a primary bearer of gendered meanings in culture (Daly 1975b; Lerner 1986). It has been the goal of feminist scholars within the field of religious studies to engage this discourse at a number of levels: to advance thoroughgoing challenges to the often rather monolithic readings of patriarchal discourse and its relationship to religious meanings produced by the field; to call into question the relationship of religious ideology to cultural experience; to attempt to cope with the dissonance that often floats up from the blending of gendered meanings of the dominant discourse with the voices speaking otherwise out of cultural experience; and to create a language more consonant with the varieties of expression of women's religious lives.

The metaphors called up by feminist critics across the disciplines—of the silence, invisibility, and erasure that have traditionally characterized women in culture—are certainly appropriate for the field of religious studies. Feminist challenges in the field of religion have called women to find their voice, to make themselves visible, and to claim their stories and their histories. It is a dual claim—to language and to memory—that provides the most impressive and potentially revolutionary dimensions to feminist critique. Feminist scholarship, then, began as a conscious digression from the dominant discourse, a discourse that took for granted a whole range of ideological assumptions about gendered meaning in religious discourse. This changing of the subject in the theological conversation was a radical act, but feminist scholarship has not remained merely in the interstices of masculinist phrasing; rather, it has led toward an articulation of "subversive memories." Because of these important metaphors—and the importance of metaphor for many feminist theologians across religious traditions, we have chosen to construct our model along the lines of language and memory. If women have been traditionally silenced in the scholarly discourse about religion, women have in the last 15 years found voices; if women have experienced the violence of obstructed memory, women have recently begun to recast the past, to reclaim memory (and therefore history). The ways in which these claims to language and memory have been shaped in the context of the field of religious studies are the objects of this explication.

METHODOLOGY

It has become a commonplace observation within the context of twentieth-century critical studies that an academic appeal to "objective" scholarship is at best an unreflective pretense. Clearly, feminist scholarship in its recognition of masculinist hegemony falls within this tradition of critical studies. Feminist scholarship is political in the sense that it articulates an explicit alternative to the ideological assumptions of the dominant culture and in the sense that it points toward social change, though the strategies recommended for attaining that change arè as varied as the feminisms they represent. Feminist critique in religious studies, as in other fields and disciplines, is grounded in the recognition that cultures have almost always organized themselves around paternal authority and that gendered meanings produced in such cultures affect women and men differently. Feminist scholarship is a call to the careful, critical work of unravelling the interweaving of gendered meanings and social structures and to the archaeology of interpreting culture in order to rethink the premises of contemporary patriarchal cultures. Perhaps the most crucial first step in this process is the taking seriously of the concept of gender.

In spite of the apparent ubiquity of the rule of the fathers across cultures, this rule does not mean the same thing at every moment and for every person in the culture. Nor does gender imagery inform all patriarchal cultures in exactly the same ways. Looking at the ways in which gender constructs social relations helps one to see the nuances, the differences. "Gender," though not used here in this sense, is often taken to be a euphemism for "women"; this presupposes, of course, that only women are gendered beings—contributing to, rather than dismantling, the dominant discourse's claim that men are normative and women are deviant. Alternatively, "gender" has also turned up as a safer alternative than "women" in some curricula; just so, there is an emerging (and as yet uninterrogated) movement for establishing "gender studies" over against "women's studies" or "feminist studies" programs. "Gender" here implies the inherent balance that critics have sometimes accused feminist studies of lacking; here "gender" means "women and men" and implies an inclusive gesture that is certainly premature politically in that it settles the question before the question has been adequately formulated.

Despite these difficulties, "gender" remains a helpful category of analysis insofar as it moves away from essentialist notions of "woman" and creates room for nuance and movement in the study of social forms and cultural experience. Historian Joan Scott has offered a provisional definition of gender in a programmatic essay on historical study:

The core of the definition rests on an integrated connection between two propositions: gender is a constitutive element of social relationships based on perceived differences between the sexes, and gender is a primary way of signifying relationships of power. (1988:42)

This definition locates gender in the social production of meaning and relationships, not in the biologies of individuals; it also provides a way of imagining gender as related to power, and in this avoids the danger of looping back into dominant modes of signifying sexual difference. It recognizes the politics of gender, but does not leave gendered meanings as archetypal or reified structures.

The recognition of the force and pervasiveness of gendered meanings in cultural formation is the first step in a feminist reading of religious traditions. This recognition and its articulation we have named the *critical* posture. Critique of the limitations of structures becomes the ground of any further feminist work in religious studies; the critical voices of religious feminists, feminist scholars, and women reflecting on their own traditions (whether they explicitly name themselves as feminists) emerged first in the discussion, and they continue to be central to the feminist agenda in rethinking religious traditions. As discussed later, the critical posture produces a range of observations about the nature of patriarchal religion and women's places in it; it also creates a space for working out of constructive alternatives to the dominant models.

Out of the critical posture emerges the paradoxical realization that, although women have traditionally been the reproducers of religious culture in its practice and transmission to generations that follow, they have rarely been part of the official history of any tradition. The profound desire on the part of religious feminists to reclaim women's historical memory, enabled by the transformations in modes of historical writing in the last two decades, has produced a burgeoning body of literature which nuances the critical observation of women's universal marginality in culture. We have chosen to call this historical work *anamnestic,* the resistance to amnesia. Anamnesia is a position, a stance of recollection and resistance. Amnesia is the absence of memory, and anamnesia is the refusal of that absence, a double negative of resistance. Double negatives are against the rules of our language system, and they produce illicit meanings. To speak in the double negative of anamnesia is a gesture of creation as well as resistance. The anamnestic posture, the resistance to amnesia/forgetfulness, offers the possibilities of recognizing a rich and varied set of traditions of women's religious lives. While these traditions probably cannot simply be appropriated by contemporary feminists as easily applied models for postmodern religious life, they do challenge the thoroughgoing character of patriarchal insistence on women's absence. Further, this anamnestic posture grounds gestures of both reform and subversive memory.

Some feminist critics argue that to liberate the multiplicity of women's voices from univocal patriarchal stereotypes requires the reformation of traditional religious contours. We designate this approach the *redemptive* posture. Although bound to their confessions of faith, these feminist theologians are "bound back" to the mythic origins of the tradition whose truths allegedly antedate its patriarchal discourse. Derived from the Latin *redemptio* or *redemere*, redemption refers to the act of buying back what has been held captive. But what is ransomed here? Most often, the term redemption implies the liberation of a person or persons. Hence, feminist theologians are faced, on the one hand, with redeeming women (i.e., themselves) from the silences of androcentric myth, language, and ritual. As confessors of faith, on the other hand, these women also feel compelled to redeem their respective religious traditions from misogynist distortions. Yet, whether the captive be women or the religious tradition or both, feminist theologians must pay the ransom price through their labors—by carefully reconstructing the record of women's voices in their own traditions and by risking the wrath of those in authority. In the eyes of other feminist critics, however, the redemptive posture which seeks the reformation rather than subversion of patriarchal religions demands too high a price—fidelity to a tradition which has historically oppressed women. These theorists prefer a third alternative to either the purely anamnestic or the redemptive.

The *anagnoretic* posture is the posture of subversive memory. It is a second form of remembering language, another double negative, a refusal not to know and therefore an insistence upon knowing. It derives from the Greek verb *anagnorizo*, which possesses a variety of meanings—active, reflexive, and causal. Its very form, ending in *-izo*, is causative. It means "to recognize, to come to knowledge about a person or thing"; it also means "to reveal oneself, to make oneself known," or "to cause another to recognize." It can mean " to acknowledge" or "to see or meet again" (Liddell and Scott 1978:101 *anagorizo*). We use it here to suggest a potentially revolutionary form of memory invoked implicitly in much contemporary feminist theology, radical memory which does not simply replicate the past but reconceives it in the image of a liberated future.

We have tried to avoid arranging these postures hierarchically, and we recognize that much of the work in feminist religious studies will fit several of these postures simultaneously. Indeed, implicitly all work in feminist religious studies will probably have taken the critical posture as a starting point. In speaking of two kinds of voices of remembrance, we tried to bring into conversation two kinds of language that have sometimes been in conflict with each other in feminist religious discourse. We do not mean to try to smooth out differences, but rather to look for points of connection between viewpoints that have sometimes seemed mutually exclusive.

Critical Posture

In the monological discourse of patriarchal religions which lend credence to male-dominated social orders, feminist scholarship appears as an insurgent force which threatens to tear the fabric of ideological legitimation. Despite the semblance of change in patriarchal societies, "one thing essentially stays the same: women are always marginal" (Daly 1985:49). Feminist scholars of religious studies, who themselves must fight for recognition within the academy, document the cultural construction of women as "outsiders" who live on the fringes of "normative," that is, male-centered, reality (Ruether 1981). At its worst, the misogynistic tendencies of patriarchal culture engender a sense of existential "otherness," "madness," or even "nothingness" among women (Christ 1980; Stange 1987). Those "anomic" narratives of women's lives which might signify an irruption of the dominant discourse have been lost, forgotten, or ignored in patriarchal religious traditions. In their stead are icons of women which defuse the potential for dissonance. In the Hindu tradition, for example, the independent, celibate goddesses are "tamed" by their transformation into consorts (O'Flaherty 1980; Hawley and Wulff 1982). In the Islamic tradition, marriage restrains a woman's dangerous potential for chaos in the social order (Mernissi 1987a). And in the Christian tradition, Mary frequently serves as an example of obedience and submission, worthy of imitation by devout women (National Conference of Catholic Bishops 1973), even in ostensibly "radical" Catholic theology.[1] Accordingly, patriarchal likenesses of women appear in many of the world's religions as models for devotion to God. The early feminist *entrée* into religious studies therefore bears the marks of those who do not recognize themselves in the ruling images of religious doctrine and practice—an experience which has "enabled women to turn private passion into a systematic feminist critique of religion" (Christ and Plaskow 1979b:3).

The challenge of feminist scholarship within the field of religious studies lies in this critique of the entrenched normative traditions of prevailing faiths and the recovery and reconstruction of women's narratives long-buried under the weight of patriarchal discourse. Within the context of male-dominated religious institutions, such scholarly endeavors appear inherently radical—even revolutionary—since they undermine hierarchical control over language, ritual, and corporate realities. Yet feminist critics cannot be construed as interlopers within the field of religious studies because, ironically, the very demand for fidelity to the standards of scholarship established by graduate institutions of religious study has led to the undoing of dominant patriarchal discourse. Its critical posture demands the anamnestic recovery of women's stories and the recasting of the world's respective patriarchal traditions into a more equitable historical account. Nevertheless, the import of feminist scholarship is not necessarily radical or revolutionary since scholars can construe their research and analyses in different ways. The purpose may simply be limited to the remembrance of women's voices in the narrative of respective religious traditions. Some feminist critics find that, in "brushing history against the grain," such scholarly endeavors suffice since they effectively deconstruct the ideological justification of patriarchal hegemony. Other feminist scholars, however, may have a more ambitious teleological purpose: to transform religious expression in contemporary cultures. Considerable disagreement exists among feminist critics in religious studies over alternative ways of conceiving the discourse of religion—from the redemption of those religious traditions in bondage to patriarchal interpretation to even alternative ways of speaking, thinking, and being (Gearhart 1976). The Roman Catholic feminist theologian Rosemary Radford Ruether, for example, argues that Christianity "cannot be discarded simply because it has been reformulated in an androcentric and ethnocentric optic" (1986:26). In the wake of this redemptive approach, proposals for the use of inclusive language in religious texts, the ordination of women, and the development of feminist liturgies and rituals abound. Yet such suggestions strike radical feminist critics like Mary Daly as an absurdity. The attempt by women to redeem patriarchal religious traditions is analogous to a "black person attempting to reform the Ku Klux Klan" (Daly 1975b:21). Daly argues that only through intentional forgetting—"false memory" and "Doublethink" (1973:146, 1984:xi)—could feminists compromise with patriarchal traditions. The deconstruction of dominant discourses begs the creation of a new reality in which women and their memories and linguistic realities hold sway. But whether critics are directed towards the redemption of existing religious faiths or the establishment of new forms of feminist spirituality, the critical posture of feminism in religious studies is founded on anamnestic scholarship—the recovery and/or reconstruction of women's stories.

Anamnestic Posture

The anamnestic posture answers the question posed early on by Carol Christ and Judith Plaskow: "Do feminists need the past—and if so, what past do they need" (1979b:9)? The answer begins with women's lives recovered from remote and recent moments in history, lives, and experiences that themselves become testimony to the partial story of dominant religious history. Yet the feminist historical work is more radical than a mere recovery of the past; it is work that reshapes the contours of the past as well, challenging the very models that have been assumed to account for human historical experience.

This work of resisting forgetfulness, the rearticulation and production of women's history, is far-reaching in its scope and its import. Acknowledging the inevitable bias of literary sources, the material conditions of whose production reflect primarily the interests and perspectives of privileged classes, historical work makes use of a variety of documentary sources and reads literary sources with an especially critical eye, reading both what is said and imaginatively reflecting on what has not been said (Schüssler Fiorenza 1983, 1984a; Brooten 1982; Kraemer 1986). Historical work often heuristically challenges the critical observation that women have always occupied the margins of culture by experimenting with methodologies of perspective: what might history look like if, for a while, we put women at the center (Schüssler Fiorenza 1983; Lerner 1986)?

Much of the historical work began by attempts to reclaim the stories of exemplary women of the past. These women are generally leaders in their traditions, privileged by means of some special relationship to an important man or by means of their extraordinary holiness or piety. Reclamations of figures in the Christian tradition like Mary Magdalene, various holy women and saints, and founders of religious movements within Christianity would fall into this category (Ruether and McLaughlin 1979). Likewise, in the Jewish tradition, one can find work that recasts the stories of the biblical matriarchs and reclaims such figures as Beruriah the Talmudic student of Torah, Glückel of Hameln, and Lily Montague (Henry and Taitz 1983; Hauptmann 1974; Umansky 1985; Goodblatt 1975). The stories of 'Aisha and Khadija as the first women of Islam and later Islamic female saints might also be included within this group (Ahmed 1986; Keddie 1972).

Among the important women who have been reclaimed through historical work are those who were the founders of traditions or companions of male founders. Feminist scholars often focus on women's contributions to the foundation of religious traditions as those foundations often point to moments of massive social transformation when women may have had greater access to leadership. Historian of religion Jane Smith summarizes this position this way: "Although women often play vital and significant roles in times of profound religious change, change accompanied by some form of social upheaval, normally these roles are substantially diminished when the upheaval has ceased and social change is gradual rather than dramatic" (1985:19). Women leaders emerge at the beginnings of religious movements, but often lose their status or position as the movement becomes more institutionalized.

In the study of Judaism and its origins scholars have focused on historical analysis of biblical texts and rethought the stories of the matriarchs Miriam, Deborah, Jael, and others.[2] Of particular concern in this work is both to reshape the telling of early history, as well as to rethink the perspectival quality of the text itself. This work has been at once anamnestic and often reformist, attempting to retrieve a usable past from the text.

In the Christian tradition, much work has been done to tease out the details of women's contributions to the founding of the religion from texts that are resoundingly androcentric.[3] One particularly poignant example is that of the woman Junia, who is greeted by Paul in his letter to the Romans. While there is no philological or onomastic evidence that the masculine form "Junius" ever existed in the Greek language, translators have traditionally resisted translating the obvious "Junia" in its feminine form because the person named in Paul's letter is also called an apostle and one who was "in Christ" before Paul. The argument has traditionally run that Paul could not mean "Junia" because women could not be apostles, though there was no proscription against female apostleship in the earliest texts. The assumption of gender-based exclusion from the apostolate colors scholars' readings of the biblical text; feminist historical reconstruction corrects the record and returns Junia to her rightful place as a leader in the early church (Brooten 1977).

Along with Junia, other early Christian leaders have been reclaimed—Phoebe, Apphia, Chloe, Priscilla, Lydia of Thyatira, Anna and Mary, and the four daughters of Philip, among others (e.g., Schüssler Fiorenza 1979:32–39). All of these are women mentioned in biblical texts and called variously "co-worker," "deacon," one who has "labored hard" in the Lord, one who prophesies. Perhaps the most important "lost" woman of the early church is Thecla, whose story is told in the Acts of Paul and Thecla; despite the fact that Thecla became the central model for later ascetic practice in the church, her story remains apocryphal, outside of the authoritative story line of the church (McDonald 1983).

The Buddhist tradition preserves the story of the Buddha's foster mother and aunt, Mahaprajapati, who pressed the Buddha to found a religious order of nuns like the one he had already founded for monks. According to the story, he refused three times and only agreed after the intervention of his companion Ananda, and only if the women agreed to live according to rules subordinating them to monks. The historicity of this particular account of the founding of women's communities has been called into question by scholars, though the figure of Mahaprajapati remains a central one for women's history in the foundation of Buddhist traditions (Barnes 1987; Willis 1985).

Historians of religious traditions have anxiously sought out the lost voices of women who contributed to their traditions as writers and as teachers. This work has resulted in the reclamation of the works of women writers and the stories of women teachers. In the Christian tradition, this journey has meant the translation and collection of sometimes obscure writings, and the reevaluation of some writing at the heart of the tradition.[4] Judaism has a rich tradition of women teachers and writers whose histories are also being uncovered (Henry and Taitz 1983). The lives, teachings, and writings of women such as Bahina Bai in the Hindu tradition and Buddhist embodiment of wisdom Yeshe Tsogyel become important testimonies to the contributions of women to their traditions (Feldhaus 1982; Klein 1985; Gross [forthcoming]). Particularly striking in the context of contemporary Buddhism is the rise of female Buddhist teachers in America (Boucher 1988; Allione 1982; Friedman 1987).

The figures of saints and martyrs appear in many religious traditions and have become a central part of feminist historical reconstruction of religion. The hagiographical traditions of many religions are particularly fruitful sources for ideas about the image of the holy woman and sometimes will provide details about women's religious life during a particular time period, even if hagiography, grounded in highly stylized conventions, is rarely a historically reliable genre.[5]

Such works are crucial to the anamnestic task of remembrance, offering tangible evidence that important women were present in the histories of traditions. They are limiting insofar as women whose names and stories have been preserved in the traditions often represent a small group of privileged women, the exceptions rather than the rule. As important as the exceptions are to challenging the rule, they reveal little about the lives of ordinary women in the traditions.

Since feminist scholars are often particularly conscious of the erasure of varieties of experience represented by focusing discussion on extraordinary persons rather than on the lives of ordinary women, much of the anamnestic gesture in feminist rereadings of religious studies has attempted to reconstruct the lives of collectivities of women. In doing so, feminist scholars have tried to move beyond the often too facile reading of women's history as a history of the victims of patriarchy. As historian Gerda Lerner has put it forcefully in her daring attempt to trace out the roots of patriarchy:

Women are the majority, yet we are structured into social institutions as though we were a minority. While women have been victimized by this and many other aspects of their long subordination to men, it is a fundamental error to try to conceptualize women primarily as victims. To do so at once obscures what must be assumed as a given of women's historical situation: Women are essential and central to creating society; they are and always have been actors and agents in history. Women have "made history," yet, they have been kept from knowing their history and from interpreting history, either their own or that of man. . . . The tension between women's actual historical experience and their exclusion from interpreting that experience . . . has moved women forward in the historical process (1986:5).

This recognition of women's central place in the acting out of history has caused many historians of religious traditions to examine the ways in which women's participation in religion historically has shaped different traditions at the same time that women's experience has also been shaped by religious ideology. This stance of revaluing ordinary women's historical experience is crucial to the feminist rereading of culture because it reconceptualizes women as more than passive objects acted upon by the forces of patriarchy. As potent as those forces often are in shaping experience, feminist historians have pointed out that patriarchy also has shaped the telling of that experience, and a retelling that insists upon female agency will fundamentally alter what we think of as "History." These historians argue that women's history must be seen as a kind of battle of interpretations and ideological constructions: as religious ideology has constructed women's religious experience, so too have women been remarkably creative in finding ways to live within such constructions with dignity and integrity, sometimes resignifying the constructions, sometimes resisting them altogether. Most important in this work is the recreation of the voices of often nameless women, those whose lived experience makes up the stories of everyday life in times past.

Women's history in religion has often included life lived in conscious, intentional religious community. Social forms emerging from this kind of communal existence are particularly fruitful sources for rereading the lives of ordinary women whose participation in religious communities of women, or women and men together, shaped the nature of the social forms themselves. The rich history of ascetical practice and its social forms in the Christian tradition has been a central topic for feminist scholars, who have tried to reconstruct the living arrangements and ideological constructions of religious women's lives in community. Whether read as liberating options or as reinscriptions of patriarchal inclosure of women's sexuality deemed dangerous and threatening to men who must contain and own it, ascetic practice and monastic life have clearly been forms of female piety from the earliest life of the church (Ruether 1979; Clark 1986; Kraemer 1980; Rousselle 1988; Hickey 1987; Castelli 1986).[6] The monastic life has shaped women's religious experience in other traditions as well, especially in Buddhism where monastic practices have been present since the foundation of the tradition (Paul 1979; Willis 1985). Here as elsewhere, the conflict between the subordination of nuns to monks must be read against the widespread participation of women in the ascetic movement. While ascetic practice and separate female communities have not been characteristic of Judaism, there is at least one notable exception in late antiquity, that of the Therapeutrides in Egypt (Kraemer 1989).

Communal existence grounded in religious conviction is a particular feature of the American scene in the nineteenth century, in the widespread utopian movements that suggested the possibility for spiritual and social renewal (e.g., Rohrlich and Baruch 1984; De Maria 1978; Proctor-Smith 1985). Women played central roles in many of these communities aimed at social transformation, and the rearrangement of sex roles was central to that change. It is perhaps not surprising that women have had a special relationship to sectarian movements since, as many historians and social theorists have argued, women tend to have more freedom to move in socially marginal movements aimed at overturning the status quo.

Social formations offer one mode of insight into the particularity of women's religious life in history. Feminist scholarship also has looked at varieties of women's religious practices and rituals as central to understanding women's historical relationship to their religious traditions.[7] Underlying much of this work is the theoretical observation that women's religious life and piety cannot be read as a simple mirror image of men's religious life in some kind of simple complementary relationship to male practice. The specificity of women's practices and rites particular to women calls for a broader rethinking of the categories defining "religion" itself (Gross 1989). In this history of Christian asceticism, women's special relationship to food asceticism has been noted by at least three feminist historians (Bynum 1987; Corrington 1986; Bell 1985). Practices that are often quite controversial, such as veiling (Haddad 1985), purdah (Papanek and Minault 1982), and suttee (Stein 1978; Mazumdar 1978), have been engaged by feminist scholars in an attempt to look at the complexities that produce historical practices which both reinforce patriarchal power relations and inscribe the reality of women's religious experience.[8]

The history of many religious practices and rites pertaining specifically to women trace out the complex relationship of patriarchal attempts to contain and control women's bodies in general and women's sexuality in particular. The relationship between the ideology of the body and religious practices is often a highly ambiguous one, and the work of feminist scholars in tracing out this complexity historically contributes not only to the anamnestic project of feminist scholars in religion but to a broader feminist theoretical rethinking of the relationship of patriarchal ideology to the lived experience of physical embodiedness.[9]

The anamnestic posture of feminist scholarship in religious studies challenges the ideological claims of patriarchal culture that women exist solely on the margin of culture. While often not their explicit goal, feminist historians in their anamnestic work help to find a usable past for those who try to make social change in the present. This historical work often becomes the ground for a redemptive stance, whether history can be used to show rupture in the apparently whole cloth of patriarchy or to argue for the continual contingency of all attempts to claim the self-evidency of patriarchal social structures. The anamnestic posture problematizes simple claims about women's relationship to ideological and social power, and opens up the possibility for gestures of reform or reconstruction, redemption, and subversive memory.

Redemptive Posture

Whereas the archaeological recovery of women's narratives satisfies some feminist scholars within the field of religious studies, other critics, particularly those who identify themselves with existing religious traditions, seek to use this knowledge in order to redeem their respective faiths from patriarchal distortion. To many secular feminists, the redemptive direction taken by these scholars may appear reformist—even conservative; yet, such judgments must be viewed in the political and sociocultural milieu of the specific religious tradition. Although the redemptive direction might have the semblance of conservatism in comparison to the program of radical feminism, this "reformist" approach becomes paradoxically revolutionary in the context of Third-World cultures. For in the redemption of indigenous religious traditions, Third-World peoples reconstitute a valuable ally in their struggle to resist encroachment by First-World corporate secularist culture. Since the forces at play in shaping the social order of First- and Third-World societies markedly differ, it is not surprising that the issues raised by redemptive intentions likewise diverge.

First-World feminists begin reflection on the normative existence of patriarchal culture from the standpoint of women's concrete experience (Robb 1987:213), for it is on the level of everyday life that the women's movement first perceived the injustices of sexism. The incongruence between the rhetoric of equality and the reality of daily life gave rise to feminist consciousness—a process of conscientization in which women became aware of the social structures of oppression and imagined an alternative vision of the way society ought to be. The redemptive posture is therefore founded on feminist ethics which serve as more than an analogue to or subdiscipline of feminist theology. "Religious authority, including Scripture, is subject to feminist norms, not *viceversa*" (Andolsen, Gudorf, and Pellauer 1987:xxi). From the redemptive standpoint, feminist ethics criticize the norms of patriarchal culture which not only oppress women but also conflict with the ethical principles which allegedly underlie that normative reality. Hence the redemptive posture seeks both to save women from the inequities of masculinist culture and to redeem the formal ethos espoused by First-World societies. Yet to succeed in this task, feminists must transform the very principles which undergird the social order.

Ostensibly, the patriarchal "democratic" cultures of the "Free World" are based upon justice, most often articulated as the "common good"—a principle which some leading feminist ethicists share (Heyward 1984; Harrison 1985). But rendered by misogynist hands, the moral tradition of the common good has all too often been translated into "the good of mankind [sic]." This deviation in the common good in patriarchal contexts is reflected in the ways in which ethical theory itself is articulated. Ethical theory may be broadly divided between theories of moral virtue and moral obligation. The theory of moral virtue holds that good people make good decisions. Therefore, ethics must analyze the "self as story" and focus on the cultivation of character (e.g., Hauerwas 1974:111–128; Hauerwas 1981). Yet, the history of character ethics is skewed by male bias in the development of such heroic virtues as courage, prudence, and temperance, popular in the ancient world as evidence of *vir* or "manliness." Likewise, theories of moral obligation frequently display masculinist distortion. Deontological approaches in which certain acts are deemed good in and of themselves are universalizable standards by which to judge conduct; yet who sets the standards? In religious cultures of the West, the deontological approach most often took the form of "Divine Command" theory; for example, the Decalogue, legitimated as the "will of God"—a theology still propagated by the Biblicist hermeneutics of Fundamentalists and conservative Evangelicals. Even the Kantian tradition of universal rules, born of Enlightenment rationalism, bears the marks of the masculinist prejudice against emotion as a legitimate resource for ethical decision making (O'Connor 1987). Alternatively, the teleological model of moral obligation strives to achieve the greatest balance of good over evil. Yet its utilitarian expression—the greatest good for the greatest number—does not necessarily advance the welfare of women. Too often women's needs have been shunted aside for the common good. Likewise, the teleological formula of *suum cuique* (i.e., "to each his/her due") frequently fails to reach women since what is due women is conceived according to masculinist needs in patriarchal culture.[10]

The bias of these approaches divulges perhaps an even more disturbing conclusion. According to feminist critics, traditional ethical theory has either ignored or, at its worst, demeaned women as moral agents. Particularly in the Western religions of Judaism and Christianity, women have been portrayed as sinful, weak, and intellectually inferior to their "virtuous" masculine counterparts. Women are deemed emotionally and mentally incapable of making the right decision, and hence are not to be trusted (i.e., they are untrustworthy). In a patriarchal culture in which men are accustomed to supervising the moral well-being of their female charges (e.g., wives and daughters) the disintegration of extended and nuclear families by the exigencies of modern corporate society has offered women the opportunity to secure their role as moral agent. However, such a possibility strikes certain sectors of American society as intolerable. Hence, coalitions of conservative Catholics, Evangelicals, Fundamentalists, and orthodox Jews call for the intervention of the state to supplant women as moral agents in the abortion controversy. Yet feminists insist on this very "right to choose" (Harrison 1983). The proposed withdrawal of legal recognition from women as moral agents is understood by the "pro-choice" movement as part of a wider misogynist violence which denies women personhood through rape, incest, and battering (e.g., Fortune 1983; Thistlethwaite 1985; Miles 1987; Fortune and Wood 1988).

Feminist ethicists seek to empower women as moral agents but not in the likeness of a patriarchal "image of God" with which women have very little resemblance. In place of the masculinist virtues of autonomy and rationality, feminist theorists find in women's narratives the values of relationship, fidelity, mutuality, friendship, and feelings—all of which transform the traditional ways of thinking about the ethics of character and obligation (e.g., Farley 1985b; Raymond 1986; Hunt 1980; Keller 1987). Moreover, within the religious traditions, feminist ethics can no longer be simply an appeal to justice upon which women must hope for change by patriarchal authorities (Robb 1985:xiv). Feminists must "do justice" and effect change themselves by identifying the sources of oppression in the culture and working towards the development of new institutional structures. From the redemptive standpoint, Christian feminists in particular have been attentive to what might be learned from radical political theory, including Marxism, as a resource for this new vision of a just social order (Harrison 1985a; Ruether 1975).

The redemptive project in First-World culture is therefore predicated on a new hermeneutical approach to the texts of Judaism and Christianity which is informed by this image of women as the "new norm" (Ruether 1985:xi). As Elisabeth Schüssler Fiorenza has argued, "The interpretation and understanding of the androcentric traditions of the Bible is therefore a major theological task" (1976:39). Following in the footsteps of Elizabeth Cady Stanton's nineteenth century project *The Woman's Bible,* feminist biblical scholarship seeks to unmask the sexist construction of theological anthropology inherent in Scripture and self-consciously to bring a woman-centered view to bear on religious texts (Ringe 1976; Schüssler Fiorenza, Brown, Barstow, Gilkes, and Hunt 1985; Farley 1985a; Brooten 1985; Osiek 1985). But, according to Schüssler Fiorenza (1983, 1984a), in order to effect such a radical change, feminist scholars must entertain a "hermeneutic of suspicion"—a methodological approach which doubts the very language of a text infused with a patriarchal world view.

Yet this approach is not without its distinctions. Some liberal feminist theologians such as Rosemary Radford Ruether and Letty Russell, argue that the Bible can be redeemed from patriarchal distortion, as if the intended meaning, made known to modern interpreters through the religious tradition, lies hidden beneath androcentric constructions. This "neo-orthodox approach" suggests that the biblical message stands behind the text itself; in other words, the text can be saved despite itself (Schüssler Fiorenza 1983:3–40). Remarkably enough, the hermeneutical approach used by liberal feminist theologians is mirrored by those whom Richard Quebedeaux has dubbed "Biblical feminists" (1987:141). Although these conservative evangelical feminists affirm the principle of biblical inerrancy, they likewise seek to reclaim the Christian tradition from patriarchy; but, instead of appealing to tradition, they invoke the authority of Christ granted believers in the "born-again" experience. Hence, the leading "Biblical feminist," Virginia Ramey Mollenkott (1977, 1983), argues that the gospel is an "ideal of humanity and egalitarian harmony in the body of Christ" by virtue of her evangelical faith.[11] On the other hand, Phyllis Trible (1973) claims that there is no Word of God outside of the text itself; nonetheless, there exists a "depatriarchalizing principle" at work in the text which, if carefully examined, unravels the thread of patriarchal claims to dominance. Schüssler Fiorenza (1983, 1984a) presents yet a third alternative to either the neoorthodox or deconstructive approaches. She suggests that a feminist reading of the Bible can neither rest in the text nor move behind it; instead, textual analysis must be supplemented by the study of the sociohistorical milieu in which these texts were written. Hence, the Bible cannot be read without some understanding of the historical oppression of women in Near Eastern and classical societies.

But whatever approach is taken—neoorthodox, deconstructive, or historical-critical—it is clear that feminist hermeneutics are motivated by more than the critical analytical methods of historical biblical scholarship. Such research is animated by what Schüssler Fiorenza has called the "theological goals of liberation theology" (1984a:85). These goals embody the emancipation of women from patriarchal constructions of the text and its concomitant androcentric rituals and concepts of women. In doing so, the redemptive approach to Judaism and Christianity implies that the original (i.e., non-sexist) face of the religious tradition had been obscured by distortions—variously described as the "masculinization of religion" (Arthur 1987) or the "patriarchal co-optation of Christianity" (Schüssler Fiorenza 1984b), so that women's narratives appear only as a palimpsest (Swidler 1974). The purpose of feminist scholarship is carefully to restore these long-hidden images to life. The attempt to resuscitate the woman-centered meaning of Judaism and Christianity takes shape through proposed changes in traditionally exclusive language, doctrine, and office.

Since the locus of sexist conditioning lies in language and religion functions as one of the primary bearers of culture, "God-Talk"—the language of theological discourse, appears as a leading concern for feminist theologians. In order to sustain their religious faith, feminist theologians must transform the very language in which they speak. As Rita Gross (1979) has argued, "The very inability to say 'God-She' is the ultimate symbol of our degradation." This concern for inclusive imagery is expressed in calls by some feminist theologians for non-sexist language in religious texts. Letty Russell (1976), for example, regards exclusive language as idolatrous since it elevates a "male" god to the level of a "graven image." Hence, biblical scholars must "liberate the Word" by adopting inclusive language not only in theological commentary but in the translation of the texts themselves. Gender-specific language, such as, "Father," "King," and "Master," should be avoided in describing the deity, unless such patriarchal terms are balanced by matriarchal images, such as, "Mother," "Nurturer." Or non-gender specific images may be employed: "God our Parent," "Spirit," "Creator," "Maker," etc. Generic use of "man" or "mankind" should be avoided, and in the specifically Christian problem of the Incarnation, the Christ should only be designated as male in his human identity as Jesus. Otherwise, the Christ ought to be described as "Savior" or "Redeemer" (Russell 1976; also Collins 1978; Thistlethwaite 1987). These recommended changes were developed by the Division of Education and Ministry of the National Council of Churches (1983) and were tentatively adopted in provisional lectionaries. Such experiments have been paralleled by Jewish feminist theologians (e.g., Janowitz and Wenig 1977–1978; Falk 1987; Cantor 1982).

Despite the progressive intentions behind these proposals, the suggestion that inclusive language should be carried over from theological discourse into the translation of religious texts themselves has not met with universal approval among feminist scholars. The elimination of androcentric bias in biblical language may be a disservice since the conspicuous absence of women's voices from the text would be effaced. The silences of the text, which speak voluminously of women's oppression, themselves are silenced. Hence, a well-intentioned reform may prematurely eliminate the very foundation of the feminist critique, thereby legitimating the very text which has denied women a voice. Consequently, Phyllis Bird (1988) argues that the text should be allowed to retain its masculine bias. And although Schüssler Fiorenza (1983) argues that

inclusive language should be employed where exclusive terminology is a product of poor translations, she also contends that androcentric language should be
kept where patriarchal intent is unambiguous. Only by dwelling on the meaning
of such silences can the reader become aware of "the reality of which they do
not speak" (Schüssler Fiorenza 1983:41).

The controversy over proposed changes in androcentric language is mirrored
in the feminist reconstruction of religious mythologies. Both Christian and Jewish feminists have sought to recast the traditions' sacred stories drawn from
religious texts according to this new critical hermeneutic. Elaine Pagels (1976)
has sought to recover maternal expressions in "God-talk," lost when gnostic
heterodox texts and their use of feminine imagery were suppressed by the early
church hierarchy (McFague 1987). Likewise, Carolyn Walker Bynum (1982)
conducted research on the use of feminine descriptors for Jesus popular during
the Middle Ages.[12] But perhaps the most controversial claim within the Christian tradition was advanced by Leonard Swidler. Swidler initiated heated debates not only among Christian theologians but also between Christian and
Jewish feminists with his argument that "Jesus was a feminist and a really
radical one" (1970–1971:177). Despite the traditional depiction of Jesus drawn
according to androcentric models of authority (e.g. "King of Kings," "Lord
of Lords") the relationship between Jesus of Nazareth and women allegedly
contradicted his patriarchal image. Swidler (1970–1971) argued that Jesus dis-
regarded the Judaic code against women—an aspect of his ministry allegedly
overlooked because of "man's intellectual myopia." Yet Swidler's rehabilitation of Jesus implied Jewish culpability for the injustices of patriarchy, since
the obverse of calling Jesus a feminist is to label Jews sexist. Hence, this
Christian feminist redemptive gesture elicited charges of anti-Semitism (Plaskow 1980; Daum 1984; "Feminists and Faith" 1980; Plaskow 1984). Indeed,
Jewish feminists became angered that Judaism was even being held responsible
for the "death of the goddess" (Daum 1980). These allegations of anti-Semitism have led to the initiation of Jewish-Christian dialogues among feminists
for mutual understanding (e.g., McCauley and Daum 1983). Christian feminist
theologians also have begun to reexamine their own tradition and acknowledge
the anti-Semitic roots which lie at the foundation of their religious faith (e.g.,
Ruether 1974a).

Although Jewish feminists were sensitive to the alleged, albeit unintended,
anti-Semitism of Christian feminists, they recognized the need to reassess their
own tradition. Like their Christian counterparts, these scholars wished to reap-
propriate religious texts for a woman-centered world view (Ozick 1985). A
critical appraisal of Torah and Talmud highlighted the traces of women's voices
which echoed, in the opinion of one commentator, the matriarchal origins of
Judaism (Litman 1982–1983). "Despite its patriarchal covenant and framework," wrote Judith Plaskow (1979), "the covenant between God and Israel
is not a covenant with men but with the whole community" (Umansky
1984a).

The feminist reappropriation of Judaism and Christianity is impeded, however, by the institutional constraints of power which lay in the hands of men (Coriden 1977; Proctor and Proctor 1976). Although 84 Protestant denominations do ordain women to the ministry, 82 still do not. And even in those churches which are open to change, like the Anglican communion, access to institutional authority has required hard-fought battles, for example, from the ordination of women into the Episcopal priesthood in 1974 to the appointment of Barbara Harris as bishop.[13] Likewise, Greek and Russian Orthodox and the Roman Catholic churches remain intransigent in their opposition to women's ordination. Although Conservative and Reformed Judaism now accept women into the Rabbinate, Orthodox Jews do not, and those women who have been ordained frequently find it difficult to win acceptance (Katz 1985–1986; Friedman 1979). Nevertheless, the painfully slow dissipation of opposition to women's ordination represents advancement to many feminists active in these respective religious traditions; yet the admission of women to clerical standing may, according to one feminist commentator, be a pyrrhic victory. In the context of a patriarchal social order, women's ordination may result in the very transvaluation of the clerical profession itself—from authority to submission, activity to passivity, prophetic judgment to the defense of the status quo (Kepler 1978). These changes undermine the revolutionary character of women's ordination by admitting women into the ranks of the clergy on patriarchal terms. If redemptive gestures are to succeed, the feminization of the clergy must be countered by the metamorphosis of the feminine into the feminist. But these demands entail a reconceptualization of the religious institution itself. And Christian feminist theologians have responded by becoming most emphatic in their call for an *"ekklesia* of women" (Schüssler Fiorenza 1983:343) or "Womanchurch" (Ruether 1983:xi)—not to the exclusion of men but for the inclusion of gynocentric perspectives.[14]

Although the redemptive approach in the First-World context may be seen as an attempt to recover women's voices in order to transform power relations in patriarchal religious institutions, the feminist movement in Third-World cultures seeks to enhance women's roles in traditional religious groupings in order to strengthen chthonic faiths. This marked difference is rooted in the resistance of indigenous cultures to the intrusive presence of a universal modern corporate culture, popularly identified with Western, secular influence. Whether in Africa, Latin America, or the pockets of Third-World cultures in First-World countries, Third-World religious movements function to maintain a culture's identity in the face of modernist forces (e.g., development, urbanization, and the flood of consumer goods). Although these religious traditions and movements (e.g., Islamic fundamentalism, Latin American liberation theology, African Christianity) may be regarded by First-World cultures as "atavistic relative to the universalizing aspect of globalization," Third-World religious groupings are paradoxically revolutionary by preserving religious traditions and *"revitalizing* individual societies or clusters of societies, especially those identified with the urban poor and peasantry" (Robertson 1985:39).

As members of their respective religious groupings, Third-World women frequently feel obliged to contribute to this revitalization process by strengthening their traditional faith which has been weakened not only by the experience of colonialism but also by sexist discrimination. Yet religious oppression of Third-World women as women is felt to be transcended by their oppression as Third-World people. In their eyes the feminist agenda of First-World women appears to fall short of an adequate social analysis which also needs to incorporate issues of class and race. "The Third World is a crossridden universe of economic, political and religio-cultural oppressions within which women are doubly or triply burdened" (Fabella and Oduyoye 1988:xi).

In an era marked by conflict between modern global culture and the indigenous religious faiths of Third-World peoples, it is not surprising that some prominent male religious figures welcome the resurgence of women's participation in hitherto patriarchal institutions. In particular, male Latin American liberation theologians have engaged in self-criticism since the viability of its peasant-based movement and grassroots "people's churches" depend greatly on the support of women (interview with Gustavo Gutierrez, in Tamez 1987:43; Alvarez 1975). Despite the conflict of "radical" liberation theologians with the Vatican on other ecclesial matters, this involvement of women in the Christian base communities is frequently portrayed by women themselves according to rather conservative patriarchal conceptions of women's role in the social order. The new woman, argues Julia Esquivel (1987), is "embodied in Mary, the Mother of Jesus" who is "a symbol of what we must become." The conservatism manifest in the Marian emphasis of Latin American liberation theology is echoed by Christocentric theological conceptions among African Christian women (e.g., Christ and Plaskow 1988; Amoah and Oduyoye 1988). Yet there is a growing awareness among Third-World women active in these churches that the liberation of the oppressed must also include the liberation of women and that therefore the Catholic Church's "option for the poor," established at the Medellín conference of Latin American bishops in 1968, must also become an ' option for women" (Aquino 1988). This call for a "women's rereading of the Bible" (Tamez 1988:173) resulted most recently in the "First Latin American Conference on Theology from the Perspective of Women" (Tamez 1989). Some women have even suggested that their full participation in the revolutionary movement is contingent upon reforms in the church; otherwise, the "call on women to cooperate would be akin to P. W. Botha calling on whites and blacks to build the South African nation while apartheid still exists" (Ramodibe 1988; also Oduyoye 1988).

Although many Latin American and African Christian communities have embraced the activism of religious women, the Islamic tradition has been much less willing to tolerate proposed reforms (Smith 1979). From the perspective of Muslim patriarchies, two models of liberation exist: pre-Islamic and modern. Neither is regarded as worthy of imitation. Each is depicted as decadent and corrupt. In Iran, where traditional Muslim life was disrupted by the Shah's modernization of the country, feminism is regarded as a foreign ideology which pollutes the Islamic body politic and religion. Its implicit rebelliousness is an affront to Allah since the submissiveness of the wife to the husband in Islamic society purportedly mimes the submission of "man" to God (Mernissi 1987b). Despite the election of Benazir Bhutto to the presidency in Pakistan, the Shi'ite "fundamentalist" groundswell continues to sweep through the Islamic world, undermining the advances made by women in Muslim societies open to change (e.g., Egypt). Particularly in the Near East, which has become increasingly important to the West, patriarchal cultures increasingly need to affirm their Arab and Muslim identities, their patriarchal character (Mernissi 1987a). Feminist scholars have noted that Islamic women reject the very notion of equality in the Western sense of the term (Higgins 1985); yet it is unclear whether women do so out of genuine conviction or because patriarchal control is so oppressive that they dare not protest. Some scholars have speculated that the emotional distress experienced by Islamic women must be expressed in publicly sanctioned religious rituals, such as, the mourning of women at the tombs and sanctuaries of Islamic saints (Mernissi 1977). In either case, Islamic women in many societies publicly endorse a religious system which, although frequently oppressive, allows them to survive within a tightly circumscribed private realm (Baried 1987).

Although they are born amidst the prosperity of advanced technological cultures, women of color who live in First-World societies likewise must learn to survive. Feminist scholars have paid particular attention to black women's religious narratives which bear witness to the myriad forms of oppression they suffer, including poverty, violence, and the daily insults to their self-esteem (Williams 1985). Despite these adversities, black women have found the inner strength to face this daily degradation of themselves and their families and to envision a more just social order (Cliff 1986; also Mitchell 1983; Cannon 1988). That hope has been the basis for the vitality of the black church in America which, despite patriarchal ministerial leadership, is heavily dependent upon black women for its day-to-day existence (Grant 1982; also Gilkes 1986). Since women embody the foundation of black religious and community life, black feminist theorists claim the right to shape the conceptual framework by which they are articulated (Williams 1987). And although black women fully appreciate the suffering caused by injustice, many suspect that white feminists cannot begin to understand them until white feminists recognize the legitimacy of the black community's concern for cultural, political, and economic survival in the face of the First-World social order. But such a development is clearly the responsibility of white feminists themselves (Grant 1984).[15]

Anagnoretic Posture

Although the redemptive posture employed anamnestic scholarship in order to reclaim dominant religious traditions for women, the anagnoretic posture holds that such reforms are clearly insufficient. Bluntly stated, "No feminist can save God" (Goldenberg 1979:10). The very notion of God is so bound up with male dominion that the feminist revolution cannot help but dethrone God with "man." Hence, as the former Roman Catholic theologian Mary Daly (1975b) commented, the women's movement is necessarily "post-Christian" and "anti-church." That is not to say that the anagnoretic posture is atheistic. On the contrary, it calls for the recovery and/or recreation of religious meanings specific to women, that is, outside of the dominant patriarchal discourse (King 1989). Most often these theorists work towards the rehabilitation of the Goddess or goddesses in some form and therefore frequently identify themselves as thealogians rather than "theologians" (Goldenberg 1979:96).

Just as such theorists have little desire to save a patriarchal deity, neither can they effect the redemption of those moral principles which, although obscured by sexist social structures, provide hope for a transformed normative reality. Whereas feminist theologians with redemptive ambitions, such as Beverly Wildung Harrison, argue that gender is not of ontological significance, thealogians often suggest that moral reasoning has a biologically and/or socially gendered foundation. Quite simply, women and men do not think alike and therefore cannot share the same normative reality. These claims are advanced largely on the basis of work by feminist research psychologists like Carol Gilligan and Mary Field Belenky.

An associate professor at the Harvard Graduate School of Education, Gilligan argues that previous psychological theory on moral development tried to "fashion women out of a masculine cloth" (1982:6). According to Freudian theory, the formation of the ego emerges out of frustrated attempts to gratify biological needs, resulting in a boundary between the self and the world and consequently the rise of culture. Disengagement begets not only distinction but also the quest for autonomy. Valued in the patriarchal world as a sign of emotional maturity, the autonomous self acts to dominate the world through aggression in order to possess that which it needs. Hence, the existence of the autonomous moral agent with the capacity for "objectivity" is based upon frustration, separation, and aggression. Although the male ego evolves according to this "normal" path of development, psychoanalytic theory accounts for women's lack of aggression as deviance, caused by narcissism and hostility to "civilized," or restrained, behavior. Yet Gilligan argues that the alleged moral inferiority of women is a patriarchal misnomer for that moral development which is unique to women. Instead of separation, women's egos are founded on connections—a progression from caring for self and caring for others to a resolution of the tensions implicit in that constellation of relationships. Hence women's moral development is predicated on a subjective ethic of caring rather than the "objective" standard of judgment. Women have difficulty articulating ethical appeals to justice, not because they are morally inferior or intellectually incompetent, but because they do not think in the same way that men do (Gilligan 1987). In the wake of Gilligan's work, one group of feminist theorists has constructed an alternative epistemological model of "women's ways of

knowing" based upon a range of responses from silence in the face of patriarchal normative reality to the connected and integrated knowledge of women's
company (Belenky, Clinchy, Goldberger, and Tarule 1986). These developments in psychological theory reflect the parallel concern of anagnoretic feminists to postulate religious mythological constructions unique to women, which
embody the desire to establish normative realities of connectedness and "sisterhood."

In the context of anagnoresis, this reappropriation of women's religious history means the "reclamation of earlier cultures" which existed before or sur-
vived in the shadows of patriarchal religion. For many feminists, these archaeological forays into the past elicit memories of goddess religions (Sjoo and Mor
1986; Spretnak 1982; Downing 1984; Gross 1978; Stone 1976, 1978; Downing
1985; Christ 1987).[16] Critics may regard such a reappropriation as a modern
anachronism, but as Sheila Collins (1979:69) has warned, "it is inadequate to
say that women want to return to the ancient world view."[17] The recovery of
goddess myth and concomitant ritual functions as a wellspring from which contemporary women can draw in order to express themselves in a religiously
meaningful way (e.g., Downing 1988). "[T]ake what is useful and important
to you and infuse it with your own spirit" (Inglehart 1983:174). The anagnoretic posture is therefore not simply the historicist remembrance of history "as
it really was" but rather the recognition of past figural elements in new mythological configurations. Since it encourages this ludic reconstruction of goddess
religions, the anagnoretic posture is freed from the limitations of anamnestic
scholarship. To the distress of some feminist scholars, this approach encourages and legitimates the efforts of countercultural feminists who draw upon
historical research in an "undisciplined" fashion or ignore it altogether and
who thereby may make "unwarranted" pronouncements, particularly on the
constitution of feminist "spirituality."[18] At its most extreme, some feminist
academics fear that such movements smack of charlatanism and discredit the
standing of the feminist critique within the university setting; however, spokes-
persons for this feminist spirituality or "womanspirit" argue that the oppression of women permits, even necessitates, the creative use of the past in order
for communities of women to survive in the present (Hunt 1983). Frequently
the words of the feminist novelist Monique Wittig are invoked: "You say there
are no words to describe this time, you say it does not exist. But remember.
Make an effort to remember. Or, failing, invent" (1969:89).

One of the earliest expressions of the anagnoretic posture was the rise of the
contemporary witchcraft movement in America. Deriving from the Old English
wicce, meaning "weaver," witchcraft was identified with weaving magical spells
in order to direct the spirits to do one's bidding. In a culture dominated by the
monotheistic, patriarchal religions of Judaism and Christianity, the purported
jealousy of the male high god would not tolerate alternative spiritual expressions. In the wake of jealousy followed wrath which fell on the heads of women
whether or not the individual was culpable. The very appearance of such resis-

tance to patriarchy met with violence (Yoshioka 1974). In the years following the "death of God" theology and the rise of new religious movements (Altizer and Hamilton 1966; Needleman 1970), it is not surprising that some women responded to the resurgence of witchcraft, symbolized in the call that "the Goddess is alive and magic is afoot!" As a founder of the wicca movement, Zsuzsanna Budapest even suggested that witchcraft was the medium by which women could be free from patriarchal religion and culture. "Feminist witches are wimmin [*sic*] who search within themselves for the female principle of the universe and who relate as daughters to the creatrix" (Budapest 1975).[19] Although wicca is a small yet diverse grassroots religious movement in Europe and the Americas, these groups share a common model of community—the coven. Like the Susan B. Anthony Coven #1 created by Budapest, these circles of women reconstruct wicca rituals of the past and engage in blessings, healings, cursings, and divination (McFarland 1975). But whereas covens are identified in the popular imagination with Satanic worship, the "Dianic practices" of these contemporary witches are self-consciously divorced from the "occult" which Budapest regards as a "male-dominated multi-million dollar business" (1975:50).

Whether redemptively conceived as "feminist base communities" or radically structured as covens (Ruether 1983:205; Starhawk 1987:256–295), these feminist groups embody the heartfelt need among some women to structure religious life and ritual around symbols and experiences that are purportedly unique to women themselves. Emerging out of the countercultural movement during the late 1960s and early 1970s, these new women's collectives experimented with a broad range of feminist expressions, from tarot, ESP, and witchcraft to more mainstream forms of religious ritual, such as meditation.[20] The development of new as well as existing rituals as the life of feminist community is an ongoing concern in feminist discussions (e.g., Washbourn 1979; Neu and Upton 1984; Umansky 1984b).

Although the formation of gynocentric religious communities is an important dimension of the anagnoretic impulse, many such "radical" feminists "do *not* see themselves as part of a religion. This larger number would characterize their interest as spiritual or psychic, but not one they seek to organize beyond occasional rituals that are often spontaneous, unconventional and irregular" (Culpepper 1987a:54). Such thealogians prefer to espouse a *philosophia*, or "love of female wisdom" as Emily Erwin Culpepper (1987b) calls it. In the construction of this new world view, feminist philosophers enlist the goddess tradition as a legitimate source of female wisdom (i.e., "the transmission of women's mysteries"). Nonetheless, Culpepper expresses concern that the monotheistic emphasis on the Goddess, derived from the mythological archetypes of C. G. Jung and Franz Neumann, may obscure the rich pluralistic pantheon of goddesses who symbolize women's experience and knowledge. Too long have these voices been silenced by sexism. Only by invoking the "Presence of their Absence'' can feminist philosophers overcome separation which so characterizes the lives of women in androcentric societies (Culpepper 1987b:12).

Drawing upon these remembered fragments, Catherine Keller has animated ''she-monsters''—those mythic females who deviated from patriarchal norms (1986:5). Since women's normative reality threatened the well-being of these cultures, masculinist oral traditions recounted these monsters as hideous creatures (e.g., Medusa, who had the power to incapacitate men by turning them to stone). Too frightening to contemplate, ''she-monsters'' were rendered harmless through their transformation into either passive maidens or defenders of patriarchal culture, such as, Athena, the ''quintessential Daddy's Girl'' (Keller 1986). Despite the superimposition of such reassuring figures, the terrifying images of these mythic females remain as a mnemonic presence for, as Keller notes, monster and Mnemosyne are derivatives of the same etymological root. The goddesses are remembered by contemporary women, particularly feminist philosophers, who are seeking to reconnect with their forgotten origins. Feminist religious philosophy therefore ''spins a web'' of ''self-composition'' in which women share a unique normative reality, anathema to androcentric cultures both ancient and modern. According to Keller, these ''sinister'' attributes must not be denied. Invoked ''for their sheer force of iconoclasm'' (Keller 1986:222), she-monsters anticipate a ''postpatriarchal time/space.''

Perhaps the most respected spinner of feminist philosophy is Mary Daly, a former Catholic theologian whose first book in 1968 followed the redemptive posture. Calling for ''radical surgery'' in the Roman Catholic tradition through the ''constant purification of doctrine and reform of practice'' (1968:73), Daly soon abandoned the premise of *The Church and the Second Sex* ''whose author I have trouble sometimes recalling'' (1975a:5). Her second book, *Beyond God the Father. Toward a Philosophy of Women's Liberation,* brooked no such compromise with the ecclesiastical patriarchate which had historically acted to oppress women, but had lost its unquestioned authority in the 1960s with the ''death of God'' and the ''second wave of feminism.'' Daly claimed that whereas the Church depicted these threats to patriarchal authority in terms of the Antichrist, the Apocalypse was really the ''second coming of women'' (1973:98). This new ''cosmic covenant'' of sisterhood would reverse the ''reversal '' of gynocentric origins effected by patriarchal discourse in a feminist dialectic of re-membering.[21] Memory here takes the form of ''hearing ourselves'' or ''our Selves'' which exist in the ''Background'' of the patriarchal ''Foreground.'' Attending to women's narratives as normative reality constitutes a ''radical feminism'' which is ''not reconciliation with the father. Rather it is affirming our original birth, our original source, movement, surge of living'' (Daly 1978:39).

If anagnoretic memory is identified with life, then the false naming of patriarchal culture means death to women, either through silence or brutality. Androcentric discourse seems ''incapable of identifying with the victims—a

subjective condition which is masked by the pose of 'objective scholarship' "
(Daly 1978:125)—a viewpoint which Daly (1987:82) later characterizes as
"methodolatry." Yet Daly also argues that, "to a radical feminist," the "death"
of God the Father is "a most unimpressive affair," for "something inherently
dead—such as a system of dead phallic symbols—cannot logically be said to
die." Accordingly, radical feminists claim that the essence of the male high
god is Absence, and therefore the Foreground of patriarchal culture will inevitably be flooded by the Presence of Elemental Spirits "crucial for the empowerment of women" (Daly 1984:11).

As the conjuring of gynocentric elemental spirits, "Feminist Erraticism"
employs metaphor in the ludic reconstruction of a world meaningful to women
(Daly 1984:xii). Daly's *Webster's First Intergalactic Wickedary of the English
Language* reverses the reversal of language in patriarchal discourse by spinning
"word-webs" which define the philosophical and mythological sources of the
radical feminist Background and mock the pretensions of the androcentric Foreground. As a "dictionary for witches," the book marks a point of departure
for "websters," that is, "female weavers" who want to "spell out" a new
normative reality as "Verb"—a new way of "Be-ing" uninhibited by masculinist culture.

Be it witchcraft, goddess worship, or radical feminist philosophy, these experiments in a gynocentric religious expression represent the active participation of women in the construction of a new reality. These anticipatory visions
are a part of an ongoing process to which feminist scholars and non-scholars
alike have made and continue to make vital contributions.

CONCLUSION

In the course of writing this chapter, the rich diversity of feminist voices in
religious studies has become clearer to us, and we have consciously tried not
to harmonize voices that often sound in striking counterpoint to one another.
At the same time, we have not heard this variety as cacophonous, nor have we
seen the varieties of positions that feminist scholars and thealogians take as a
problem to be resolved. Whether speaking from a critical, anamnestic, redemptive, or anagnoretic position, each thinker's articulation contributes to a conversation among people who respect and often embrace one another's differences. The very existence of such variety itself is radical, for it challenges the
dominant Western philosophical tradition's fixation on monolithic claims to truth.
As two feminist theorists have put it: "We are accustomed to think in terms of
powers associated with accumulation and identity rather than the powers associated with dispersion and rupture precisely because the conventions of discourse, based on binary oppositions that preserve identity, insist that we do"
(Doane and Hodges 1987:141).

The most radical critique of Western patriarchal culture is brought by feminists who assert the power of the critique as plural. This is not a simple em-

bracing of "pluralist," cafeteria-style theorizing. Rather, it is a recognition that there is not a singular, monolithic, correct critique of the force of patriarchy on women's lives. It is a recognition that, just as there are differences in the material and spiritual effects of patriarchy, so there are varieties of strategically effective feminist stances in response. The recognition of these differences constitutes feminism's most radical critique, and it is just this kind of radical critique that is embodied in the diverse work of feminist scholars and thealogians in religion. It is the creative interplay of differences that empowers feminist work in religious studies—work that promises to remake traditions and create new ones.

NOTES

We would like to acknowledge the invaluable assistance of Andrea Castner, currently a graduate student at Harvard Divinity School, whose bibliographical research helped us immensely in uncovering innumerable articles and books in this emerging field within the religious studies discipline.

1. See for example the "virginal attitude" of Leonardo Boff's liberation theology: "Mary is also our model for the basic attitude that we all ought to have before God, the only attitude worthy of a creature: openness and total acceptance" (1987:151).

2. The literature here is quite extensive (e.g., Teubal 1984; Crawley 1986; Exum 1986; Schungel-Straumann 1984; Burns 1987). For more extensive bibliography on the Hebrew Bible in general, see also Laffey (1988).

3. Elisabeth Schüssler Fiorenza (1983) is the classic work and reclaims both those women whose names we know and also those—including the women in whose memory the book is named—whose names have been lost through the androcentric transmission of tradition. See Part I for the theoretical framework of this reconstructive work.

4. There has been a great deal of work done in this area, though more remains to be done. For earliest Christian writers, see Patricia Wilson-Kastner et al. (1981), which includes the writings of Perpetua, Proba, Egeria, and Eudokia; also Clark and Hatch (1981). Female authorship has been argued for the apocryphal acts of the apostles by Davies (1980). The writings of medieval women appear in a number of collections: Dronke (1983); Petroff (1986); Thiébaux (1987); Wilson (1984). There are also books by individual medieval women, including autobiographies and visionary works, and here the bibliography is extensive; representative works include Hadewijch of Antwerp (1980); Hildegard of Bingen (1986); Kempe (1940). See also Atkinson (1983); Shahar (1983); Shank and Nichols (1984, 1987). For women writers in the Renaissance and Reformation, see Wilson (1987). In more contemporary historical recovery of women writers in the Christian tradition, see Humez (1981) and Andrews (1986).

5. Feminist work on the hagiographical tradition in Christianity includes that of Clark (1979, 1984); Brock and Harvey (1987); Barstow (1986); and numerous other works on medieval saints.

6. While many of the more common sources have been collected and anthologized widely, a forthcoming volume of previously untranslated primary documents relating to ascetic practices will fill out the picture in interesting ways; see Wimbush (1990), which includes a sizable number of texts relating to women's ascetic lives. Publications relat-

ing to women's communities in the medieval period are many (Bennett, Clark, and Westphal-Wihl 1989 for a helpful introduction).

7. An excellent cross-cultural anthology of studies may be found in Falk and Gross (1989).

8. Das (1986) sets the historical construction of suttee within the larger context of British colonial discourse.

9. Here the work of a number of feminist scholars working within the Christian tradition is particuarly helpful, given the highly problematic split in Christian thought between body and spirit (King 1988; Pagels 1988; Borresen 1981; in Judaism, see Baskin 1985; Neusner 1979, 1980). The complexity of the relationship between patriarchal understandings of women's sexuality and women's own experience of sexuality and embodiedness in Islam is traced out in Mernissi (1987a).

10. Patriarchal and moral norms are particularly virulent when conflated with racism. See Cannon (1988).

11. Although there exists a small number of "Biblical feminists" in American conservative Christianity, Fundamentalists and Evangelical women, by and large, have little sympathy for the feminist project (Pohli 1983; Kwilecki 1987).

12. Yet according to Bynum, the discovery of this imagery should not be confused with the feminist program since "the female (or woman) and the feminine are not the same" (1982:167).

13. See for example Hiatt and Wondra (1975). For a biographical account by one of the first women ordained, see Heyward (1976).

14. A valuable collection of homilies by Jewish, Catholic, and Protestant feminists may be found in *Spinning a Sacred Yarn* (1982).

15. Such problems also plague the relationship between Anglo and Hispanic feminists in the United States (Isasi-Diaz 1987; Mercadante, Riggs, Byerly, Weems, and Andolsen 1988). For an analysis of the response among First-World feminists see Heyward (1985).

16. Emily Erwin Culpepper (1987a) has expressed concern that the feminist appropriation of the goddess has been ethnocentrically weighted towards the Western tradition, particularly Hellenistic goddesses. This bias has been addressed by the recent appearance of anthologies on goddesses from Western and non-Western religions, for example, Olsen (1987). Although scholarly books and articles have increasingly appeared in the literature within religious studies, one feminist scholar (Olds 1986) fears the idolatrous potential in goddess worship and suggests an alternative image of a divine androgyne.

17. See also Christ: "Whatever God the Mother and the Goddess may have meant in ancient civilization, today God the Mother and Goddess symbolize the emerging power of women" (1987:156).

18. See for example the criticism of Mary Daly whose "elemental feminist philosophy" is closest to the mainstream of scholarly discourse: "[T]he quality of Daly's scholarship leaves much to be desired, especially in light of the growing amount of competent feminist research available on some of the history periods about which she writes" (Harrison 1985:269, n. 4).

19. See also the writings of King (1987a) and Starhawk (1979a, 1979b): "[R]emember the power of the Mother—reown the ground upon which you stand, the longing and the terror, make it yours with consciousness" (Starhawk 1979b:79).

20. For a brief overview of these developments, see Grimstad and Rennie (1975);

also Turner (1978). For an extended discussion of one such ritual, see Minerva (1975), in which one women's collective, Minerva, created a feminist astrology center by reclaiming this mantic discipline from alleged patriarchal distortions.

21. See the discussion of "Dismemberment by Christian and Postchristian Myth" (Daly 1978:73–105), and the entry under reversal, "Word-Web One" (Daly 1987:93).

REFERENCES

Ahmed, Leila. 1986. "Women and the advent of Islam." *Signs* 11:665–691.

Allione, Tsultrim. 1982. *Women of Wisdom*. London: Routledge and Kegan Paul.

Altizer, Thomas J. J., and William Hamilton. 1966. *Radical Theology and the Death of God*. Indianapolis: Bobbs-Merrill.

Alvarez, Olga Lucia. 1975. "Latin American women, the Church and Liberation Theology." *Radical Religion* 2 (1): 14–21.

Amoah, Elizabeth and Mercy Amba Oduyoye. 1988. "The Christ for African women." Pp. 35–46 in *With Passion and Compassion: Third World Women Doing Theology*, edited by V. Fabella and M. Oduyoye. Maryknoll, NY: Orbis.

Andolsen, Barbara H., Christine E. Gudorf, and Mary D. Pellauer (editors). 1987. *Women's Consciousness, Women's Conscience: A Reader in Feminist Ethics*. San Francisco: Harper and Row.

Andrews, William L. (editor). 1986. *Sisters of the Spirit. Three Black Women's Autobiographies of the Nineteenth Century*. Bloomington: Indiana University Press.

Aquino, Maria Pilar. 1988. "Women's participation in the Church, II: a Catholic perspective." Pp. 159–164 in *With Passion and Compassion: Third World Women Doing Theology*, edited by V. Fabella and M. Oduyoye. Maryknoll, NY: Orbis.

Arthur, Rose Harmon. 1987. "The wisdom goddess and the masculinization of Western religion." Pp. 24–37 in *Women in the World's Religions: Past and Present*, edited by U. King. New York: Paragon.

Atkinson, Clarissa W. 1983. *Mystic and Pilgrim: The Book and the World of Margery Kempe*. Ithaca: Cornell University Press.

Atkinson, Clarissa W., Constance H. Buchanan, and Margaret R. Miles (editors). 1987. *Shaping New Vision: Gender and Values in American Culture*. Ann Arbor: UMI.

Baried, Bororoh. 1987. "Muslim women and social change in Indonesia: the work of Aisyiyah." Pp. 203–209 in *Speaking of Faith: Global Perspectives on Women, Religion, and Social Change*, edited by D. Eck and D. Jain. Philadelphia: New Society.

Barnes, Nancy Schuster. 1987. "Buddhism." Pp. 105–133 in *Women in World Religions*, edited by A. Sharma. Albany: SUNY.

Barstow, Anne Llewellyn. 1986. *Joan of Arc: Heretic, Mystic, Shaman*. Lewiston, NY: Edwin Mellen.

Baskin, Judith. 1985. "The separation of women in rabbinic Judaism." Pp. 3–18 in *Women, Religion and Social Change*, edited by Y. Haddad and E. Findly. Albany: SUNY.

Belenky, Mary Field, Blythe McVicker Clinchy, Nancy Rule Goldberger, and Jill Mattuck Tarule. 1986. *Women's Ways of Knowing: The Development of Self, Voice, and Mind*. New York: Basic.

Bell, Rudolph. 1985. *Holy Anorexia*. Chicago: University of Chicago Press.

Bennett, Judith M., Elizabeth A. Clark, and Sarah Westphal-Wihl (editors). 1989.

"Working Together in the Middle Ages: Perspectives on Women's Communities." *Signs* 14 (2): 255–517.

Bird, Phyllis. 1988. "Translating sexist language as a theological and cultural problem." *Union Seminary Quarterly Review* 40 (1 & 2): 89–95.

Boff, Leonardo. 1987. *The Maternal Face of God. The Feminine and its Religious Expressions*. San Francisco: Harper and Row.

Borresen, Kari Elisabeth. 1981. *Subordination and Equivalence: The Nature and Role of Woman in Augustine and Aquinas*. Washington: University Press of America.

Boucher, Sandy. 1988. *Turning the Wheel: American Women Creating the New Buddhism*. San Francisco: Harper and Row.

Brock, Sebastian P., and Susan Ashbrook Harvey. 1987. *Holy Women of the Syrian Orient*. Berkeley: University of California Press.

Brooten, Bernadette. 1985. "Early Christian women and their cultural context: issues of method in historical reconstruction." Pp. 65–91 in *Feminist Perspectives on Biblical Scholarship*, edited by A. Collins. Chico, CA: Scholars.

———. 1982. *Women Leaders in the Ancient Synagogue*. Chico, CA: Scholars.

———. 1977. "Junia . . . outstanding among the Apostles (Romans 16:7)." Pp. 141–144 in *Women Priests*, edited by L. Swidler and A. Swidler. New York: Paulist.

Budapest, Zsuzanna. 1975. "Witch is to woman as womb is to birth." *Quest* 2:50–56.

Burns, Rita J. 1987. *Has the Lord Indeed Spoken only Through Moses? A Study of the Biblical Portrait of Miriam*. Decatur, GA: Scholars.

Bynum, Carolyn Walker. 1987. *Holy Feast and Holy Fast: The Religious Significance of Food to Medieval Women*. Berkeley: University of California Press.

———. 1982. *Jesus as Mother: Studies in the Spirituality of the High Middle Ages*. Berkeley: University of California Press.

Cannon, Katie Geneva. 1988. *Black Womanist Ethics*. Atlanta: Scholars.

Cantor, Aviva. 1982. "An egalitarian Hagada." *Lilith* 9:9–24.

Castelli, Elizabeth. 1986. "Virginity and its meaning for women's sexuality in early Christianity." *Journal of Feminist Studies in Religion* 2 (1): 61–88.

Christ, Carol. 1987. *The Laughter of Aphrodite: Reflection on a Journey to the Goddess*. San Francisco: Harper and Row.

———. 1980. *Diving Deep and Surfacing. Women Writers on Spiritual Quest*. Boston: Beacon.

Christ, Carol, and Judith Plaskow (editors). 1988. "The Christ-Event from the viewpoint of African women": Thérèse Souga, "I: a Catholic perspective" and Louise Tappa, "II: a Protestant perspective." Pp. 22–34 in *With Passion and Compassion: Third World Women Doing Theology*, edited by V. Fabella and M. Oduyoye. Maryknoll, NY: Orbis.

———. 1979a. *Womenspirit Rising: A Feminist Reader in Religion*. San Francisco: Harper and Row.

———. 1979b. "Introduction." Pp. 1–17 in *Womenspirit Rising: A Feminist Reader in Religion*, edited by C. Christ and J. Plaskow. San Francisco: Harper and Row.

Clark, Elizabeth A. 1986. *Ascetic Piety and Women's Faith: Essays on Late Ancient Christianity*. Lewiston, NY: Edwin Mellen.

———. 1979. *Jerome, Chrysostom, and Friends*. Lewiston, NY: Edwin Mellen.

———. (translator). 1984. *The Life of Melania the Younger*. Lewiston, NY: Edwin Mellen.

Clark, Elizabeth A., and Dianne Hatch (translators). 1981. *The Golden Bough, the*

Oaken Cross. The Virgilian Cento of Faltonia Betitia Proba. Chico, CA: Scholars.

Cliff, Michelle. 1986. "I found God in myself and I loved Her/I loved Her fiercely: more thoughts on the work of black women artists." *Journal of Feminist Studies in Religion* 2 (1): 7–39.

Collins, Adela Yarbro. 1978. "An inclusive biblical anthropology." *Theology Today* 34:358–369.

———— (editor). 1985. *Feminist Perspectives on Biblical Scholarship.* Chico, CA: Scholars.

Collins, Sheila. 1979. "Reflections on the Meaning of Herstory." Pp. 68–73 in *Womenspirit Rising: A Feminist Reader in Religion.* San Francisco: Harper and Row.

Coriden, James (editor). 1977. *Sexism and Church Law: Equal Rights and Affirmative Action.* New York: Paulist.

Corrington, Gail Peterson. 1986. "Anorexia, asceticism, and autonomy: self-control as liberation and transcendence." *Journal of Feminist Studies in Religion* 2 (2): 51–62.

Crawley, Joanne. 1986. "Faith of our mothers: the dark night of Sarah, Rebeka, and Rachel." *Review for Religious* 45:531–537.

Culpepper, Emily Erwin. 1987a. "Contemporary Goddess Thealogy: A Sympathetic Critique." Pp. 51–71 in *Shaping New Vision: Gender and Values in American Culture,* edited by C. Atkinson, C. Buchanan, and M. Miles. Ann Arbor: UMI.

————. 1987b. "Philosophia: feminist methodology for constructing a female train of thought." *Journal of Feminist Studies in Religion* 3 (2): 7–16.

Daly, Mary. 1987. *Webster's First New Intergalactic Wickedary of the English Language.* Boston: Beacon.

————. 1985. *The Church and the Second Sex. With the Feminist Postchristian Introduction and New Archaic Afterwords by the Author.* Boston: Beacon.

————. 1984. *Pure Lust. Elemental Feminist Philosophy.* Boston: Beacon.

————. 1978. *Gyn/ecology: The Metaethics of Radical Feminism.* Boston: Beacon.

————. 1975a. *The Church and the Second Sex: With a New Feminist Postchristian Introduction by the Author.* New York: Harper and Row.

————. 1975b. "The qualitative leap beyond patriarchal religion." *Quest* 1 (Spring): 20–40.

————. 1973. *Beyond God the Father. Toward a Philosophy of Women's Liberation.* Boston: Beacon.

————. 1968. *The Church and the Second Sex.* New York: Harper and Row.

Das, Veena. 1986. "Gender studies, cross-cultural comparison and the colonial organization of knowledge." *Berkshire Review* 21:58–76.

Daum, Annette. 1984. "A Jewish feminist view." *Theology Today* 41:294–300.

————. 1980. "Blaming the Jews for the death of the goddess." *Lilith* 7:12–13.

Davies, Stevan. 1980. *The Revolt of the Widows. The Social World of the Apocryphal Acts.* Carbondale: Southern Illinois University Press.

De Maria, Richard. 1978. *Communal Love at Oneida: A Perfectionist Vision of Authority, Property and Sexual Order.* Lewiston, NY: Edwin Mellen.

Doane, Janice, and Devon Hodges. 1987. *Nostalgia and Sexual Difference: The Resistance to Contemporary Feminism.* New York: Methuen.

Downing, Christine. 1988. *Psyche's Sisters: Re-Imagining the Meaning of Sisterhood.* San Francisco: Harper and Row.

————. 1984. *The Goddess: Mythological Images of the Feminine*. New York: Cross-roads.

Downing, Mary May. 1985. "Prehistoric goddesses: the Cretan challenge." *Journal of Feminist Studies in Religion* 1 (1): 7–22.

Dronke, Peter. 1983. *Women Writers of the Middle Ages*. New York: Cambridge University Press.

Eck, Diana L., and Devaki Jain (editors). 1987. *Speaking of Faith: Global Perspectives on Women, Religion, and Social Change*. Philadelphia: New Society.

Esquivel, Julia. 1987. "Christian women and the struggle for justice in Central America." Pp. 22–32 in *Shaping New Vision: Gender and Values in American Culture*, edited by D. Eck and D. Jain. Ann Arbor: UMI.

Exum, J. Cheryl. 1986. "The mothers of Israel: the patriarchal narratives from a feminist perspective." *Bible Review* 2 (1): 60–67.

Fabella, Virginia, and Mercy Amba Oduyoye (editors). 1988. *With Passion and Compassion: Third World Women Doing Theology*. Maryknoll, NY: Orbis.

Falk, Marcia. 1987. "Notes on composing new blessings: toward a feminist Jewish-reconstruction of prayer." *Journal of Feminist Studies in Religion* 3 (1): 39–53.

Falk, Nancy Auer, and Rita M. Gross (editors). 1989. *Unspoken Worlds: Women's Religious Lives*. Rev. ed. Belmont, CA: Wadsworth.

Farley, Margaret. 1985a "Feminist consciousness and the interpretation of Scripture." Pp. 41–51 in *Feminist Interpretation of the Bible*, edited by L. M. Russell. Philadelphia: Westminster.

————. 1985b. *Personal Commitments: Making, Keeping, Breaking*. San Francisco: Harper and Row.

Feldhaus, Anne. 1982. "Bahina Bai: wife and saint." *Journal of the American Academy of Religion* 50:591–604.

"Feminists and faith: a discussion with Judith Plaskow and Annette Daum." 1980. *Lilith* 7:14–17.

Fortune, Marie. 1983. *Sexual Violence, the Unmentionable Sin: An Ethical and Pastoral Perspective*. New York: Pilgrim.

Fortune, Marie M., and Frances Wood. 1988. "The center for the prevention of sexual and domestic violence: a study in applied theology and ethics." *Journal of Feminist Studies in Religion* 4 (1): 115–122.

Friedman, Lenore. 1987. *Meetings with Remarkable Women: Buddhist Teachers in America*. Boston: Shambala.

Friedman, Reena Sigman. 1979. "The politics of women's ordination." *Lilith* 6:9–15.

Gearhart, Sally. 1982. "Womanpower: energy re-sourcement." Pp. 194–206 in *The Politics of Women's Spirituality*, edited by Charlene Spretnak. New York: Doubleday.

Gilkes, Cheryl Townsend. 1986. "The roles of church and community mothers: ambivalent American sexism or fragmented African familyhood?" *Journal of Feminist Studies in Religion* 2 (1): 41–59.

Gilligan, Carol. 1987. "A different voice in moral decisions." Pp. 236–256 in *Speaking of Faith: Global Perspectives on Women, Religion, and Social Change*, edited by D. Eck and D. Jain. Philadelphia: New Society

————. 1982. *In a Different Voice: Psychological Theory and Women's Development*. Cambridge: Harvard University Press.

Goldenberg, Naomi. 1979. *Changing of the Gods: Feminism and the End of Traditional Religions*. Boston: Beacon.

Goodblatt, David. 1975. "The Beruriah traditions." *Journal of Jewish Studies* 26(1–2):68–85.

Grant, Jacquelyn. 1984. "A black response to feminist theology." Pp. 117–124 in *Women's Spirit Bonding*, edited by J. Kalven and M. Buckley. New York: Pilgrim.

———. 1982. "Black women and the church." Pp. 141–152 in *But Some of Us Are Brave: Black Women's Studies*, edited by G. T. Hull, P. B. Scott, and B. Smith. Old Westbury, NY: Feminist Press.

Grimstad, Kristen, and Susan Rennie. 1975. "Spiritual explorations cross country." *Quest* 1:49–51.

Gross, Rita M. [forthcoming]. "Yeshe Tsogyel: enlightenment consort, great teacher, female role model." *Tibet Journal*.

———. 1989. "Menstruation and childbirth as ritual and religious experience." Pp. 257–266 in *Unspoken Worlds: Women's Religious Lives*, edited by N. A. Falk and R. M. Gross. Belmont, CA: Wadsworth.

———. 1979. "Female God language in a Jewish context." Pp. 167–173 in *Womanspirit Rising: A Feminist Reader in Religion*, edited by C. Christ and J. Plaskow. San Francisco: Harper and Row.

———. 1978. "Hindu female deities as a resource for the contemporary rediscovery of the goddess." *Journal of the American Academy of Religion* 46:269–291.

Haddad, Yvonne Yazbeck. 1985. "Islam, women and revolution in twentieth century Arab thought." Pp. 275–306 in *Women, Religion and Social Change*, edited by Y. Y. Haddad and E. B. Findly. Albany: SUNY.

Hadewijch of Antwerp. 1980. *The Complete Works*, translated by Mother Columba Hart. New York: Paulist.

Harrison, Beverly Wildung. 1985. *Making the Connections: Essays in Feminist Social Ethics*, edited by C. S. Robb. Boston: Beacon.

———. 1983. *Our Right to Choose: Toward a New Ethic of Abortion*. Boston: Beacon.

Hauerwas, Stanley. 1981. *Community and Character: Toward a Constructive Christian Social Ethic*. Notre Dame, IN: Notre Dame University Press.

———. 1974. *Vision and Virtue: Essays in Christian Ethical Reflection*. Notre Dame, IN: Fides/Claretian.

Hauptmann, Judith. 1974. "Images of women in the Talmud." Pp. 184–212 in *Religion and Sexism: Images of Women in the Jewish and Christian Traditions*, edited by R. R. Ruether. New York: Touchstone.

Hawley, John Stratton, and Donna Marie Wulff (editors). 1982. *The Divine Consort. Radha and the Goddesses of India*. Boston: Beacon.

Henry, Sondra, and Emily Taitz. 1983. *Written Out of History. Our Jewish Foremothers*. 2nd rev. ed. Fresh Meadows, NY: Biblio.

Heyward, Carter. 1985. "An unfinished symphony of liberation: the radicalization of Christian feminism among U.S. white women." *Journal of Feminist Studies in Religion* 1 (1): 99–118.

———. 1984. *Our Passion for Justice: Images of Power, Sexuality and Liberation*. New York: Pilgrim.

———. 1976. *A Priest Forever: The Formation of a Woman and a Priest*. New York: Harper and Row.

Hiatt, Suzanne R., and Ellen K. Wondra. 1975. "On the politics of Episcopal ordina-
    tion: a conversation." *Radical Religion* 2 (1): 45–53.
Hickey, Anne Ewing. 1987. *Women of the Roman Aristocracy as Christian Monastics.*
    Ann Arbor: UMI.
Higgins, Patricia. 1985. "Women in the Islamic Republic of Iran: legal, social and
    ideological changes." *Signs* 10:477–494.
Hildegard of Bingen. 1986. *Scivias,* translated by Bruce Hozeski. Santa Fe: Bear.
Humez, Jean McMahon (editor). 1981. *Gifts of Power. The Writings of Rebecca Jack-
    son, Black Visionary, Shaker Eldress.* Amherst: University of Massachusetts Press.
Hunt, Eleanor Humes. 1980. "What is feminist ethics: a proposal for coming discus-
    sion." *Journal of Religious Ethics* 8:115–124.
Hunt, Mary E. 1983. "Beyond the academy gates: sources for feminist liberation the-
    ology." *Journal of Women and Religion* 3 (1): 7–16.
Inglehart, Haillie. 1983. *Womanspirit: A Guide to Women's Wisdom.* San Francisco:
    Harper and Row.
Isasi-Diaz, Ada Maria. 1987. "Toward an understanding of *Feminismo Hispano* in the
    U.S.A." Pp. 51–62 in *Women's Consciousness, Women's Conscience: A Reader
    in Feminist Ethics,* edited by B. H. Andolsen, C. E. Gudorf, and M. D. Pel-
    lauer. San Francisco: Harper and Row.
Janowitz, Naomi, and Maggie Wenig. 1977–1978. "Selections from a prayerbook where
    God's image is female." *Lilith* 1:27–29.
Katz, Raye T. 1985–1986. "Exploring the link between womanhood and the rabbin-
    ate." *Lilith* 14: 19–24.
Keddie, Nikki R. (editor). 1972. *Scholars, Saints, and Sufis.* Berkeley: University of
    California Press.
Keller, Catherine. 1987. "Feminism and the ethic of inseparability." Pp. 251–264 in
    Women's Consciousness, Women's Conscience: A Reader in Feminist Ethics,
    edited by B. H. Andolsen, C. E. Gudorf, and M. D. Pellauer. San Francisco:
    Harper and Row.
———. 1986. *From a Broken Web: Separation, Sexism and Self.* Boston: Beacon.
Kempe, Margery. 1940. *The Book of Margery Kempe,* edited by Sanford Brown Meech.
    Oxford: Oxford Univeristy.
Kepler, Patricia Budd. 1978. "Women clergy and the cultural order." *Theology Today*
    34:402–409.
King, Karen (editor). 1988. *Images of the Feminine in Gnosticism.* Philadelphia: For-
    tress.
King, Ursula. 1989. *Women and Spirituality: Voices of Protest and Promise.* New York:
    New Amsterdam Books.
———. 1987a. "Goddesses, witches, androgyny and beyond? Feminism and the trans-
    formation of religious consciousness." Pp. 201–218 in *Women in the World's
    Religions: Past and Present,* edited by U. King. New York: Paragon
———. 1987b. *Women in the World's Religions: Past and Present.* New York: Para-
    gon.
Klein, Anne C. 1985. "Nondualism and the Great Bliss Queen: a study in Tibetan
    Buddhist ontology and symbolism." *Journal of Feminist Studies in Religion* 1
    (1): 73–98.
Kraemer, Ross S. 1989. "Monastic Jewish women in Graeco-Roman Egypt: Philo Ju-
    daeus on the Therapeutrides." *Signs* 14:342–370.

————. 1986. "Hellenistic Jewish women: the epigraphical evidence." Pp. 183–200 in *Society of Biblical Literature Seminar Papers 1986*, edited by K. H. Richards. Atlanta: Scholars.

————. 1980. "The conversion of women to ascetic forms of Christianity." *Signs* 6:298–307.

Kwilecki, Susan. 1987. "Contemporary Pentacostal clergywomen: female Christian leadership old style." *Journal of Feminist Studies in Religion* 3 (2): 57–76.

Laffey, Alice L. 1988. *An Introduction to the Old Testament. A Feminist Perspective.* Philadelphia: Fortress.

Lerner, Gerda. 1986. *The Creation of Patriarchy.* New York: Oxford University Press.

Liddell, Henry George, and Robert Scott. 1978. *A Greek-English Lexicon.* revised by H. S. Jones. Oxford: Oxford University Press.

Litman, Jane. 1982–1983. "Is Judaism a matriarchal religion?" *Lilith* 10:32.

Mazumdar, Vina. 1978. "Comment on suttee." *Signs* 4:269–273.

McCauley, Deborah, and Annette Daum. 1983. "Jewish-Christian feminist dialogue: a wholistic vision." *Union Seminary Quarterly Review* 38 (2): 147–190.

McDonald, Dennis Ronald. 1983. *The Legend and the Apostle. The Battle for Paul in Story and Canon.* Philadelphia: Westminster.

McFague, Sally. 1987. "God as mother." Pp. 97–123 in *Models of God: Theology for an Ecological, Nuclear Age.* Philadelphia: Fortress.

McFarland, Morgan. 1975. "Witchcraft: the art of remembering." *Quest* 1:41–48.

Mercadente, Linda, Marcia Riggs, Victoria Byerly, Renita J. Weems, and Barbara H. Andolsen. 1988. "Racism in the women's movement." *Journal of Feminist Studies in Religion* 4 (1): 93–114.

Mernissi, Fatima. 1987a. *Beyond the Veil. Male-Female Dynamics in Modern Muslim Society.* Rev. ed. Bloomington: Indiana University Press.

————. 1987b. "Femininity as subversion: reflection on the Muslim concept of Nushuz." Pp. 95–108 in *Speaking of Faith: Global Perspectives on Women, Religion, and Social Change*, edited by D. Eck and D. Jain. Philadelphia: New Society.

————. 1977. "Women, saints and sanctuaries." *Signs* 3:101–112.

Miles, Margaret R. 1987. "Violence against women in the historical Christian West and in North American secular culture: the visual and textual evidence." Pp. 11–28 in *Shaping New Vision: Gender and Values in American Culture*, edited by C. W. Atkinson, C. H. Buchanan, and M. R. Miles. Ann Arbor: UMI.

Minerva. 1975. "Chart your self." *Quest* 1:66–71.

Mitchell, Mozella G. 1983. "The black woman's view of human liberation." *Theology Today* 39:421–425.

Mollenkott, Virginia Ramey. 1983. *The Divine Feminine: The Biblical Image of God as Female.* New York: Crossroads.

————. 1977. "Evangelicalism: a feminist perspective." *Union Seminary Quarterly Review* 32:95–103.

National Conference of Catholic Bishops. 1973. "Behold your mother. woman of faith." A Pastoral Letter on the Blessed Virgin Mary. 21 November.

National Council of Churches in the U.S.A. 1983. *An Inclusive Lectionary: Readings for Year A.* John Knox; New York: Pilgrim; Philadelphia: Westminster.

Needleman, Jacob. 1970. *The New Religions.* Garden City, NY: Doubleday.

Neu, Diann, and Julia Upton. 1984. "Guidelines for planners of rituals." Pp. 347–238 in *Women's Spirit Bonding,* edited by J. Kalven and M. I. Buckley. New York: Pilgrim

Neusner, Jacob. 1980. *The Mishnaic Order of Women.* 5 vols. Leiden: Brill.

———. 1979. "Thematic or systemic description: the case of Mishnah's division of women." Pp. 79–100 in *Method and Meaning in Ancient Judaism.* Missoula, MT: Scholars.

O'Connor, June. 1987. "On doing religious ethics." Pp. 265–284 in *Women's Consciousness, Women's Conscience: A Reader in Feminist Ethics,* edited by B. H. Andolsen, C. E. Gudorf, and M. D. Pellauer. San Francisco: Harper and Row.

Oduyoye, Mercy Amba. 1988. "Be a woman and Africa will be strong." Pp. 24–53 in *Inheriting Our Mothers' Gardens: Feminist Theology in Third World Perspective,* edited by L. M. Russell, K. Pui-lan, A. M. Isasi-Diaz, and K. G. Cannon. Philadelphia: Westminster.

O'Flaherty, Wendy Doniger. 1980. *Women, Androgynes and Other Mythical Beasts.* Chicago: University of Chicago Press.

Olds, Linda E. 1986. "The neglected feminine: promises and perils." *Soundings* 69:226–240.

Olsen, Carl (editor). 1987. *The Book of the Goddess Past and Present: An Introduction to Her Religion.* New York: Crossroads.

Osiek, Carolyn. 1985. "The feminist and the Bible: hermeneutical alternatives." Pp. 93–105 in *Feminist Perspectives on Biblical Scholarship,* edited by A. Y. Collins. Chico, CA: Scholars.

Ozick, Cynthia. 1985. "Torah as the matrix for feminism." *Lilith* 12/13:47–48.

Pagels, Elaine. 1988. Adam, Eve, and the Serpent. New York: Random House.

———. 1976. "What became of God the mother? conflicting images of God in early Christianity." *Signs* 2:292–303.

Papanek, Hanna, and Gail Minault (editors). 1982. *Separate Worlds: Studies of Purdah in South Asia.* Delhi: Chanakya; Columbia, MO: South Asia Books.

Paul, Diana Y. 1979. *Women in Buddhism: Images of the Feminine in the Mahayana Tradition.* Berkeley: Asian Humanities.

Petroff, Elizabeth (editor). 1986. *Medieval Women's Visionary Literature.* New York: Oxford University Press.

Plaskow, Judith. 1984. "Anti-Semitism: the unacknowledged racism." Pp. 89–96 in *Women's Spirit Bonding,* edited by J. Kalven and M. I. Buckley. New York: Pilgrim.

———. 1980. "Blaming the Jews for inventing patriarchy." *Lilith* 7:11–12.

———. 1979. "Bring a daughter into the covenant." Pp. 179–184 in *Womanspirit Rising: A Feminist Reader in Religion,* edited by C. Christ and J. Plaskow. San Francisco: Harper and Row.

Plaskow, Judith, and Joan Arnold Romero (editors). 1974. *Women and Religion.* Missoula, MT: Scholars.

Pohli, Carol Virginia. 1983. "Church closets and back doors: a feminist view of moral majority women." *Feminist Studies* 9:529–558.

Proctor, Priscilla, and William Proctor. 1976. *Women in the Pulpit: Is God an Equal Opportunity Employer?* Garden City, NY: Doubleday.

Proctor-Smith, Marjorie. 1985. *Women in Shaker Community and Worship: A Feminist Analysis of the Uses of Religious Symbolism.* Lewiston, NY: Edwin Mellen.

Quebedeaux, Richard. 1987. "We're on our way, Lord! The rise of evangelical feminism in modern American Christianity." Pp. 129–44 in *Women in the World's Religions: Past and Present*, edited by U. King. New York: Paragon.

Ramodibe, Dorothy. 1988. "Women and men building together the church in Africa." Pp. 14–21 in *With Passion and Compassion: Third World Women Doing Theology*, edited by V. Fabella and M. A. Oduyoye. Maryknoll, NY: Orbis.

Raymond, Janice G. 1986. *A Passion for Friends: Toward a Philosophy of Female Affection*. Boston: Beacon.

Ringe, Sharon. 1976. "Biblical authority and interpretation." Pp. 23–28 in *The Liberating Word: A Guide to Nonsexist Interpretation of the Bible*, edited by L. Russell. Philadelphia: Westminster.

Robb, Carol S. 1987. "A framework for feminist ethics." Pp. 211–234 in *Women's Consciousness, Women's Conscience: A Reader in Feminist Ethics*, edited by B. H. Andolsen, C. E. Gudorf, and M. D. Pellauer. San Francisco: Harper and Row.

————. 1985. "Introduction." Pp. xi–xxii in *Making the Connections: Essays in Feminist Social Ethics*, by Beverly Wildung Harrison; edited by C. S. Robb. Boston: Beacon.

Robbins, Thomas, William C. Shepherd, and James McBride (editors). 1985. *Cults, Culture, and the Law*. Chico, CA: Scholars.

Robertson, Roland. 1985. "Relativization, religion, and globalization." Pp. 31–42 in *Cults, Culture, and the Law*, edited by T. Robbins, W. C. Shepherd, and J. McBride. Chico, CA: Scholars.

Rohrlich, Ruby, and Elaine Hoffman Baruch. 1984. *Women in Search of Utopia: Mavericks and Mythmakers*. New York: Schocken Books.

Rousselle, Aline. 1988. *Porneia: On Desire and the Body in Antiquity*, translated by Felicia Pheasant. Oxford: Blackwell.

Ruether, Rosemary Radford. 1986. "Recontextualizing theology." *Theology Today* 43 (April): 22–27.

————. 1985. *Womanguides: Readings Toward a Feminist Theology*. Boston: Beacon.

————. 1983. *Sexism and God-Talk: Toward a Feminist Theology*. Boston: Beacon.

————. 1981. "The feminist critique in religious studies." *Soundings* 64 (Winter): 388–402.

————. 1979. "Mothers of the church: ascetic women in the late patristic age." Pp. 71–98 in *Women of Spirit: Female Leadership in the Jewish and Christian Traditions*, edited by R. R. Ruether and E. McLaughlin. New York: Touchstone.

————. 1975. "The first and final proletariat: socialism and women's liberation." *Soundings* 58:310–328.

————. 1974a. *Faith and Fratricide: The Theological Roots of Anti-Semitism*. New York: Seabury.

———— (editor). 1974b. *Religion and Sexism: Images of Women in the Jewish and Christian Traditions*. New York: Touchstone.

Ruether, Rosemary Radford, and Eleanor McLaughlin (editors). 1979. *Women of Spirit. Female Leadership in the Jewish and Christian Traditions*. New York: Touchstone.

Russell, Letty M. (editor). 1976. "Changing language and the church." Pp. 88–94 in *The Liberating Word: A Guide to Nonsexist Interpretation of the Bible*, edited by R. Russell. Philadelphia: Westminster.

Schungel-Straumann, Helen. 1984. "Tamar." *Bibel und Kirche* 39:148–157.

Schüssler, Fiorenza Elizabeth. 1984a. *Bread Not Stone. The Challenge of Feminist Biblical Interpretation*. Boston: Beacon.

———. 1984b. "Claiming the center: critical feminist theology of liberation." in *Women's Spirit Bonding*, edited by J. Kalven and M. I. Buckley. New York: Pilgrim.

———. 1983. *In Memory of Her. A Feminist Theological Reconstruction of Christian Origins*. New York: Crossroads.

———. 1979. "Word, spirit, and power: women in early Christian communities." Pp. 29–70 in *The Liberating Word: A Guide to Nonsexist Interpretation of the Bible*, edited by L. Russell. Philadelphia: Westminster.

———. 1976. "Interpreting patriarchal traditions." Pp. 39–61 in *The Liberating Word: A Guide to Nonsexist Interpretation of the Bible*, edited by L. Russell. Philadelphia: Westminster.

Schüssler Fiorenza, Elisabeth, Karen McCarthy Brown, Anne Llewellyn Barstow, Cheryl Townsend Gilkes, and Mary E. Hunt. 1985. "On feminist methodology." *Journal of Feminist Studies in Religion* 1 (2): 73–88.

Scott, Joan Wallach. 1988. "Gender: a useful category of historical analysis." Pp. 28–50 in *Gender and the Politics of History*. New York: Columbia University.

Shahar, Shulamith. 1983. *The Fourth Estate. A History of Women in the Middle Ages*. New York: Methuen.

Shank, Lillian Thomas, and John A. Nichols (editors). 1987. *Medieval Religious Women*. Vol. II: *Peaceweavers*. Kalamazoo, MI: Cistercian.

———. 1984. *Medieval Religious Women*. Vol. I: *Distant Echoes*. Kalamazoo, MI: Cistercian.

Sharma, Arvind (editor). 1987. *Women in World Religions*. Albany: SUNY.

Sjoo, Monica, and Barbara Mor. 1986. *The Great Cosmic Mother*. San Francisco: Harper and Row.

Smith, Jane I. 1985. "Women, religion and social change in early Islam." Pp. 19–35 in *Women, Religion and Social Change*, edited by Y. Y. Haddad and E. B. Findly. Albany: SUNY.

———. 1979. "Women in Islam: equity, equality, and the search for the natural order." *Journal of the American Academic of Religion* 47:517–537.

Spinning a Sacred Yarn: Women Speak from the Pulpit. 1982. New York: Pilgrim.

Spretnak, Charlene (editor). 1982. *The Politics of Women's Spirituality*. Garden City, NY: Anchor.

Stange, Mary Zeiss. 1987. "Treading the narrative between myth and madness: Maxine Hong Kingston and contemporary women's biography." *Journal of Feminist Studies in Religion* 3 (1): 15–28.

Starhawk. 1987. *Truth or Dare: Encounters with Power, Authority, Mystery*. San Francisco: Harper and Row.

———. 1979a. *Dreaming the Dark*. Boston: Beacon.

———. 1979b. *The Spiral Dance*. Boston: Beacon.

Stein, Dorothy K. 1978. "Women to burn: suttee as a normative institution." *Signs* 4:253–268.

Stone, Merlin. 1978. "The three faces of goddess spirituality." *Heresies* 2:2–4.

———. 1976. *When God Was a Woman*. New York: Harcourt Brace Jovanovich.

Swidler, Leonard. 1974. "Is sexism a sign of decadence in religion?" Pp. 167–175 in

Women and Religion, edited by J. Plaskow and J. A. Romero. Missoula, MT: Scholars.

―――. 1970–1971. "Jesus was a feminist." *Catholic World* 212:177–183.

Swidler, Leonard, and Arlene Swindler (editors). 1974. *Woman and Religion.* Missoula, MT: Scholars.

Tamez, Elsa. 1988. "Women's rereading of the Bible." Pp. 173–180 in *With Passion and Compassion: Third World Women Doing Theology,* edited by V. Fabella and M. A. Oduyoye. Maryknoll, NY: Orbis.

―――. 1987. *Against Machismo.* Oak Park, IL: Meyer-Stone.

―――― (editor). 1989. *Through Her Eyes: Women's Theology from Latin America.* Maryknoll, NY: Orbis.

Teubal, Savina. 1984. *Sarah the Priestess. The First Matriarch of Genesis.* Athens: Ohio University.

Thiébaux, Marcelle (translator). 1987. *The Writings of Medieval Women.* New York: Garland.

Thistlethwaite, Susan Brooks. 1987. "Inclusive language and linguistic blindness." *Theology Today* 43:533–539.

―――. 1985. "Every two minutes: battered women and feminist interpretation." Pp. 96–107 in *The Liberating Word: A Guide to Nonsexist Interpretation of the Bible,* edited by L. Russell. Philadelphia: Westminster.

Trible, Phyllis. 1984. *Texts of Terror: Literary-Feminist Readings of Biblical Narratives.* Philadelphia: Fortress.

―――. 1978. *God and the Rhetoric of Sexuality.* Philadelphia: Fortress.

―――. 1973. "Depatriarchalization in biblical interpretation." *Journal of the American Academy of Religion* 41(1):30–49.

Turner, Kay. 1978. "Contemporary feminist rituals." *Heresies* 2:20–26.

Umansky, Ellen. 1985. *Lily Montague and the Development of Liberal Judaism: From Vision to Vocation.* Lewiston, NY: Edwin Mellen.

―――. 1984a. "Creating a Jewish feminist theology: possibilities and problems." *Anima* 10:125–135.

―――. 1984b. "Reflections on the creation of a ritual meal." Pp. 351–352 in *Women's Spirit Bonding,* edited by J. Kalven and M. I. Buckley. New York: Pilgrim.

Washbourn, Penelope. 1979. "Becoming woman: menstruation as spiritual challenge." Pp. 246–258 in *Womenspirit Rising: A Feminist Reader in Religion,* edited by C. Christ and J. Plaskow. San Francisco: Harper and Row.

Williams, Delores. 1987. "Black womanist theology." Pp. 66–70 in *Christianity and Crisis* 47: 2 March.

―――. 1985. "Women's oppression and life-line politics in black women's religious narratives." *Journal of Feminist Studies in Religion* 1 (2): 59–71.

Willis, Janice D. 1985. "Nuns and benefactresses: the role of women in the development of Buddhism." Pp. 59–85 in *Women, Religion and Social Change,* edited by Y. Y. Haddad and E. B. Findly. Albany: SUNY.

Wilson, Katharina (editor). 1987. *Women Writers of the Renaissance and Reformation.* Athens: University of Georgia Press.

―――. 1984. *Medieval Women Writers.* Athens: University of Georgia Press.

Wilson-Kaster, Patricia, et al. 1981. *A Lost Tradition. Women Writers of the Early Church.* Lanham, MD: University Press of America.

Wimbush, Vincent (editor). 1990. *Ascetic Behavior in Graeco-Roman Antiquity: A Sourcebook*. Philadelphia: Fortress.

Wittig, Monique. 1969. *Les Gu rill res,* translated by David Le Vay. New York: Avon.

Yoshioka, Barbara. 1974. "Whoring after strange gods." *Radical Religion* 1:6–11.

9

The Emergence of New Voices:
Women in Architecture

N. Jane Hurt

Women have always been involved in the making of the spatial environment.
It was not until the spatial environment was designated as needing professional
designing that women's efforts were devalued. As architecture grew in stature
as a profession, women's involvement became more and more limited and architecture as a professional endeavor was limited to men practitioners. Through
the years there have been a few "maverick" women who have entered the
field. Much of their work has been notable for its creativity. It has not been
until after World War II that women truly began to enter the profession. And
it took until the mid-1960s for women to enter in sufficient numbers to now
have a voice. It was to search for women's emerging voices, their voice of
experience and their voice of creativity, that this research was begun.

The following chapter focuses upon the experiences of 20 women architects
who were interviewed as a beginning search for a voice of collective experience.[1] My own experiences as a woman student of architecture and as a professional architect have been used to corroborate what I have heard from my
respondents. The women architects were informally interviewed to initiate a
search for meaning within our common experiences. The majority of the interviews were conducted at three national conferences held during the 1988–1989
academic year. The interviews were based upon three questions to which the
women were encouraged to respond however they wished. What I have recognized from the start was that this was not to be a definitive statement of the
experiences of a significant cross-section of women in the profession, but an
initial exploration of the issues with which women in architecture have had to
deal or may still face during their professional lives. What I have found leads

to a poignant comment on an emerging women's voice calling for the freedom to be creative individuals.

The three conferences at which most of the interviews took place included the 8th Congress of the Union Internationale des Femmes Architectes (UIFA), the Architectural Research Centers Consortium (ARCC) Research Conference, and the 6th Annual Conference on the Beginning Student. The UIFA Congress was held in Washington, DC, 28, 29, and 30 September 1988. It was at the UIFA Conference that I was able to interview 15 of the 20 women. Among this group were three women from China, one black woman from South Africa, one woman from New Zealand, and one from New South Wales, Australia. Of these six women all have been practitioners, and several have taught design at various points in their careers. The remaining nine women were from various parts of the United States.

My interview plan was to sit down with women during breaks in the conference proceedings and tape-record informal responses to my questions. It is from these tape recordings that the women's responses are quoted. One of my first interviews was of a group consisting of five women architects and one woman engineer who is involved in the building industry. These women came from various parts of the United States: one practicing in New York City; one practicing and doing research in Cambridge, MA; two who practice in Los Angeles; another practicing in St. Helena, CA; and the sixth woman, an engineer from Northridge, CA. Another group interview was conducted which included a woman from the Midwest and the black South African, with the Australian woman joining us. This was unfortunate timing and circumstances because the South African was reserved in her participation and there was insufficient time to hold an individual interview as I would have hoped there would be. Having learned a valuable lesson from this frustration, I conducted the remaining interviews at this and the other two conferences with individual women. Of the two additional women interviewed during this conference, one practices in Washington, DC and the other is from the Pacific Northwest.

The ARCC Research Conference was held at the University of Illinois at Urbana–Champaign, IL, 13, 14, and 15 November 1988. The four women interviewed at this conference were from various parts of the United States— three from the Midwest and one from the Northeast. All four are involved with architectural research and three teach design and/or research; the other one is a full-time researcher. Also interviewed at this conference were two men professors, both of whom have been involved in architectural education and research. Both men had come to me stating their desire to have their comments included in my research as both felt most positive about the women students with whom they had worked over the years. Their comments were not included because of what I consider a valid warning extended by several women respondents and colleagues. What one must constantly be aware of is that, however sincere the men respondents may be, women's reactions to their comments often will be to search for implicit condemnation by omission. So, although I had no doubt of the sincerity of my men respondents, when both had stated that their "women students were better researchers," women to whom this statement was repeated reacted negatively. The women's rejection was to say that implicit in men saying that women are better researchers is what is left off: "therefore they are not good designers."

The third conference attended was the 6th Annual Conference on the Beginning Student held at Tulane University in New Orleans on 7 and 8 April 1989. The final woman interviewed was met at this conference. Although she has studied and practiced in the eastern and northeastern regions of the United States, she is now teaching in the Deep South. Looking back at the description of the field studies, I recognize that the nature of the conferences attended may have put me in touch with women who may not be representative of all women working as architects. However, this study is a search for appropriate topics for research into women's experiences and makes no claims to being a definitive study of collective experience.

The issue of collective experience is one of utmost importance as one looks back on experiences trying to make sense of them. How do women architects really feel about their experiences—as students and as professionals? How do we really feel about our work? How much of the negative aspects of our experiences has been sublimated in order to deal with events (both past and present) without losing our tempers, our jobs, or our dignity? How can we come to an understanding of how we feel about our work, particularly when that work is being done in a field wherein women often have to fight to be allowed to study, work, and to be taken seriously?

The three questions asked of my colleagues (and me) were:[2]

1. Do you think/feel that there are masculine versus feminine aspects to design?
2. Do you think/feel that you were treated differently from your male counterparts when you were a student—because of being a woman student of architecture?
3. Considering your answers to the first two questions, how do you think/feel your ideas or experiences concerning your responses affect your work as a professional (your work as a professional managing projects and/or as a designer)?

At times, we will consider the answers to the three questions as a whole when looking at the women's responses since there is often little or no way to separate the narratives. What also becomes apparent when looking at the responses is that the women interviewed did not separate their lives into compartments but amalgamated into their responses details of how their lives—as women with husbands, families, and other obligations and interests—did or did not fit together.

UNDERSTANDING CONTEXT

In order to take an informed look at women in architecture one must have some understanding of the context in which they work. Architectural design is never without context. Context refers to not only the physical environment in which a building is built, but also to the ideological stance of the people involved in the design of the building. Design is always a reaction to context whether that reaction is positive, neutral, or in opposition to it.[3] Thus, in order for an architect to divorce his or her design work from its context still requires that that context (the physical setting, society, and culture), be understood even more thoroughly than when the context has been accepted as the basis for design.

Throughout the following study, women refer to several fundamental issues: rational thinking, intuition, and a male-dominated profession. The majority of the women interviewed come from Western cultures in which the primary bases for their architectural designs have been modernist ideas that are based on rational thinking; thus rational thinking is a part of the context. That the women interviewed repeatedly include rational thinking as contrasted with intuitive thinking in their discussions of how they see their experiences as students of architecture and as professional architects designing buildings attests to its importance. Rationalism might be defined as "knowledge superior to and independent of sense perceptions" (*Webster's Dictionary* 1985:977) and as a rejection of nonrational thinking in favor of reason and experience as criteria fundamental to problem solving. In the interviews, the term "rational thinking" generally referred to reasoning based on stages of understanding issues organized in a logical sequence.

In contrast, the term "intuitive thinking" generally referred to an approach to problem solving that, while it does not ignore prior knowledge of the background describing an issue, nevertheless does not require a sequential analysis and synthesis of that background in order to come up with a solution. In his "Introduction" to Jung's *Man and His Symbols*, John Freeman describes Jung and his colleagues' dialectical methods:

They convince not by means of the narrowly focused spotlight of the syllogism, but by skirting, by repetition, by presenting a recurring view of the same subject seen each time from a slightly different angle—until suddenly the reader who has never been aware of a single, conclusive moment of proof finds that he has unknowingly embraced and taken into himself some wider truth.

Jung's arguments (and those of his colleagues) spiral upward over his subject like a bird circling a tree. At first, near the ground, it sees only a confusion of leaves and branches. Gradually, as it circles higher and higher, the recurring aspects of the tree form a wholeness and relate to their surroundings. (Jung 1964:14)

This might describe the intuitive design experience. Similar to the manner in which the bird gains understanding of the tree, intuitive design requires looking at the issues from multiple points of view. Moreover, the final understanding of a design solution—or its insolubility— comes upon the designer in a series of intuitive "leaps," or what one might describe as one long crescendo of inspiration.

The final issue fundamental to the women's discussion of their experiences is male domination of the architectural profession. This introduction alludes to the manner in which women have been limited in their participation in the making of the built environment. In *Women in American Architecture: A Historic and Contemporary Perspective*, Susana Torre (1977:157) described the numbers of women in practice, stating that the percentages given in the American Institute of Architects' (AIA) 1975 study showed that "women represent only 1.2 percent of all registered architects and 3.7 percent of the total U.S. 'architectural population'." Footnoting this statistical information, Torre quotes a letter from Ellen Perry Berkeley:

these statistics are meaningless now, and were probably meaningless at the time. The total population should have been 59,484 registered architects [according to Samuel T. Balen of the National Council of Architectural Registration Boards], not 42,043 [as indicated by the AIA], and no one knew (or was telling) how many of these 59,484 were women. (1977:215)

This quotation calls into question not only the percentages but the actual numbers registered as professional architects. The higher figure came from the NCARB, the National Council of Architectural Registration Boards, a nongoverning council of state registration boards that has as one of its main missions the development of a nationally recognized registration exam for architects in all states,[4] and it is the NCARB's statistics that would have the higher credence in this case. The same study by the AIA described women as generally being placed in stereotyped positions with limited opportunities for advancement and little regard for their qualifications. This study also pointed out a great disparity in salaries, namely that male architects' average incomes were "61.22 percent higher than that of female architects" (Torre 1977:157). This same study continues, saying that while men were encouraged to take time to teach, women employees who take time off for child-care responsibilities "risk losing their jobs" (Torre 1977:157).

Another quote from Torre is from a poster found at the New York Chapter of the AIA's 1974 exhibition, "Women in Architecture." The poster (whose authors are unknown) quotes a 1973 survey saying, "70 percent of women interviewed acknowledged discrimination, and 95 percent of the men denied it" (1977:157). The point of linking the seemingly disparate aspects of female versus male numbers and experiences is to highlight what are sources of frustration to the female professionals. Inequality of numbers indicates male domination of the field (as of 1975). Lower salaries, job stereotyping, and limitations gave a clear signal of what women could expect should they risk entering a field where they were not wanted.

Doctoral research by Rochelle Martin entitled "The Difficult Path: Women in Architecture'' was completed in 1986. For this study she conducted in-depth interviews of women architects regarding their experiences as professionals; she has summarized some of her findings in a recent article:

> Women continually express a lack of confirmation as architects; they lack the sense of belonging that accompanies an accepted and welcome member of the professional community . . . ; establishing credibility as experts is one of the most problematic areas of professional identity. Women must accommodate themselves to the male determined standards or be found lacking in the qualities attributed to a professional. . . . In situations with colleagues, clients, and construction workers, women architects continually encounter stereotypes of women as less competent than men. (1989:206–207)

Martin's research points out potential results of women entering male-dominated professions. They risk disempowerment by their male colleagues who seek to retain the status quo. That women may have different approaches to design thinking and problem solving further complicates their quest for professional credibility. The disempowerment of women by males seeking to block their entry into the profession by limiting the definition of what is "good" ("good design" or "good design thinking") is an issue of primary importance to women seeking to improve their credibility.

BACKGROUND STUDIES

One of the issues addressed in this chapter is whether or not women architects recognize differences in the way they address architectural design in comparison with the work of their male colleagues. Research by Carol Gilligan (1977), Anne Wilson Schaef (1985), Anne Fausto-Sterling (1985), and Mary Field Belenky et al. (1986) addresses the issue of women's thinking. The work of these researchers and many others is cited by numerous women architects now writing about what it means to be female in this profession. The writings of Doris Cole (1973), Susana Torre (1977), Jennifer Bloomer (1988a, 1988b), Karen Kingsley (1988), Martin (1989), Karen Franck (1989), and many others focus not only upon the condition of women in the workplace; their work explores issues of feminist approaches to design and to feminist design thinking as contrasted with masculine design thinking. What is perhaps most important to this chapter is the issue of how women deal with differences in approach to design thinking—particularly if their approach is not in keeping with the expectations of their male colleagues and employers.

Anne Wilson Schaef (1985) makes informed generalizations about the implicit meanings underlying how we think in our society. Her main idea is to describe a "White Male System" (W.M.S.) that "drives" our society and the emergence of a "Female System" as women question their perception of the world versus that of the existing system in power. In discussing the W.M.S., Schaef describes her experiences as a psychologist/therapist counseling women, helping them to understand their responses to our society in contrast to how men perceive society. According to Schaef, in our W.M.S. dominated or "driven" society, women are seen as nonrational because they most often do multivariate thinking, using a more multifocused, multidirectioned approach. In contrast, the men's approach is seen, in Schaef's analysis, as the rational, logically sequenced thinking that typifies Modernist thinking and Modernist design approaches.

In a recent article, Karen Franck (1989) seeks to "help women identify and understand qualities and concerns in themselves that are often unrecognized or suppressed in architectural education, research, and practice." Her research defines masculine versus feminine relationships to the world as follows:

Women's underlying relationship with the world is one of connection while men's is one of separation. . . . This difference in the nature of identity between men and women is reinforced by socialization where girls learn nurturing and caretaking roles and boys learn more abstract, less person-oriented skills. That masculinity is defined in terms of the denial of connection and femininity is defined as self-in-relationship has important implications for cognitive activities and hence for western science, philosophy, and architecture. (1989:2)

Franck continues in her description of "feminist ways of knowing and analysing," listing seven basic qualities characteristic to feminist thinking. Briefly summarized, they are:

underlying connectedness . . . and a sensitivity to the connectedness of categories, . . . a desire for inclusiveness . . . to overcome opposing dualities . . . a responsibility to respond to the needs of others . . . acknowledgement of the value of everyday life and experience . . . acceptance of subjectivity as a strategy for knowing and of feelings as part of knowing . . . acceptance and desire for complexity [and] acceptance of change and a desire for flexibility. (1989:4-5)

The research cited above points to distinct differences in the way men and women think. Rational thinking has long been held up as desirable in comparison to intuitive thinking. It comes as no surprise that rational thinking goes hand in hand with a male-dominated Modernist approach to architecture. Appropriate at this point is to describe how women continued to express feminist, intuitive approaches to architecture, often in spite of the rational Modernist world around them.

KEEPING WOMEN IN THEIR PROPER PLACE

Women have long been involved in making shelters. As is apparent from the research described, women bring to the design of the environment an approach to thinking about the world that can be very different from that of their male colleagues. Doris Cole's *From Tipi to Skyscraper* (1973) narrates women's changing role in the creation of shelters. Gwendolyn Wright (1977), Dolores Hayden (1977a, 1977b), and Polly W. Allen (1988), among others, describe women's involvement with the design of the home environment. And the women of the British group known as Matrix 1984 published *Making Space: Women and the Man Made Environment*. While several of these are more factually dispassionate accounts of events, most have an undercurrent of intense feelings of injustice that manifest themselves when the authors begin to discuss events previously ignored or underplayed in their significance. The Matrix group openly declares its rage at the manner in which women's ideas have been dismissed without fair scrutiny and the way women's achievements have been ignored. By way of illustrating this, Matrix has included illustrations of house plans designed by men, but critiqued by women evaluating the efficacy of their design. The text accompanying these illustrations describes the battles waged and lost by women attempting to alter these plans to be more suited to family needs. That women's opinions were noted at all has been attributed (by Matrix) in part to maneuvering by politicians seeking to defuse uneasy feelings concerning public housing schemes. Many of the examples cited were from the turbulent times of 1920s Britain.

Allen's *Building Domestic Liberty: Charlotte Perkins Gilman's Architectural Feminism* (1988) describes Gilman's attempts to alter the home setting by radically changing the physical environment to be supportive of more communal sharing of domestic tasks. That Gilman's work subtly influenced neighborhood design is evinced by present-day housing projects that include shared domestic work areas (such as laundry rooms), community rooms, child care facilities, and playgrounds. Her ideas are also evident in current planning of housing for the elderly. Allen's critique of Gilman's work focuses on her strength as a planner of environments for everyday living, stating that any weaknesses in her work occurred when Gilman began to develop philosophical grounds for her design ideas. Allen also points out that Gilman, like many present-day white middle-class feminists, never resolved what to do with her "legitimate anger"—anger perhaps at being limited to domestic planning, anger never dealt with by a woman living in a male-dominated Victorian world.

Doris Cole (1973) describes how women from the nineteenth century carried on vigorous and enthusiastic studies of how to improve the home environment, including everything from how to design the house to be most appropriately heated and ventilated to the best interior surfaces for improved cleaning to what forms were best for what functions. These studies were focused on provision of the most healthful environment possible. Notable amongst the women publishing handbooks on architecture (Cole 1973) were Harriet Beecher Stowe and her sister, Catherine Beecher, whose books appeared in the mid-nineteenth century.

At the time of the Beecher sisters' writing, women's domain might have been centered in the home and church, but what is apparent from the content of the nineteenth-century publications was that they worked within the restrictions placed upon "respectable" women by society. These restrictions relegated these women to involvement with home and family and their work within the church. The popularity of these homemaking publications demonstrated that women's voice in evaluating the physical environment was never silent. It also indicates how intelligent women, who because of their respectability were "trapped" into limited means of expression, found outlets for their creativity. The outcome was to take a fervent interest in what *was* their concern—their homes and families.

What becomes apparent in all of these descriptions of domestic architecture is that while women were (and still are) more accepted as designers of domestic environments, many more homes have been designed by men practitioners than by women since architecture became a profession. The question of how women architects feel about being relegated to the domestic scene is perhaps one clue to their feelings about their role as professional designers. Is designing homes to be avoided at all costs—as "the kiss of death" to a woman's career? Or are women architects happy to be involved, finding great satisfaction in carrying through their ideas on domestic organization? The question that of necessity follows has to be: have they had any choice?

THE WOMEN'S RESPONSES

In the interviews, women architects discuss their experiences as students and professionals and finally address aspects of masculine versus feminine design. In the text that follows I have clustered the answers to each of the questions to reinforce the message I have received from the interviews. The women's responses should be read keeping in mind that their experiences have shaped what is now their professional credibility.

The Shaping of a Woman's Experience through Education

In response to the question, "Do you think/feel that you were treated differently from your male counterparts when you were a student—because of being a woman student of architecture?," the women interviewed described their experiences as follows.

The first woman interviewed at the UIFA Conference is a native of Washington, DC, where she has gone to college, raised a family of four children, and practiced architecture. Describing her experiences as a student in the late 1940s:

They sort of dared you to succeed. . . . I think they did give us [the women] probably the severest criticism because the hierarchy had said that they should take in women, the architectural school itself didn't particularly want them—they took in blacks before they took in women.

   The same three questions were asked of three women architects from China interviewed at the UIFA Conference. Their responses to the questions have been included as an example of the contrasts and similarities between Western and non-Western cultures. One woman interviewed was from Shanghai and the other two were from Beijing. These women were confident that all are treated equally regardless of gender. "Before 1949 it [China] was very different, but now it is equal."

   Also interviewed at the UIFA Conference was a woman landscape architect from New South Wales, Australia, originally from New Zealand. After raising four children, she returned to take a postgraduate course in landscape architecture instead of resuming her architectural practice. When asked if women students were treated differently from their male colleagues, she responded by describing her experiences as an undergraduate:

A little. I was the only woman in the class, and I think I was a bit of a rarity, something unusual. We went away for a weekend to look at a site and because I was the woman, I had to have a separate tent from everyone else who were all in together. . . . There were things like that where they felt a bit nervous, I think, about a woman being there. . . . I wasn't aware of any discrimination, it seemed to me quite OK. Unless I was just not listening to them, I don't remember any issues. . . . It was only later on when I went to work that I became more aware of those things. As a student I really didn't find any great problem.

   At the conference a woman architect from Missouri was also interviewed. She had attended Bryn Mawr followed by graduate study at Columbia University, a school deliberately chosen because its architecture program had the highest number of women students at that time (mid-1970s). In a discussion of student experiences on American campuses, the respondent described her experiences with fellow students (both male and female) as having been positive. On the other hand, most of the studio professors were male and the respondent's experiences with some indicate that they had difficulty dealing with women students. The prejudice described in this interview was more subtle than that often experienced by the women respondents. This woman's male professors made it very difficult to "elicit a genuine response from a professor or get . . . genuine criticism, because I was . . . being patted on the head and told 'that's nice'." For the most part, the respondent reported that her professors kept their sexist prejudices under wraps. What she found much more difficult was dealing with their egos:

It was their response to me of saying, a very paternalistic, "oh, isn't this sweet" and refusing to give me any genuine feedback on a project, or when I would question what they had said or try to engage them in some sort of dialogue, just being so horrified and offended that I should even ask them a question that they would just blow up and start yelling and screaming. . . . But that didn't happen very often. . . . In third year there I had a guy tell me I had no sense of space. . . . In a private review . . . my professor had this one guy going over our work for the semester, he said something about my project that I didn't agree with and I said so and he blew up and started telling me all this shit. Well, I knew at the time that it was his ego we were dealing with and not my work. But that was more unusual. Most of the professors, 75 percent of them were male, most of them were real good.

The New Zealand architect described one of the most negative aspects of her student experiences as having been told when she entered (as were all of the women architecture students) that:

three out of four women will fail—will not make it through to the end of the course. They never told the men what their failure rate was . . . . They would deliberately tell the women what their failure rate was. . . . You were neurotic to begin with. . . . Am I going to be one of the ones? We never heard about women architects at all, they didn't exist, . . . I was told, "you don't need to know about this kind of stuff, don't worry your pretty little head about it."

The first woman interviewed at the ARCC Research Conference noted that her experiences were different from those of most of her colleagues, since she entered as an adult in her mid-30s and had already had careers in other fields. Those experiences included participation in the feminist movement from the late 1960s to early 1970s (she began her architectural studies in the mid-1970s). This woman had always wanted to be an architect but had been actively discouraged by persons counseling her on her choices. She had been told that no one would hire her, and that if they did, she would not get very challenging work and would be "relegated to designing kitchens." She also was told that if she did choose architecture as a career she would have to give up any ideas of having a marriage and a family and dedicate her life to her work since architecture was "a real calling."

Despite this apparent discouragement, this respondent was not bitter about how her plans had been delayed; rather, she stated that she had felt that her counselors had her best interests at heart. A positive note in her narrative came when she described how her having come to architectural studies so late resulted in her having a "different perspective from that of an 18-year-old." Moreover, from having been active in the women's movement, she "showed up with a whole set of support systems," recognizing sexism and how it works, and not as a student to be "molded by willful teachers."

In the 1970s, when this woman began her architectural studies, the faculty included only one woman. The respondent's assessment of architectural school was that it was a "grueling, difficult experience to go through." She observed:

When I went to architecture school . . . there seemed to be a great deal of difference in terms of how women students were dealt with. . . . Women had to meet certain requirements that were sort of unwritten requirements. One of the most interesting was that you had to be, have some level of physical attractiveness—and that those women students who were too fat or ugly, I'm talking about in terms of male assessment . . . would get a lot of pressure. They were told in all sorts of direct and indirect ways that they weren't architecture material. If you didn't meet this sort of minimum requirement for physical attractiveness you were really forced out of the school—in subtle kinds of ways.

The other thing is the metaphors—the ways in which men would talk about skills needed for architecture or skills that could be transferred into architecture—were all from the male world. I had a teacher, for example, who thought that you couldn't be an architect unless you knew how to work on cars, that sort of thing. So there was a whole value system that was perhaps invisible some of the time but . . . or at least not explicit some of the time that operated in the architecture school which made life as a student more stressful for women.

Another woman interviewed at the ARCC Research Conference, now a professor of architecture at a midwestern university, described how her having married while she was in school gave her a different perspective on education. She refused to devote all of her time to working in the design studio, preferring instead to seek a balance between personal life and professional life. She has now been married 22 years. She noted that on one studio project they were given an extended deadline and she decided to use the extra time to do a "really good perspective drawing." After spending the day completing the drawing, she got very good reactions from all of her professors but one. After the review she asked him, "Why didn't you give me an 'A'?" He responded, "women can't draw that well."

My own experiences as a student of architecture include similar confusing and sometimes painful experiences. One that occurred very early in my education (sophomore year perhaps) was to have a professor tell me that I was "taking a deserving young man's place" by being a student in the architecture program. I reacted by telling this professor that "when he makes my grades he can have my spot!" Even as early as high school I had already learned that there was great opposition to women entering the profession. As an entrant in a regional science fair in the "architecture" category, I had been told by a woman judge who had overheard the judges discussing my project that the judges had all been in agreement that my project was the best but they wanted to encourage a young man, so he got first place. That had been an eye-opening year for learning about discrimination on a personal level—earlier, the architect judging my high school science fair told me he had had to give the first place to me but to never come to him looking for a job as he would never hire a woman.

What has been described focuses on the negative aspects of what we as women students in what has been a male-dominated profession have experienced. That all of the respondents had continued on to develop into contributing professionals attests to their belief in their ability, intelligence, and that they have something to contribute to the field. What we did not realize until much later, if at all, was that the denigration of our work by our professors devalues it. Many of the women respondents recognize now that they have learned to think, design, and act as professionals in a masculine way, "playing the game" as their male professors deemed suitable and perhaps losing something of themselves along the way.

Women as Professional Architects

In responding to this question, the women's discussion of their experiences as professional architects included elements of their personal lives that we have all had deleted from our professional lives. In stark contrast to this, it seems that males rarely discuss family matters with colleagues unless that person is a close personal friend and/or somehow knows the family. Regardless of whether or not it is discussed, the family, personal relationships, and outside interests and distractions were repeatedly brought up in the women respondents' descriptions of their professional experiences. While this may appear to be a relatively minor difference, I suspect that its inclusion is indicative of its importance and impact. The question as stated was, "Considering your answers to the first two questions, how do you think/feel your ideas or experiences concerning your responses affect your work as a professional (your work as a professional managing projects and/or as a designer)?"

In the statistical data cited by Torre (1977:157), she quotes the AIA research into the status of women, noting that while men were encouraged to take time out from work to teach, if women took time out for child-care activities they risked their jobs. The respondents' inclusion of their family corroborates the above, as the women describe what they faced as wives and mothers juggling career and homemaking. As clearly as if they had stated aloud, "You can be an architect, but only if you finish all of your other chores first," their employers had established another hurdle to block the women's professional development. Differences in male versus female interests are apparent in the respondents' descriptions of every aspect of their professional lives, including casual dialogues with colleagues.

Asked how women's discussion topics differ from the men's, especially at conferences, the midwestern architect commented:

[women from] countries . . . in which the feminist movement perhaps hasn't had as much effect as it has in the United States, I found those people speaking more about their roles as mothers or mentioning it in their talks, saying that as women architects we are professionals. . . . A French woman talked about how we had to be professionals, we had to be mothers, we had to be wives and above all to be seductive and I thought that would never be said in an American woman's group. For better or for worse, that is not acknowledged, that that's an aspect of our life—our professional lives. At a professional conference like this, no one would say that . . . because we're trying to be like men.

What some of my women respondents have had to do in order to do their work and raise families, rarely with formal help from society in the form of day-care centers, illustrates one of the stumbling blocks they have had to overcome in order to enter the profession. It becomes part of the test of worthiness that demands that women run farther, jump higher, and endure longer than what is expected of their male counterparts. In view of this it is no wonder that inclusion of their family circumstances is a necessary part of the story. Examples of this were the experiences of the Washington, DC respondent as a young architect practicing throughout her years of child raising as related with good humor: "If you want to get a building permit fast, take your 4-year-old little boy with you and take a buddy of his. . . . They get you through fast." She and her partner, who was not an architect,[5] used to have to take their children along on jobs, often having to "play pass the baby" while measuring for drawings.

In describing their experiences as women professionals, one of the three Chinese women commented:

woman is tired . . . we have to do housework, so we are tireder than men. . . . My husband hates my job. He said to me "you love your job but don't like me." My daughter loves my job . . . they will learn the same. . . . She is a student [of architecture]—I told her she will be tired.

Because Chinese homes have few if any labor-saving appliances and because Chinese women are still expected to take care of the housework, these architects experience perhaps an even more difficult situation than their American counterparts.

Another topic producing great frustration, disillusionment, and anger has been unfair treatment by employers, clients, and colleagues concerning wages, job assignments, and opportunities for advancement. For example, describing what occurred after she began working, the woman from New South Wales responded:

The first thing that struck me as really unfair was that there were three of us who joined at the same time . . . and I started getting less money after about six months . . . and that was something that I just couldn't accept, couldn't understand, 'cause I was better than the other two fellows anyway. And to be paid less just seemed to me quite absurd. . . . But, apart from that, I wasn't aware of any great problems when I was working in this firm.

Continuing, describing her experiences having her own practice for five years:

I think you do meet a bit of discrimination once you start working for yourself. There are certain jobs you get and certain jobs you don't get and I think that's related to where you meet the clients. . . . I don't think I got much commercial or industrial work. I

got a lot of work for schools, a certain amount of domestic work, but very little industrial or commercial work.

The woman architect from New Zealand worked in a four-person (all-female)
firm. The founder had done so in response to becoming "fed up" with her
previous employers' lack of support when two of her former clients had re-
quested that she be removed from their jobs, because they did not want a
woman working on their projects. The previous firm's partners did not support
her work and made the situation even worse by telling her exactly why she was
removed from the jobs, thus undermining her confidence.

The woman boss also found that she had been getting relatively less important contracts as well. The "young guys" had been getting better work while
she was confined to more mundane jobs for which the fees were relatively
lower, justifying her having a lower wage than her colleagues. Both the respondent and her female colleagues had experienced their male colleagues being
supportive when they first arrived at the firm and the rapid cooling of the atmosphere when these same men came to the realization that the women's work
was as good as theirs.

Her reaction to this lack of consideration and faith was to start her own firm
into which she brought only women employees. The women in the firm realized that the all-female policy was "kind of illegal" but the head had realized
how much time she had spent "boosting their [male] egos all the time, telling
them they'd done a wonderful job." Being an all-female firm did have its
humorous moments:

the good thing about being an all-woman firm is that clients come to us very aware that
it's all woman. And they know, so we don't get any problems. We only had one
problem, being an all-woman firm, and that was trying to figure out how high to hang
a wall-hung urinal in a men's toilet in a hotel. That's the only problem we had. It
wasn't in our graphic standards, so we actually rang up the manufacturer who burst out
laughing—saying, "well it depends on the height of the joker, doesn't it?" So we left
it up to the guys on site in the end. . . . How the hell did we know?

That these women architects have had to endure professional jealousy and
egotistical behavior on the part of male colleagues might be dismissed as something anyone—male or female—might have to tolerate. However, these women
have observed how their male colleagues act among themselves in contrast to
what they have experienced in similar situations. To hear a woman say "he
wouldn't have said that to me, or acted like that, if I'd been a man" brings a
sigh of recognition and agreement from most women colleagues. A colleague's
husband explained to me that underlying the man's reluctance to "let fly" his
temper at male colleagues is the threat that if pushed too far, they will literally
hit back. The woman colleague who gets the brunt of her male colleague's
temper—is perhaps the recipient because she is perceived as not willing or not
capable of hitting back.

The women architects' responses have included many examples of open discrimination on the part of their employers and colleagues. They also have brought up the conflicts introduced into their personal lives by the demands placed upon their time and energy and family and home life by the work itself. Interestingly, none of the respondents has wanted to get rid of that responsibility, for they recognize it as a vital part of their selves.

This may be a clue to the question of whether or not women architects consider domestic design projects as work to which they are relegated. It seems, though, that the design of intricate spaces demanding detailed knowledge of functional requirements as well as the spatial needs of activity and inspiration are fascinating to female architects. As noted below, the women architects interviewed for this study explain why the field of architecture fascinates them and why they believe they have a unique contribution to make to the profession. Interesting also is that although women want equal pay for equal work and do want interesting projects, none of the respondents described the less interesting work as being unworthy of their attention and best efforts. That their male colleagues often make this distinction is suggested in the earlier comments that describe relegation to designing less important work as a way male employers kept their female employees from advancing.

Masculine Versus Feminine Aspects of Design

As stated the question was: Do you think/feel that there are masculine versus feminine aspects to design? What becomes apparent from the respondents' reactions to this question is that they have very definite ideas about what makes design masculine or feminine. Regardless of the fact that many of the respondents acknowledge that their design thinking and approaches to problem solving may have been unduly influenced by their male professors and employers, the characteristics of feminine ways of knowing and analyzing described by Franck (1989) are repeatedly restated in the following interviews. Franck's (1989) concluding statement reiterates these characteristics:

Although this essay follows earlier feminist thinking in architecture and other fields, it is still only part of a fledgling effort to outline a feminist approach to architecture. Connectedness and inclusiveness, the ethic of care and the value of everyday experience, subjectivity and feelings, complexity and change are only some of the qualities that a feminist approach to architecture might well encourage.

With this in mind, the respondent's reactions may be searched for contradictions and additional concepts that focus on differences in male versus female approaches to design thinking. Asked if there are masculine versus feminine aspects to design, the architect from Missouri responded:

When I look at a building I can't say . . . that was designed by a woman or that it was designed by a man, possibly if we weren't all trained in the same schools to do the same sort of architecture one might find differences—maybe we all do masculine architecture. I don't know. My personal feeling is that men and women don't naturally design things differently or think differently—maybe that's because we all get taught to think like men and if somehow we were trained differently we might do different architecture. I don't know. But I've certainly never thought looking at a building—oh, that must have been designed by a woman.

However, reasons for apparent anonymity of building design should not be considered primarily as the result of all architects having been taught by male professors, and thus being expressions of some masculine approach; the client's circumstances and aspirations also have been contributing factors—and are often the most powerful factor. Discovering implicit gender-related meaning in design is an intriguing notion, sometimes explored by individual women out of their own personal quests for meaning in their work. The architect from New Zealand, who had worked in the all-woman firm, described one example of personal exploration:

I ran some women-only studio programs at the School of Architecture in Auckland . . . and it was really interesting. . . . When I was going through school, people kept on sort of saying, "Ah well, women design differently to men." And that's all they'd say. They'd never sort of said why or how, they'd mutter something about, "Ah, woman's work's a bit softer, got more curves in it," or something like that, and I just wanted to explore what it might be women designing without men being in the group or men being around them. So I used to take the group off and we'd be quite separatist for the three or five weeks that we were away. It was really quite interesting because they produced really interesting and really strong work. . . . I don't think you can look at architecture and say, "A woman did that or a woman didn't do that. . . ." I think people look at a lot of women's work and they see a lot of curves, and they sort of go, "Ah well, it's sensual, it's the body, it's harking back to the womb," and all that kind of stuff. I used to think that, but I don't think that so much any more. I think curves have got more to do with openness, with wanting to break out. And I think that is what women's work is about, they're actually wanting to break out of the confines of architecture that men have dictated for them. Like men have built them great tower blocks that they've never had to live in or they've built them isolated suburban homes for women to live these sort of isolated places. And I think women's work is about trying to break out of these things.

This theme of design by men for women recalls what was noted at the beginning of this chapter, that women were limited or denied a place in the decision-making realm of the architectural profession. And it was the time during which the architectural profession had its coming of age that Modernism developed as an architectural design rationale. Several of the respondents' comments in the following quotes point to Modernism as a masculine approach to design thinking. That researchers such as Schaef (1985) have described rationalist thinking as characteristic of masculine thinking, and as contrasted with intuitive, multivariate thinking being feminine, corroborates this idea. Another respondent, who works as a researcher at a school of architecture, noted that:

as there are now more women faculty, the whole ambience is changing, but part of that is because the models for architectural thinking have been changed a lot. I went to a school where the Modern Movement was still very much alive. And that from my point of view, the Modern Movement in architecture is a male period—architect as controller, as hero, the value system that operates in Modernism is a gender-specific value system. . . . What was difficult in the education I received, was that Modernism and the maleness that it implies, the maleness approach to architecture, was presented as Architecture and not as one version of architecture. And I think that has changed somewhat, because Modernism has certainly been called into question in the last few years in various ways so I think that . . . the change in attitude that allows more approaches to architecture has been helpful to women students. I think that the pluralism in architecture helps me create a different kind of environment.

Another issue raised by the interviews was that of how men versus women conceptualize spatial solutions. When I asked the same questions of a group of six women (five architects and one engineer) at the UIFA Conference, one responded:

I had heard another aspect of that recently at the AIA Convention—the idea that men and women are essentially the same, they design the same, they can deal with construction, they can deal with the math and the art, all that at the same level, and I agree with that, but she [the speaker was a woman architect who teaches in New York] was talking about women—women design from the outside in—that they are much more conscious of other people's reaction to them. . . . Maybe that's a result of socialization—as a person first, they design from the outside in so they are more concerned with conceptualizing spaces. They are more aware of outsiders—how people perceive spaces. We are more aware of trying to socially design spaces as to how they are used rather than as to freestanding monuments or sculpture, or an art piece of itself, whereas men create from the inside out, they want to make a statement that stands alone and they are not so concerned with the social uses of that art—architecture.

Another woman added, "a result of that is that men think in elevation. They are looking at the building, the image of it, from the outside, and these women students are thinking in plan, how you get in, where do you go." A third commented:

To me this is an attitudinal difference not a real difference. The men are quick to know what makes them famous. They're quick to know what makes a project a magazine publication type of project . . . and care, and so they are looking at it like the creation of a work of art because they know that's what's going to get published and they know that's going to win the awards and they give a higher priority to that than the social issues because, well because they've got to be successful. And how do you be successful in the design field? If I'm going to be successful in the design field I'm going to do the same thing, [even though] I'm a woman. . . . . If I want to put other things before my career, and other things before my success, and other things before my design recognition, I'll play it differently. But if I want the design recognition—I'm going to play it like the men play it. That's the way the game's played. I think it's wrong that it is played that way but. . . .

A colleague in the group continues:

It's a different morality. I still argue because it's the same issue of intuition versus non-intuition. It's always been thought, when I was brought up, that intuition was bad because it was feminine and it was irrational and therefore it was not a viable tool. Well in my adult life, I've watched the whole attitude towards intuition change. It's now a valid tool, men use it, it's now all right for men to be intuitive. . . . I sense in the last five years, it's actually for men a valuable tool and if they can demonstrate that they're intuitive they've got a real leg up over the other guys. And that's a real recent phenomena, and I've watched this whole social attitude change on the issue of intuition. My male partner, which I had for 14 years, used to say, "Well, Beverly's intuitive, and I'm willing to accept that and I'm willing to go along with her decisions because I feel that I'm willing to accept that."

It may be intriguing to hypothesize that architectural design might also represent the femininity or masculinity of the author. As has been suggested before, several of the women respondents have said that they see no real difference between their work and that of male colleagues. Also noted earlier was the fact that this could be the result of the design being done for a client (whose needs must be satisfied) and the possibility that this has resulted from most of the women having (so far) been taught to design by men. The women respondents have, however, described a gender difference in attitude that relates to the manner in which they have been acculturated. What is apparent from the discussion of differences in approach to career advancement is that several women respondents have linked their difference in approach to career to their commitments outside of their careers. Recognizing the limitations of this idea coming from so few respondents leads to the suggestion that this might be a most intriguing and enlightening topic for future research. This difference in attitude and its resultant variations in approach to problem solving manifest themselves most powerfully in the educational experiences of women architecture students and later in their careers when their work is judged using male rules to evaluate what is "good design".

A woman architect who teaches design at a midwestern university responded to the question about masculine versus feminine aspects of design when interviewed at the ARCC Research Conference:

as a starting point, I think that women do tend to think from the inside out, and I think it comes out of women's concerns for the social network and also the role that women have played in the home as looking out on the world—versus the male role from out in the world looking into the home . . . that there is this difference in the two. . . . But I don't know whether it's biological or cultural, and that's not necessarily important except in our society . . . that is one difference.

Another difference is that I think, as a rule, women tend to be more process-oriented and the men are more product-oriented. And that also reinforces then the outside-inside, because a product is something that you deal with from an image perspective, you deal with a product in a very superficial way. Whereas a process you really have to engage in it, and so it tends to go on—the internal workings of a building would become much more of a process orientation concerned with that.

This respondent's comments reinforce those stated earilier, even though there is a reversal of terminology as regards "inside versus outside." The concept put forward in both focuses on the connectedness referred to by Franck (1989). The respondent continues, describing her way of bringing a female approach to design thinking into the educational setting, the design studio:

women students and male students are treated differently . . . and I think it comes out of architecture being a male profession. Values are male values. So, a male values the exterior of the building, and if [the male architectural designer] does value the interior, but it really is not something that is dwelt on, at least in schools, although people think it has to work because, obviously, in the pragmatic sense you can't design a building that doesn't work that way. There is not . . . an understanding among women practitioners that the meaning comes from this exterior thing. The exterior thing is given meaning from the way the interior thing operates—the process. Often women are spending a lot of time with students in dealing with the thing they feel is going to create the most meaning and then it isn't valued in the product. So, obviously it takes more practice as a teacher, because I feel that part of my role is to really deal with the process of the way things are done in the studio. And I think it does support women, not necessarily by actively going out saying I'm going to work with the women, but if you can support those ideas, women's projects suddenly start looking really good. Whereas if you don't value those ideas, women can learn to operate in that arena and they learn to deal with the male values, but I think it suppresses certain rich things that women have to offer to the field, if that isn't dealt with.

Several different issues have surfaced in response to the question of masculine versus feminine aspects of design. The first and perhaps more obvious issue focuses on the design work itself; that is, whether spatial forms reflect gender. The interviews indicate that there are many ways of addressing this issue. One would be to focus on the archaeological/anthropological basis of traditional shapes and forms, materials and functions of buildings and sites. Rounded, curvilinear forms, and softness of texture have all been suggested as perhaps traditionally feminine in their design qualities. However, one must then ask whether these design elements have been deliberately defined by males to represent feminine aspects of design. Another way to focus on this issue is to examine how the persons constructing the buildings and sites were influenced by their local materials; for example, Cole (1973) describes Native American and pioneer women using whatever materials they had available to fashion whatever was suitable to the family's needs.

Perhaps the most intriguing issue raised by the respondents has been the notion that architects design in the way they have been taught. The majority of women architects interviewed for this paper, and the majority of women architects in practice today, have been taught by men. Add to this the notion that between women and men architects there are fundamental differences in approach to design and to social and cultural issues, and the question arises, how much do women students have to sublimate of themselves in order to complete their design education? There are positive as well as negative aspects to this issue. To label as ineffectual the manner in which architects are educated and trained through apprenticeship to full professional status is a misnomer. A better assessment would be to say that for some persons seeking to become professional architects the educational/apprenticing sequence is limiting. Women do have a contribution to make to what has, so far, been a male-dominated profession. Looking back at women's continuous involvement in the creation of shelters, one might say that women entering the architecture profession are staging a sort of "home coming."

The question that arises here is how the educating of architects is dominated by masculine notions of what is "good" design and "good design thinking." If one accepts Schaef's (1985) ideas that gender differences in socialization manifest themselves in thinking and problem solving then it makes sense to look more carefully at the education of what is fundamentally a problem-solving profession. Women students of architecture as well as women professionals need to address the issue of how much of their professional selves has been sublimated in order to have their work considered "good." This exercise should not be limited to women architects only. One respondent had stated earlier that being able to design intuitively—long disdained as "not good" and "unsuitable" and as a feminine/woman's domain—has now become accepted as "good," "desirable," and a "way to get a leg up" on colleagues who cannot. What is ironic about this final coming of age of intuitive thinking is its sometimes unsuitable pairing with logical problem-solving sequences. The entire education system, with its math and science based problem-solving skills, still leaves one inherently leery of the multivariate thinking that best accompanies intuitive thinking.

The midwestern architecture professor described her role as a professional designer, focusing on differences between herself and a male colleague concerning what was suitable, or "good" information for presentation in a seminar:

I'm a person who has taken the tack that I want to use my feminine side of myself as an asset, so I did not repress that and learn to think like a man, which I see probably 50 percent of the women or more do that in order to function in the profession. It means that . . . the research is integrated. I don't separate the different aspects of my [work]. I don't separate teaching from research nearly the way men do. . . . I just did a presentation the other day in someone's class. . . . Afterwards he criticized what I did and I realized that what I was trying to present were all the connections between all different aspects of the research and he didn't want me to talk about the connections. He wanted me to talk about the different pieces of it.

Because my approach is more integrated or holistic, I have experienced similar disagreements with colleagues who evaluate my work as "not good" because it is not what they do nor does it fit into the mold they have experienced as students and later as professionals. Specifically, one difference is that I wait a very long time before establishing categories. Recently, this difference between my approach and that of my colleagues has become more glaringly apparent. While I am capable of exploring (and often do explore) my research topics and problem-solving activities in a logical, sequential fashion, I often do not want to when beginning a project. After numerous years of multivariate thinking, using intuition to temper research explorations, I feel limited when categorization and labeling is required at an early stage of the work.

Likewise, the architecture professor from the Midwest noted:

In the normal woman's way of categorizing, I think that women, when they do do categories, they wouldn't just start at the beginning by labeling them and men would start from the very first thing devising these labels. And so I think often that that's what women have to contribute is to get out structure [get rid of], hold back, because we want to find the structure before we get to the labels, whereas the men feel that the label is the structure. . . . And they'll force things into these categories even if they don't like them. And then many men won't even stand back and realize that they've forced something into the categories because of the way they started. I think a woman, most women would not.

This professor thought that women researchers and designers approach design related to the way that they see the environment and in the way that they see things through their relationships with people, whereas the men's approach is more concerned with the making of a thing symbolic of something. What Schaef (1985) has pointed out is that relationships are central to women's universe and they are not central to men's. This would seem to corroborate the above comments on the focus of feminine versus masculine aspects of design.

Another professor of architecture from the Northeast discusses masculine versus feminine aspects of design, describing what Franck (1989) included as a necessary characteristic of a feminist approach to design, that of accepting "subjectivity and feelings, complexity and change," as well as "connectedness." The northeastern professor stated:

I think there are masculine and feminine aspects of design. I think in a very blatant way if you take conventional ways of looking at what masculine means and feminine means, masculine is often aggressive, pushing, and feminine is much more receptive. . . . [Now] we're looking at things as objects. I think the object orientation is not a female . . . way of looking at things. . . . As we attempt to isolate as opposed to pull to- gether—I think that's a more masculine way of looking at things as opposed to feminine way of looking at things. . . . I don't think that the whole feminine notion is after all this separation, I think it is about connection. And so I think that it also has to do with loss of control over many things. I'll say modes of production, what is going on in the world at large. . . . If it was a feminine response it would be more to accept the level of chaos, level of ambiguity, . . . and sort of work with that and actually look very deeply into why we have this . . . futility. How could we transform it in a very easy way?

What we might focus upon as women searching for understanding of our roles as architects and architectural educators is hinted at in the interviews, where the respondents have described masculine versus femine approaches to design thinking. Looking at what they have described as masculine approaches could help me to understand my confusion when, as an undergraduate student of architecture, a professor complimented my work, saying, "You do very masculine design." My first reaction was to take his assessment as the compli- ment it was meant to be. My silent reaction was to wonder, "What the hell does he mean by that?" Thinking back on this, I realize that the power of this comment was that it overlooked my gender. My work can never be truly mas- culine. How frustrating to always be trying to live up to a goal that can never be achieved. As several women noted, since women architects were taught by men, they were taught to think like men. In retrospect, my professor's compli- ment affirmed this. I now see my professor's assessment as a dissolution disem- powering me as a designer. Although I was aware as a student of the potential discrimination I faced in my chosen profession, nothing prepared me for the pain of being considered inadequate because I am of the "wrong" gender.

Awareness of being denigrated or disempowered by male professors or by colleagues always comes as an unexpected and unnecessary distraction to a person's work. As students, some of us have handled it by fighting back and by playing the game by "masculine" rules, designing according to what was considered appropriate. As many respondents have stated, women have suc- ceeded by learning the masculine rules.

This raises a more fundamental question. If there truly are differences in how men and women perceive the world, how they function in relationships, and how they solve problems, how may women architects recognize these dif- ferences in their work as practitioners and as professors of design? As architec- tural theorists explore and propose alternatives to Modernism as the basis for design thinking, the formula by which Modernist design has been taught—its problem-solving methodology and thus the tenets of "rational thinking"—is being challenged. In a pluralistic society, groups other than white males assume leadership responsibilities. In looking for these new voices, women's ap- proaches to thinking and exploration of ideas hopefully will come to be valued.

CONCLUSIONS

What I have learned about women colleagues since the inception of this research has allowed me to come to some understanding of the collective experience of the women architects interviewed. For example, one emotion shared by the respondents was that it truly helps to know that each has not been the only one to feel as she has. This awareness of a shared history does not remove the anger felt concerning inequities in the workplace and university setting, but it does help to have someone say, ''I have shared your rage, you are not crazy, and you are not alone.'' This does not necessarily lead to acceptance, but it is the first step in a search for new directions to be taken in architectural education, and perhaps a greater understanding of differing approaches to professional practice and design.

At one time, I had intended to limit the interviews to women from roughly the same age group as myself, because younger academic generations may have had a less sexist experience as students, since open verbal discrimination has become illegal. The focus on masculine versus feminine may have been altered as well, as acceptance of intuitive thought is given more credence. However, as I transcribed the interview tapes it became apparent that several of the younger women interviewed had had experiences that made it appear that, although it is now illegal to discriminate based on a person's sex, the practice continues. That issues of sex discrimination in architectural education have perhaps become more covert may make it even more important to discuss their effects and consequences.

A goal of this research has been to identify issues faced by women architects. The most desirable outcome would be to suggest solutions to remove some of the present barriers faced by women architecture students that might hinder their having good experiences as students and later as professionals. It is apparent from the interviews that understanding and learning to cope with our experiences have been important parts of the professional lives of many of the women architects. Often just understanding the reasons for those experiences can lessen or alleviate their pain. Better still, we may be able to alter or eliminate some of the causes completely. In addition, this focus on women in architecture should also lead to a better understanding of the needs of men in the profession. For example, male students also may reject the formal approaches to design thinking espoused by a school. So the focus should be upon looking at multivariate ways of thinking about design issues; not eliminating Modernist rational thinking but allowing other intuitive voices to speak as well.

One of my final interviews was with a woman who teaches architecture at a university in the Deep South. She recommended that all architects become more sensitive to both the content of design teaching and to the manner in which it is taught. In the interviews, several of the women expressed dismay at the brutality of the manner in which students' work is evaluated. If we are to begin recognizing the other voices in design thinking, we have to learn to listen to ideas in a different way as there is undoubtedly more than one way to approach design.

What is needed now is a serious look at those other voices, those of women architects, both as students and as working professionals. There are other ways to think about design; there are other ways to approach problem solving. What is needed is to open an already pluralistic society to accepting what it already has—pluralistic thinking—by recognizing and validating those other approaches. To begin by looking at women working as professionals in male-dominated fields is one way to do this.[6]

It is my hope that the silencing of the creative voices of women designers through the negation of their power to think and solve problems will end. This negation of women's power to design and to decide too often has been the norm. The assumption that masculine thinking and problem solving is superior because it is rational and a part of the tradition of male domination of the architectural profession ignores the pluralism of our society. Since intuitive reasoning has become more accepted as a viable aspect of design thinking, this indicates a shift of focus from the rigidity of rational, Modernist solutions. Women in architecture have an eloquent voice. It is my hope that they will be heard.

NOTES

I wish to acknowledge all the women I have interviewed. Their candor and eloquence is evident on the preceeding pages. Also, I wish to thank the women who have sent me their articles and have suggested background readings.

1. Not all of the women interviewed are quoted here.
2. The three questions were not always asked in this exact way.
3. To further define this, a "positive" reaction to context would include buildings and outdoor environments designed to fit in to their setting, and this could be either as focal point(s) or as background to other buildings and landscape. What is meant by "neutral" context could best be defined by the anonymous style of modern buildings found in numerous cities where there are numerous International Style buildings. An example of "opposition" or "negative" reaction to context would be buildings and/or outdoor environments that seem out of place or inappropriate to their setting, forming neither background nor focal points in keeping with their setting. Regardless, architectural design always establishes some relationship to context.
4. Ellen Perry Berkeley is the editor of a forthcoming book, *Architecture: A Place for Women* for which two of the reviewed articles were written. Berkeley's writings on women in architecture include articles for major architectural publications. The NCARB mission includes not only the development of a registration exam but also the development with the AIA of guidelines for professional practice to be followed by apprenticing architects that soon will be mandatory in all states for persons seeking registration. The NCARB also facilitates reciprocity between state registration boards for registered architects wishing to practice in states other than those in which they are licensed. Their involvement with all state registration boards gives their statistical data a stronger base.

5. The respondent's partner was a school teacher who is now the chairperson of the speech and drama department of a local junior college.

6. The 1989 Annual Meeting of the Association of Collegiate Schools of Architecture (ACSA) has established a task force to "gather information about women's experiences" with a stated focus that their findings will "promote equitable policies and practices within the schools" (*ACSA News,* April 1989:3).

REFERENCES

ACSA News. 1989. 18 (8): 3.

Allen, Polly W. 1988. *Building Domestic Liberty: Charlotte Perkins Gilman's Architectural Feminism.* Amherst: University of Massachusetts Press.

American Institute of Architects Task Force on Women in Architecture. 1975. "Status of women in the architectural profession." Washington, DC: American Institute of Architects.

Belenky, Mary Field, et al. 1986. *Women's Ways of Knowing: The Development of Self, Voice, and Mind.* New York: Basic Books.

Bloomer, Jennifer. 1988a. "In the museyroom." *Assemblage: A Critical Journal of Architecture and Design Culture* 5:59–64.

———. 1988b. "Failed attempts to heal an irreparable wound." Paper presented at the Association of Collegiate Schools of Architecture forum, Chicago.

Cole, Doris. 1973. *From Tipi to Skyscraper: History of Women in Architecture.* Boston: MIT Press.

Fausto-Sterling, Anne. 1985. *Myths of Gender: Biological Theories About Women and Men.* New York: Basic Books.

Franck, Karen. 1989. "Towards a feminist approach to architecture." Unpublished manuscript.

Gilligan, Carol. 1977. "In a different voice: women's conceptions of self and morality." *Harvard Educational Review* 47:481–517.

Hayden, Dolores. 1977a. "Catherine Beecher and the politics of housework." Pp. 40–49 in *Women in American Architecture: A Historic and Contemporary Perspective,* edited by S. Torre. New York: Whitney Library of Design: Watson-Guptill Publications.

———. 1977b. "Challenging the American domestic ideal." Pp. 32–39 in *Women in American Architecture: A Historic and Contemporary Perspective,* edited by S. Torre. New York: Whitney Library of Design: Watson-Guptill Publications.

Jung, Carl G. (editor). 1964. *Man and His Symbols.* London: Aldus Books.

Kingsley, Karen. 1988. "Gender issues in teaching architectural history." *The Journal of Architectural Education* 41 (2): 21–25.

Martin, Rochelle. 1989. "Out of marginality: toward a new kind of professional." Pp. 205–211 in *Architecture: A Place for Women,* edited by E. P. Berkeley et al. Blue Ridge Summit, PA: Smithsonian Institution Press.

Matrix. 1984. *Making Space: Women and the Man Made Environment.* London: Pluto Press.

Schaef, Anne Wilson. 1985. *Women's Reality: An Emerging Female System in a White Male Society.* New York: Harper and Row.

Torre, Susana (editor). 1977. *Women in American Architecture: A Historic and Contem-*

porary Perspective. New York: Whitney Library of Design: Watson-Guptill Publications.

Webster's Ninth New Collegiate Dictionary. 1985. Springfield, MA: Merriam-Webster.

Wright, Gwendolyn. 1977. "The model domestic environment: icon or option?" Pp. 18–31 in *Women in American Architecture: A Historic and Contemporary Perspective*, edited by S. Torre. New York: Whitney Library of Design: Watson-Guptill Publications.

10

Art and Artist as Mediators and Creators of Paradox

Margaret Ford
(Introduction by Pamela R. Frese)

INTRODUCTION

Margaret Ford states that:

The very language of art suggests that nothing can be seen without its context; hence the terms figure/ground relationship, positive/negative space, and even male/female. As an artist I seek to understand the relationship between polar extremities and to find the ties that bind them together.

It is through herself as artist and through her art that Margaret identifies and mediates these polar categories.

One dilemma for the artist is the recognition that scholars will use her and her work as data and draw from it their own interpretations based upon their own perspectives of art and artist. The artist is also aware that she mediates between this interpretation and her unconscious selection of artistic forms and the symbols that give them meaning. For Margaret, the creation of art just happens, a product of inspiration and talent. Much later she could, if she wanted, sit back and analyze why she used particular elements in each work. But this is not her goal as artist, as creator. She views herself and her art as vehicles that mediate between unconscious cultural categories and our perceptions of the art work. But the artist also recognizes that she and her work are vehicles for the recreation of these cultural categories and paradoxes through our interpretations.

John Berger (1987 [1972]) has made a similar point in his seminal consideration of art and advertising. Our "way of seeing" is never settled; rather, our understanding of a reality is constantly being negotiated and reinterpreted. Most importantly: "We never look at just one thing; we are always looking at the relation between things and ourselves. Our vision is continually active, continually moving, continually holding things in a circle around itself, constituting what is present to us as we are" (Berger 1987 [1972]:9). In this sense, the editors of this volume perceive that Margaret's work reflects historical and mythical influences on the underlying structure of meaning in American culture. Her sculptures could be described as statements of gender domains, reflecting the natural complementarity of gendered oppositions, often through a "game" metaphor.

As a concluding pictoral essay, Margaret Ford summarizes in image the necessary complementarity of the genders. For a complete understanding of gender, one needs both masculine and feminine perspectives. One needs also to view gender as plastic, as shaped and defined in various contexts. "Seeing" gender, as it were, through the eyes of an artist presents a thought-provoking and eloquent conclusion to the discussion of gender in multidisciplinary perspective.

THE ARTIST'S VIEW

Over time I have made many attempts to create a figurative presence without being limited to strict anatomical representation. The composite nature of the work allows the figure to exist in relationship to other living forms or architectural settings. For example, in "Heartwood Home," the tree stump becomes a wooden structure which contains a figure becoming a tree—a cycle of living and dying.

This figure did not satisfy the quality of presence which I was seeking, so I eliminated the anatomical parts and was left with the garment or coat. While suggesting human presence and proportion, the coats in "Honeycomb" and "Gown of Thorns" allowed the exploration of inside/outside relationship—the contrast of external surface and inner space.

By 1981, after three years of exploring variations on this theme with "Moonglow" and "Two Step," the usefulness of the metaphor had run its course. I sensed that it would be necessary to confront once again a more direct rendering of the figure, but I had no idea how to accomplish this technically without changing the materials with which I worked.

Some experiments with tree branches showed me the possibilities of combining wood and clay. It took three years to develop the technical processes seen in "Blue Masquerade" and Fountain" and to hone the expressive urge which had required this change into a coherent idea.

These first figures were small in scale but they contain the basic format which is the focus of my work today. Each figure stands on a ground, a landscape. This place, a gameboard, a map, a horizon between land and sky, defines the arena in which the human being struggles to define an aspect of its identity.

While these figures are still composites, the tree branches provide an anatomy which is organic if not specifically of human proportion as in my sculpture "Pan Returns to a New Tune." Finding these figures in the natural growth of a tree allows me to discover distortions far more expressive than I would contrive on my own. In "Checkmate" and "Hecate's Doublecross," this expressiveness articulates the ideas which intrigue my intellect and stimulate my imagination: the nature of human bonding and separation, a sense of historical time and the process of change, the connection between a sense of self and a sense of place.

In two final examples of recent work I will share some details of my personal understanding of their meaning. "Fission/Fusion" refers to the sources of atomic energy. It seemed paradoxical that these two opposing actions—splitting apart and fusing together—both release great amounts of energy. This seems to be true of human relations as well. This dance of joining and separating is creative but we may also be burned. The format of the composition has antecedents in both medieval and Renaissance art. While it is not necessary for the viewer to play art-history detective, I hope that these references stir, at least subliminally, a sense of historical time and changing world views.

Since childhood I have known the story of Penelope from the Odyssey. In "Penelope Unravels Her Dreams," Penelope's right foot rests on Ithaca in the eastern Mediterranean. Having shared this island home with Ulysses, she kept it intact during his long journey of return from Troy. In the face of aggressive encroachment she kept her autonomy with wit and handicraft, weaving by day and unraveling at night, never reaching the deadline set for her acceptance of a new husband.

Many contemporary Penelopes are caught between their daytime hopes and dreams and the dissolution of their unconscious night. To grow beyond this dilemma we have to dismantle the dream that Ulysses will come to rescue us. By reversing the process of the classical Penelope we may use her courage and our own wit to unravel our nightmares and reweave a new reality.

REFERENCE

Berger, John. 1987 [1972]. *Ways of Seeing*. London: Penguin.

Illustration 10.1
"Heartwood Home"
by Margaret Ford, 1979; wood and clay, 62″ × 18″ × 12″. Photograph by Margaret
Ford

Illustration 10.2
''Honeycomb''
by Margaret Ford, 1979; ceramic, 20″ × 16″ × 9″. Photograph by Ed Marquand

Illustration 10.3
"Gown of Thorns"
by Margaret Ford, 1980; ceramic with rose thorns, 12″ × 14″ × 8″. Photograph by
Colleen Chartier

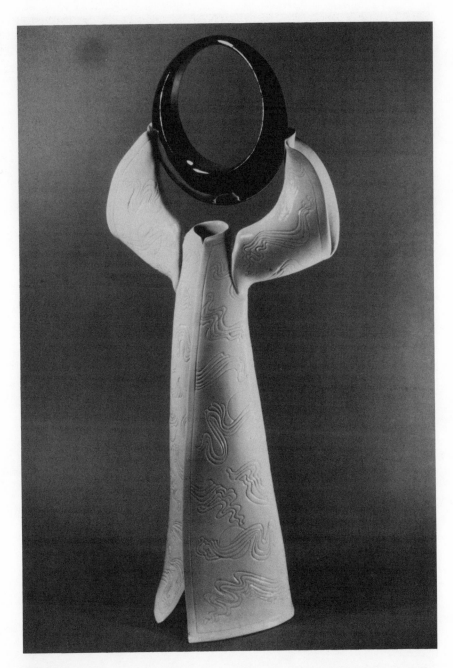

Illustration 10.4
"Moonglow"
by Margaret Ford, 1979; ceramic, 22½″ × 10″ × 6″. Photograph by Margaret Ford

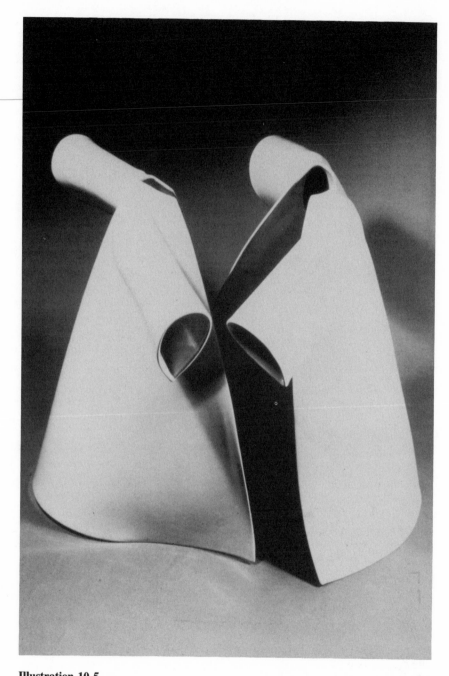

Illustration 10.5
"Two Step"
by Margaret Ford, 1981; ceramic, 17″ × 20″ × 13″. Photograph by Margaret Ford

Illustration 10.6
"Blue Masquerade"
by Margaret Ford, 1984; wood and clay, 25½″ × 16″ × 11½″. Photograph by Margaret Ford

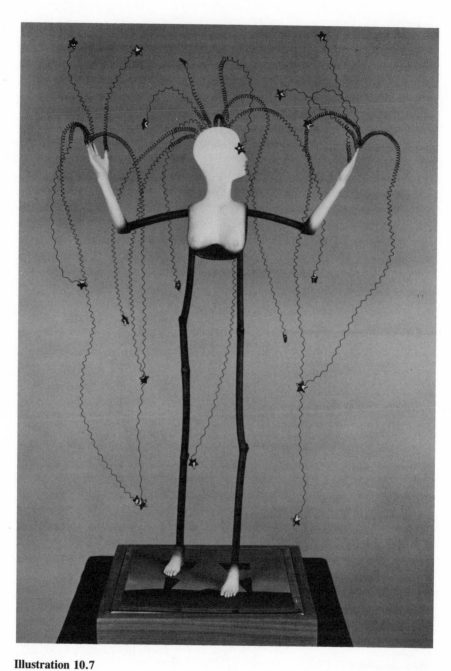

Illustration 10.7
''Fountain''
by Margaret Ford, 1984; clay, wood, and wire, 25½″ × 15″ × 9¼″. Photograph by
Eduardo Calderon

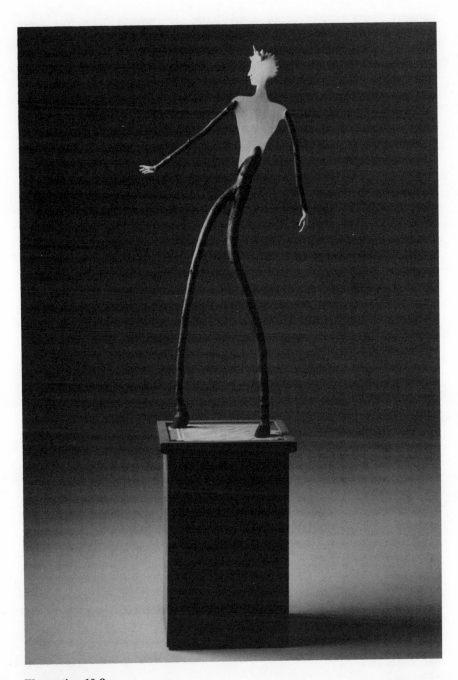

Illustration 10.8
"Pan Returns to a New Tune"
by Margaret Ford, 1986; wood and clay, 68″ × 21″ × 15″. Photograph by Anil Kapahi

189

Illustration 10.9
"Checkmate"
by Margaret Ford, 1986; wood and clay, 5′ × 33″ × 18″. Photograph by Margaret Ford

Illustration 10.10
"Hecate's Doublecross"
by Margaret Ford, 1989; mixed media. Photograph by Anil Kapahi

Illustration 10.11
"Fission/Fusion"
by Margaret Ford, 1986; wood and clay, 48″ × 24″ × 8″. Photograph by Margaret Ford

Illustration 10.12
"Penelope Unravels Her Dreams"
by Margaret Ford, 1986; wood, clay, and rayon cord. Photograph by Margaret Ford

Afterword

This book recognizes the power inherent in approaching the subject of gender from a multi-disciplinary perspective. In this book we use the term "gender" in its broadest sense to include an understanding of male and female as discrete yet interrelated cultural constructs. This allows us to include more diverse views in feminist discourse through the use of language that is not the jargon of a particular discipline but is a common parlance unifying disparate voices. We recognize that there are significant distinctions made by some scholars between the terms "gender" and "feminism." And we do not wish to diffuse this important discussion through our use of "gender" in the way that Castelli and McBride accuse some scholarly discourse of doing:

> "gender" has also turned up as a safer alternative than "women" in some curricula; just so, there is an emerging (and as yet uninterrogated) movement for establishing "gender studies" over against "women's studies" or "feminist studies" programs. "Gender" here implies the inherent balance that critics have sometimes accused feminist studies of lacking; here "gender" means "women and men" and implies an inclusive gesture that is certainly premature politically in that it settles the question before the question has been adequately formulated. (this volume, pp. 114–115)

The contributors to this volume represent a diversity in gender research, so the text in general explores various facets of the opposition of male and female modes of thought and how those modes are reflected in and are perpetuated by expressive culture, social institutions, and disciplinary epistemology.

It is a particularly Western desire to perceive new directions of investigation in terms of a promised mastery over a pristine, fertile wilderness. Women's studies, men's studies, gay studies, and the crucial arguments made by feminists of color are all engaged in some dimension of research into gender constructs and herald the opening of new frontiers of investigation. And all are essential elements of any holistic understanding of gender constructs.

There is an unfortunate tendency towards fragmentation within this rich and promising research on gender—indeed, even within disciplines—over the various uses of the term "feminist" and the differing understandings ascribed to a study of "gender." This fragmentation of a complex and multi-variate subject is accompanied by its frequent omission in disciplinary discourse; and institutional structures of other relevant perspectives that threatens to marginalize the entire topic.

There are certainly many different definitions of feminism and every discipline supports several interpretations of the relationship between gender and feminist thought. Consequently, every discipline can contribute an exciting diversity of perspective to any discussion of gender. It is important, however, that we not favor any one kind of disciplinary knowledge or theoretical perspective over another, or treat any particular view of feminism and gender as the only legitimate approach, but that we encourage a continued diversity of voices. It may be important to recognize that the study of gender may not "evolve" linearly, either within or outside of disciplinary territory, but rather in ever-increasing, all-encompassing spheres of complexity, a product of the critical thinking that emerges in intellectual frontiers.

Frontiers are inherently powerful areas of knowledge and Western culture depends on these metaphors to precipitate change. Our use of gender is designed to mark a frontier—and to help provide a bridge necessary to explore in exciting new directions.

GENDER AND FEMINISM IN ANTHROPOLOGY

Both editors of this volume are anthropologists. Although our work reflects two different dimensions of the anthropological study of gender, we feel that both of our chapters fit firmly within the current anthropological discourse on gender. More generally, it is possible to view this entire book as a "text" within the context of contemporary feminist anthropology.

Two related positions, both published in 1988, present excellent overviews on the anthropological treatment of gender constructs. Henrietta Moore and Judith Shapiro consider gender as a central issue in anthropological discourse but differ in their emphases on the importance of this term in relation to feminist concerns.

Henrietta Moore posits a three-stage development for the anthropological concern with gender that began in the 1970s: 1) a founding of women's studies in anthropology to critique male bias on a number of levels; 2) an expansion into gender studies and a recognition of the cultural definitions of male and female; and 3) the recent emergence of gender research as part of a feminist anthropology. Feminist anthropology, while incorporating all previous levels, holds a critical awareness of the interrelationships between gender, race, and class. Moore continues:

Feminist anthropology is not, however, the same thing as the "anthropology of gender." . . . The problem is really one of terminology, because it is perfectly possible to make a clear distinction between the study of gender identity and its cultural construction (the anthropology of gender) and the study of gender as a principle of human social life (feminist anthropology). (1988:188)

In addition, Shapiro argues for a broader understanding of gender, one that does more than merely recognize the "differentness of women and men" (1988:2). She urges us to examine critically our understanding of those differences in order to avoid prescribing gender roles and appropriate gendered (and disciplinary) perspectives.

Even within anthropology, this maturing of the discussion of feminism is not uniform in all scholarly work, but this does not devalue the gender issues which are raised. For example, the Frese and Coggeshall chapters in this book illustrate the study of gender in anthropology, and both authors acknowledge that they themselves are products of Anglo-American culture and disciplinary discourse. Coggeshall examines gender from a male perspective, but his work illustrates the power of culture to redefine gender. Even in the absence of a female gender, Coggeshall argues that the predominant male image of female becomes incarnated in submissive males, reflecting the status and power differences between genders in American culture in general, over and above race and class distinctions. Frese examines the prescribed gender roles and the perceived gender qualities that are perpetuated through time in expressive culture and ritual performance. The symbolism and ritual process of the American wedding reflects the dominant patriarchal Anglo-American culture and thus affects the actions and beliefs of all classes and ethnic groups to some degree.

Our book emphasizes disciplinary diversity and with few exceptions does not include an explicit consideration of the relationship between race, class, and gender. But this does not mean we consider those issues trivial, irrelevant, or unknowable. Rather our text attempts to address these concerns at the level of disciplinary epistemology and to indicate the varied levels of sophistication of feminist discourse in a number of intellectual perspectives. The absence of important discussions on race and class in this volume vividly reflects the many biases in Western culture, in social institutions, and at the level of disciplinary epistemology.

Let us learn from our intellectual diversity and seek an understanding of gender that allows all voices to be represented in this essential discussion. Let us go beyond many different boundaries in our attempt to comprehend the complexity of gender constructs in any society and the social institutions and cultural beliefs that perpetuate them. And most of all, let us be wary of traditional disciplinary paradigms that exclude those who explore and are a part of the frontiers. For, as Moore so persuasively argues:

The justification for doing feminist anthropology has very little to do with the fact that "women are women the world over," and everything to do with the fact that we need to be able to theorize gender relations in a way which ultimately makes a difference. (1988:198)

Readers may now ask, or in fact demand, of their own disciplines the depth of feminist discourse already existing in others. A conscious, critical awareness of the role that American culture and society play in gender constructs can also help to precipitate change. Indeed, whether in novels, in courtrooms, in theoretical formulations, or in the training of professionals, gender differences need not be transformed into gender subordination. Only by transcending the boundaries of disciplines can we begin to see how far we have come, or how far we still need to go.

REFERENCES

Moore, Henrietta L. 1988. *Feminism and Anthropology.* Minneapolis: University of Minnesota Press.
Shapiro, Judith. 1988. "Gender Totemism." Pp. 1–9 in *Dialectics and Gender: Anthropological Approaches,* edited by Richard R. Randolph, David M. Schneider, and May N. Diaz. Boulder, CO and London: Westview Press.

Index

About the Editors and Contributors

PAMELA R. FRESE received her Ph.D. from the University of Virginia. She is Assistant Professor of Anthropology at the College of Wooster in Wooster, Ohio. She conducts research and has published on religious symbolism, cross-cultural marriage beliefs and practices, American life-cycle rituals and ritual foods, and the ornamentation of American yards.

JOHN M. COGGESHALL obtained a Ph.D. from Southern Illinois University–Carbondale. He is an Assistant Professor of Anthropology at Clemson University, Clemson, South Carolina. Publications include a monograph on the German-Americans of southwestern Illinois, a volume (with Jo Anne Nast) on the area's vernacular architecture, and several other articles on midwestern folklore/folklife. His research interests also include prison culture and approaches to teaching ethnographic methodology.

MARYANN E. BRINK is an Assistant Professor of Medieval History at the College of William and Mary, Williamsburg, Virginia.

BARBARA S. BURNELL is an Associate Professor of Economics at The College of Wooster.

ELIZABETH CASTELLI is an Assistant Professor of Religious Studies at the College of Wooster.

MARGARET FORD, with an M.S.A. from the University of Washington, is a well-recognized sculptor residing in Seattle.

N. JANE HURT is an Associate Professor in the Department of Architectural Studies at Clemson University.

JAMES McBRIDE, Ph.D., is an Assistant Professor of Religion and Social Ethics at Fordham University in New York City.

SUSAN JARET McKINSTRY is an Associate Professor of English at Carleton College in Northfield, Minnesota.

SUSAN NEWTON is presently a Visiting Professor of Sociology at the Louisiana Scholars College at Northwestern State University of Louisiana, Natchitoches.

KAREN TAYLOR is an Assistant Professor of American Cultural and Women's History at the College of Wooster.

CLAUDIA THOMPSON is an Associate Professor of Psychology at the College of Wooster.

MARK WEAVER is an Associate Professor of Political Science at the College of Wooster.